Rameau is ... of the hero of
the communist Rev. He is against ... because
he has none. He sees a corrupt order
with sycophants and privilege. He is The
great actor → the product of the Baroque
period. Diderot's Rameau is the prototype
of The Revolutionist. He is somewhat
nihilistic. He has to revolt against everything.
Mind, as well as emotion, works in him.
He is also against the chaotic principle,
The motion principle, the principle of
Becoming, flux of life.

    Rabelais was constructive as well as
destructive (Abbe Theleme), not like Diderot.

    Rousseau tried to harmonize his soul
into the universe, unlike Diderot's Rameau.

    This is the birth of the modern
idea of Tragedy: Tragedy springing out of
man's nature itself. Man is alone, free,
but that is his damnation. We should learn
what man's nature is — (the job of
Humanism)

DIDEROT:
INTERPRETER OF NATURE

DIDEROT
INTERPRETER OF NATURE

Selected Writings

Translated by
JEAN STEWART AND JONATHAN KEMP

Edited, and with an Introduction,
by
JONATHAN KEMP

NEW YORK
INTERNATIONAL PUBLISHERS

" If ever anybody dedicated his whole life to the ' enthusiasm for truth and justice '—using this phrase in the good sense—it was Diderot."

FRIEDRICH ENGELS.

" . . . and here
Nature's Secretary, the Philosopher."

JOHN DONNE.

CONTENTS

CONTENTS

INTRODUCTION

IN 1936 on the Fourteenth of July, the anniversary of the
storming of the Bastille, the historic site in Paris was
decorated for the huge Popular Front demonstrations with
monster portraits of great Frenchmen of the Revolution
of 1789. Among those honoured by this great political
movement of human emancipation and defence against
Fascism, was Denis Diderot.

What does Denis Diderot mean to-day, in the present
situation of social flux ? Were these Frenchmen, members
of the Radical, Socialist and Communist Parties, leading
French writers and scientists, celebrating only a past triumph
and its heroes ? Or does Diderot mean something more ?
Does his creative genius and passionate humanity still exert
influence ? Who are his spiritual heirs ?

The masterpieces of world literature have a permanent
value, however far we may be from the period and conditions that gave rise to them. Until recently Diderot has
been read and studied almost exclusively as literary artist,
man of letters, editor of the *Encyclopedia* and writer on
æsthetics, expressing more vividly than any other writer the
thought of the Age of Enlightenment and the intellectual
atmosphere which prepared and reflected the great French
Revolution of 1789. Thus Diderot could be studied aca-
demically, as a museum-piece, and a post-mortem dissection made of his work for the light it throws on the intellectual ferment of that pregnant epoch, when the bourgeoisie
was a revolutionary class engaged in the overthrow of
feudalism.

In preparing this selection of Diderot's writings, the object
was not, however, that they should be read only from this

aspect, as marking the greatness of a past age. Diderot himself wrote :

" This is the fate of all men of genius : they are not at the level of their own time, they write for the succeeding generation."*

In retrospect we know that Diderot himself did indeed write for his own time, preparing men's minds for the revolution which he did not live to see. But he was also writing for succeeding generations ; his work has a practical value more evident to-day than for many years past. The study of dialectical materialism, the philosophical basis of revolutionary Marxism, is reaching a greater magnitude than ever before in this country, while another social revolution is maturing. Modern dialectical materialism and the new humanism of Marxism is the spiritual heir of Diderot.

Diderot is one of the great line of materialist philosophers ; his successors were Feuerbach, Marx and Engels. This side of Diderot's work has been very little studied, and in general the importance of his philosophical work has been subordinated, by those who have studied him hitherto, to the other manifold aspects of his writings, and to the interest of his rich and vivid personality.

A primary object in preparing this selection of his writings was to assist the study of modern dialectical materialism. For this reason the notes in this book are confined almost exclusively to relating Diderot's work to more recent materialist writings. These notes are not intended to replace the full commentary on Diderot's philosophic work which could and should be undertaken by modern materialists, but are intended only as indications of points of contact and for further reading. Modern dialectical materialism has, of course, a developmental history like any other scientific law or generalization. Without a knowledge of the developmental stages in philosophy cul-

* *Letter on the Publishing Trade*, " Œuvres Complètes," XVIII, 16.

minating in the Marxian synthesis of dialectical materialism, the understanding of the latter is made unnecessarily difficult. It is like attempting to study modern atomic physics without knowing how the present state of development of the science was reached, without knowing the successive stages in the deepening and widening of scientific knowledge about the atom.

Writing on the necessity for natural science to recognize the dialectical character of natural phenomena, Engels said :

"It is, however, precisely the polar antagonisms put forward as irreconcilable and insoluble, the forcibly fixed lines of demarcation and distinctions between classes which have given modern theoretical natural science its restricted and metaphysical character. The recognition that these antagonisms and distinctions are in fact to be found in nature, but only with relative validity, and that on the other hand their imagined rigidity and absoluteness have been introduced into nature only by our minds—this recognition is the kernel of the dialectical conception of nature. It is possible to reach this standpoint because the accumulating facts of natural science compel us to do so ; but we reach it more easily if we approach the dialectical character of these facts equipped with the consciousness of the laws of dialectical thought. In any case natural science has now advanced so far that it can no longer escape the dialectical synthesis. But it will make this process easier for itself if it does not lose sight of the fact that the results in which its experiences are summarized are concepts ; but that the art of working with concepts is not inborn and also is not given with ordinary everyday consciousness, but requires real thought, and that this thought similarly has a long empirical history, not more and not less than empirical natural science. Only by learning to assimilate the results of the development of philosophy during the past two and a half thousand years will it be able to rid itself on the one hand of any isolated natural philosophy standing apart from it, outside it and above it, and on the other hand also of its own limited method of thought, which was its inheritance from English empiricism." (Engels. *Anti-Dühring*, p. 19.)

Diderot marks one of the great stages of development in philosophy in general and in the philosophy of natural science. The study of his work is essential for the proper understanding of modern dialectical materialism. For natural science itself Engels's characterization remains in large measure true, and the dialectical synthesis still awaits conscious general application. A beginning is now being made by those younger scientists who have discovered the liberating and co-ordinating power of dialectical materialism. Diderot's work is one of the cardinal stages in pre-Marxist materialism.

For very good reasons, materialist philosophy is practically untaught in academic courses in philosophy ; generally speaking, a materialist philosophy has been the ideological reflection and weapon of revolutionary classes. Always the forces of reaction against progress have viewed with horror any materialist, or "atheist" doctrines, and have fought their propagation with every weapon, from misrepresentation to physical terror. At the same time, some form of idealist philosophy together with religion and superstition has always been the ideological expression of non-progressive classes or social groups.

To prevent confusion in what follows it is well to make certain that the meaning of materialism and idealism in philosophy is understood, since they are two words often used in quite another sense, the first as a term of abuse, and the second as a term of praise, by those wishing to misrepresent and defame the ideologists of revolution.

There is

" a traditional philistine prejudice against the word materialism resulting from the long-continued defamation by the priests. By the word materialism, the philistine understands gluttony, drunkenness, lust of the eye, lust of the flesh, arrogance, cupidity, avarice, miserliness, profit-hunting and stock-exchange swindling—in short, all the filthy vices in which he himself indulges in private. By the word idealism he understands the belief in virtue, universal philanthropy and in a general way a ' better world,' of which he boasts before others, but in which he himself at the utmost believes only so long as he is going through the depression or bankruptcy consequent upon his customary ' materialist ' excesses. It is then that he sings his favourite song, ' What is man ?— Half beast ! Half angel ! ' " (Engels. *Ludwig Feuerbach*, p. 41.)

In philosophy the words materialism and idealism have quite different meanings from the perversions trenchantly described by Engels.

One of the great basic questions of philosophy is that concerning the relation of thinking and being, the relation of spirit or mind to nature. The differentiation of materialism from idealism in philosophy may be described as follows :

" The question of the position of thinking in relation to being, a question which . . . had played a great part also in the scholasticism of the Middle Ages, the question : which is primary, spirit or nature—that question, in relation to the church, was sharpened into this : ' Did God create the world or has the world been in existence eternally ? ' "

" The answers which the philosophers gave to this question split them into two great camps. Those who asserted the primacy of spirit to nature and, therefore, in the last analysis, assumed world creation in some form or another . . . comprised the camp of idealism. The others, who regarded nature as primary, belong to the various schools of materialism. The two expressions, idealism and materialism, primarily signify nothing more than this." (Engels. *Ludwig Feuerbach*, p. 31.)

The distinction was understood in this sense also by idealist philosophers. Thus the view of the dialectical idealist Hegel was :

" Generally speaking, empiricism finds the truth in the outward world ; and even if it allow a supersensible world, it holds knowledge of that world to be impossible and would restrict us to the province of sensation. This doctrine when systematically carried out produces what latterly has been termed materialism. Materialism of this stamp looks upon matter *qua* matter, as the genuine objective world." (Hegel. *Enzyclopädie der philosophischen Wissenschaften in Grundrisse.* Werke. 1843., vol. IV, 83. *Quoted in* Lenin, *Materialism and Empirio-Criticism.* Collected Works. Vol. XIII, p. 99.)

The modern dialectical materialist interpretation of the relation of man's thinking to his own existence and to surrounding nature is shown in Lenin's words :

" Knowledge is the eternal infinite approach of thought to the object. The *expression* of nature in man's thought must be understood not in a ' dead ' ' abstract ' way, not *without movement*, not without contradictions, but in an eternal process of movement, of the springing up of contradictions and their solution." (Lenin, quoted by Fox.)

Diderot was a materialist in this sense : he believed in the primacy of nature and derived the infinitely complex structure of the universe from the motion and organization of matter. Man is a product of nature and man's mind, his thinking, depends upon the existence of his body, and is a function of the brain or a reflection of the outer world. Diderot's philosophical development shows a consistent movement to this position (see p. 20) which he thenceforward held in his maturer work.

For the rest, let Frederick Engels, himself one of the great materialists and co-worker with Marx in the development of dialectical materialism, write Diderot's epitaph :

" The conviction that humanity, at least at the present moment, moves on the whole in a progressive direction has absolutely nothing to do with the antithesis between materialism and idealism. The French materialists equally with the deists, Voltaire and Rousseau, held this conviction to an almost fanatical degree, and often made the greatest personal sacrifices for it. If ever anybody dedicated his whole life to the ' enthusiasm for truth and justice '—using this phrase in the good sense— it was Diderot." (Engels. *Ludwig Feuerbach*, p. 41.)

Many of Diderot's scientific conceptions have become out of date after nearly two hundred years ; it could hardly be otherwise, since they were necessarily conditioned by the knowledge then available. Yet also germs and foreshadowings of what are now modern scientific ideas can be found in his work. He was always eager to understand and to incorporate into his writing the results of the most recent scientific work. Only a philosophy like Diderot's, an embryonic dialectical materialism, was able to grow and develop continuously ; new scientific facts did not wreck his "theory," but only provided a further enlargement of knowledge for the testing and shaping of his generalizations and his materialism based on the primacy of nature. His recognition of the dialectics of nature, clearly shown in the *Conversation between d'Alembert and Diderot*, and in *D'Alembert's Dream* placed him far in advance of the contemporary materialist philosophers who were seeking to work out consistently materialist theories of biological phenomena (see p. 30). His political and moral ideas bear the marks of his period ; but here also many progressive conceptions reaching beyond his time may be found, which are real and living ideas for to-day.

A coherent philosophic materialism ; a dialectic method, only embryonic in the philosophic and scientific fields, but brilliantly developed in the social criticism of *Rameau's Nephew* ; a militant and witty atheism ; a constant urge towards the future sustained by a tremendous thirst for new knowledge, new ideas, and an intense love for humanity —these things characterize Diderot. They make him a living figure for to-day when another major social revolution, an even more decisive movement of human emancipation, is maturing in all the capitalist states of the world. The modern revolutionary movement stands for the full use of science and industry for the benefit of all, for the corresponding free development of human thought ; and against the tyranny of Fascism, with its destruction and thwarting of creative human thinking and against the horrors and waste of war. History has set before the modern working-class the task of superseding capitalism and building socialism. All progressive and liberal thinkers must ally themselves with this revolutionary class of the mid-twentieth century, as Diderot and his co-workers did with the revolutionary class in their epoch, since it is the only class which can break the barriers that decaying capitalism places in the way of further human betterment. All those characteristic qualities of Diderot's genius must find embodiment to-day in a correspondingly great intellectual movement, reflecting and helping the socialist revolution.

i. THE LIFE OF DIDEROT

Only a brief sketch of the life of Diderot can be given here as an indication of the personal background of his work.

Denis Diderot was born at Langres, Haute Marne, France, in October 1713. His father was a cutler ; the Diderot family had been artisans, some entering the Church, for more than a century. Diderot went first to a school conducted by Jesuits, where he proved himself a brilliant pupil. It was decided that he should enter the Church and an uncle was prepared to leave his living to him. At one period Diderot wished to forsake this career and become a cutler, but he returned to his studies and at the age of 12 was tonsured. For some reason unknown, the design that he should succeed to his uncle's living was vetoed by the Chapter. When the time came to leave school Diderot was determined to continue his studies and made secret preparation to go to Paris, possibly with the connivance of the Jesuits. When this was discovered by his father the latter agreed that he should continue and took him to Paris where he entered the Jesuit college of Louis-le-Grand. He was a brilliant student and obtained his master of arts degree. But his feelings for the religious vocation had cooled, probably because the contacts he made and the free discussions he heard in the capital city showed him that there were wider fields for his abilities and developing tastes than were offered by a career in the Church. He began to study law ; this was about 1730.

About the next formative ten years of his life practically nothing is known. There is evidence that his father refused further support because of his failure to continue at law. His mother supplied the deficiency as much as possible, sending a servant on foot several times to Paris with money for him. It is conjectured that he led a very bohemian life at this time, doing odd jobs of teaching, translating and writing, living on credit and probably also getting money by fairly dubious means, as was the lot of many of the writers of the Enlightenment.

Nothing is known of his intellectual development during this period, but it is evident that he must have mixed with the crowd of writers and thinkers who were the intellectual expression of the maturing revolution. He must have read widely in Voltaire, Locke, Montaigne, Montesquieu, Toland and other progressive and free-thinking writers, for the first personal work that is known to be his is a translation and adaptation, appearing in 1745, of Shaftesbury's *Inquiry Concerning Virtue*. In this Diderot clearly showed that he had emerged from the deadening bonds of religious dogma (see p. 21).

Diderot frequented the cafés, gardens and book-sellers where the intelligentsia of Paris met and discussed all the questions of that period of intellectual ferment, making many friends among them and rapidly becoming one of the foremost.

He married Antoinette Champion in 1743. His life with her was not happy, chiefly owing to differences in temperament : Diderot, bohemian, brilliant and short of money, his wife no doubt embittered by domestic in-security and burdened by housekeeping cares, unable to understand or appreciate his interests. Diderot lived by doing badly-paid translating work. In the winter of 1746 the publishers for whom he worked, knowing him to be almost penniless, proposed that he should undertake the translation and adaptation from the English of *Chamber's Encyclopedia*, which they wished to publish in conjunction with the printer Le Breton. Diderot was only too glad to have the opportunity to get a regular wage.

It is evident that the offer of this work was the nucleus that was needed to crystallize all the ideas and discussions that Diderot had had with his friends of the group known as the " philosophers," who represented the ideological front of the coming revolution. It is only necessary to mention Voltaire, Rousseau, Condillac, d'Alembert, Condorcet, Montesquieu, Fontenelle, Buffon, Daubenton, d'Holbach, Helvétius, Gassendi, Galiani, Raynal, to indicate the brilliant quality of the flower of intellectual France, which, in one way or another, made up the liberating movement of the Enlightenment. Most of these, with many others, Diderot was able to enlist in the production of the *Encyclopedia*.

If ever a man seized an opportunity and brilliantly exploited it to forward an ideological revolution that man was Diderot. He planned and directed the writing of the *Encyclopedia* so that it became the beacon and the monument of the Age of Reason, and a unique intellectual achievement. How well this work was suited to the man and the man fitted for the work is shown by this, that the direction and production of the *Encyclopedia* became the main theme of Diderot's life for the next twenty years. Until beginning the *Encyclopedia* when he was thirty-three, Diderot's life had been like that of any of his circle ; much reading of the new work that was being produced, much discussion of social, moral, philosophic and scientific problems, translating to make a living and some writing. In the project of the *Encyclopedia* Diderot seems to have recognized his life-work, which he thenceforward pursued with a tenacity rarely equalled.

The *Encyclopedia* was begun in 1746 and for the next twenty years there was a struggle of varying intensity against the often violent attacks of reaction, led by the Jesuits, before the work was completed. During this long period many contributors withdrew their support through fear and discouragement, the chief one being d'Alembert, who had been co-director with Diderot. The latter kept to the work to the end, and when it became necessary, organized the illegal printing and distribution of the last volume. He did not follow the advice of Voltaire to emigrate and finish the work abroad. There is no space here to describe more fully the extremely interesting history of the *Encyclopedia*, reflecting as it does the conflicting forces and cross-currents in the contemporary class-struggle. The *Encyclopedia* was completed only through the energy, courage and tenacity of Diderot.

At the period of the beginning of the *Encyclopedia*, Diderot published work of his own which involved him in trouble with the authorities. The *Philosophic Thoughts* (1746) was condemned and publicly burnt. He wrote the *Promenade of a Sceptic* (1747) which was denounced to the police, who searched for, but could not find, the manuscript. The denouncer was the abbé Pierre Hardy, curé of Saint Médard, who said that Diderot was " a man without any accomplishments, who played the wit and gloried in blasphemy." Diderot changed his dwelling-place, and wrote the essay on *The Sufficiency of Natural Religion*. Other work, particularly the *Letter on the Blind, for the Use of Those who See* (1749), and allegations about still other " dangerous writings " brought further police interference.

The police were active everywhere then, repressing by terror the rising popular anger against the increasing taxation needed to pay for the Seven Years' War, the luxury of the Court and the extravagance of the King's mistress, Madame la Pompadour.

Many writers and learned men were imprisoned in the Bastille and elsewhere, often without trial, for indefinite periods under a *lettre de cachet*. Similar repressive measures in India at the present time enable us to visualize the conditions in France under which Diderot worked. The French monarchy during Diderot's lifetime used repression by terror against the progressive intellectuals, among whom the group of " philosophers " around Diderot and d'Holbach were in the forefront. At that stage of historical development the bourgeoisie was a revolutionary class, working for the overthrow of feudalism, which was preventing the fuller development of human potentialities. To-day the bourgeoisie has developed to its limit in the capitalist class, and further advance demands, in turn, its supersession. Capitalism, especially as expressed through Fascist governments as in Italy, Germany and elsewhere, now plays the role of the French monarchy of Diderot's time. The repression of all the liberal and progressive thought which is the ideological weapon and reflection of the modern revolutionary class, the workers and their allies ; the curtailment of civil liberties ; all these features with which we are acquainted in this period of decaying capitalism, make real to us the conditions under which Diderot and his co-workers had to carry on the work for which they are honoured to-day as great emancipators of humanity. The repression used by the French monarchy was less well organized than it is to-day in Fascist countries ; among other reasons because the historical stage had then been reached when the ruling class no longer knew how to rule and was itself internally divided and beginning to disrupt. Many of its own servants were untrustworthy and gave help to the progressive movement.

Diderot, who was looked upon as one of the leaders (a police-agent said that he was " a clever fellow, but extremely dangerous ") was among those arrested. He denied authorship of everything of which he was accused, except the *Promenade of a Sceptic*, which he acknowledged. With the prospect of seeing the *Encyclopedia* destroyed at birth and his family reduced to poverty, he appears to have made humiliating vows and promises. For this, and in default of any concrete evidence against him, he was released after three months, and allowed to continue with the direction of the *Encyclopedia*, but always under the difficulty of writing and editing so that it should pass the censor (see p. 16).

In 1773, after the completion of the *Encyclopedia*, Diderot travelled to the court of Catherine II of Russia, who had bought his library from him in 1767, allowing it to remain with him during his life-time. He returned to France in 1774 and the remaining ten years of his life were relatively uneventful, with the temporary easing of the social tension after the death of Louis XV, during the beginning of the reign of Louis XVI, although there is evidence that the police were still anxious to embroil him. Thus Restif de la Bretonne, in his autobiography *Monsieur Nicolas* under the date 1775–6, when describing his own troubles with the police censorship says :

" I received a note from the police-agent Desmarolles, ordering me to come to his office. He told me that the sale of the *The School for Fathers* was suspended ; and that a new secret censor had been appointed to examine it with extreme rigour. ' Your *Paysan*,' he added, ' has already caused enough trouble. A magistrate has written to me about it ; here is his report : " This is a coherent and unified system of philosophy for overthrowing all religion, all morality, . . . etc." '

" This magistrate was the famous d'Epresmesnil, who, having imagined that the work was by Diderot, wished to involve the philosopher in a quarrel with the *Parlement*." (Restif de la Bretonne. *Monsieur Nicolas*, X, 136.)

The police interference apparently came to nothing, however, and Diderot was left alone. He died in 1784, five years before the outbreak of the revolution of which he was the highest ideological expression.

The best biography of Diderot is probably that by André Billy (1932) which uses newly discovered material. This book is concerned almost exclusively with his personal life and is not a study of his philosophical work.

The study of Diderot by John Morley (1878, 1886), is the best available in English and is on the whole sympathetic, at least to Diderot the man, but much hampered by Victorian prudishness. It does not give prominence, for this reason, to the most mature of Diderot's philosophical writings, (e.g., the *Conversation between D'Alembert and Diderot*, and the complementary pieces and other dialogues) nor is it able to show Diderot's work as one of the great stages in the development of materialism ; rather it tries to explain away or to excuse his atheism and materialism.

There is an interesting and very appreciative essay on Diderot in *The New Spirit*, by Havelock Ellis. The only study of Diderot's philosophy from the point of view of modern dialectical materialism is that by I. K. Luppol (1936). Another study of Diderot, by Jean Luc, is announced in the same series, *Socialisme et Culture*, as Luppol's book. For the bibliography, see p. 357.

ii. THE WRITINGS OF DIDEROT

The production of the *Encyclopedia* formed the main thread of Diderot's activity during more than twenty years of his life. He intended that the *Encyclopedia* should be an organized whole, embracing all the sciences, not as so many unconnected fields of knowledge, but in their interconnections, showing the ways in which one science was related to another, the ways in which science was investigating all the various parts of nature, and the impossibility of understanding a few isolated parts without reference to the whole.

The *Encyclopedia* was to apply consistently the principle of freedom of thought and criticism of authority. Further, it was aimed to give complete descriptions of the arts, crafts and manufactures of the period, thus giving a detailed picture of contemporary industry. It was intended that the *Encyclopedia* should be not simply a work of reference for specialists but rather an instrument of universal education, and to this end the articles were deliberately written so that the trades, sciences and philosophy should be accessible to everybody. The *Encyclopedia* was deliberately planned to be of great social significance, and shows Diderot, in the historical conditions, under a despotic monarchy, as a creative genius of brilliant imagination and foresight, admirably reflecting the revolutionary ideological forces that were ripening within the effete social structure. Besides the general directing and editorial work, Diderot himself contributed many articles, dealing particularly with the history of philosophy, and with mechanical arts and crafts. For the latter, he spent much time studying them practically in the workshops, and supervised the making of the drawings for the three to four thousand plates illustrating the work. The artisan tradition of his family, of which he was very proud, stood him in good stead here, and it was characteristic of him that he studied the crafts and manufactures practically, as well as by voluminous reading. Björnstahl, a Swedish professor who met him at the Hague in 1774 on his return from Russia, records interesting details illustrating the practical side of Diderot's character. Björnstahl said :

" He has views extending over an incredibly wide field, possesses a vivacity I cannot describe, is pleasant and friendly in intercourse, and has new and unusual observations to make on every subject. Who could fail to prize him ? He is so bright, so full of instruction, has so many new thoughts and suggestions, that nobody can help admiring him. But willingly as he talks when one goes to him, he shows to little advantage in large companies, and that is why he did not please everybody at St. Petersburg. You will easily see the reason why this incomparable man, in such companies, when people talk of fashion, of clothes, of frippery and all other sorts of triviality, neither gives pleasure to others, nor finds pleasure himself. . . . He often told me that he never found the hours pass-slowly in the company of a peasant, or a cobbler or any handicraftsman, but that he had many a time found them pass slowly enough in the society of a courtier. ' For of the one,' he said, ' one can always ask about useful and necessary things, but the other is mostly, so far as anything useful is concerned, empty and void.' " (Quoted in Morley's *Diderot*, Vol. II, Chapter IV.)

Diderot studied science practically in the laboratory of Rouelle, who was Lavoisier's teacher.

Owing to the necessity, if the *Encyclopedia* were to be

produced at all, of avoiding interference by the censorship, the articles for it had to be written very circumspectly. Furthermore, the large number of contributors drawn upon did not all hold identical political and social views. It was the co-operative effort of a " united front " of progressive thinkers with the main general objective of enlightenment in all fields of knowledge.

For these reasons the *Encyclopedia* articles do not always live up to the high standard planned in the *Prospectus*. In correspondence with Voltaire, d'Alembert put forward various reasons for the blemishes which the former found in the *Encyclopedia*. He explained that Diderot was not always in a position to reject and prune articles that were offered him, for reasons of general expediency. A writer who was valuable for some excellent articles might insist, as the price of good work, on the inclusion of some of his bad work, too :

" No doubt we have bad articles in theology and metaphysics, but with theologians for censors and a privilege,* I defy you to make them any better. There are other articles less exposed to the daylight and there everything is repaired." (Quoted by Morley, *op. cit*, Vol. II, p. 142.)

The tyranny of ecclesiasts and ministers made dissimulation necessary, and a veil had to be drawn over direct expressions of opinion and criticism, the writer's true opinions being revealed by

" a piquant phrase, an adroit parallel, a significant reference, an equivocal word of dubious panegyric." (Morley, *op. cit*. II, p. 143.)

In the article " Encyclopédie " Diderot himself said :

" In all cases where a national prejudice would seem to deserve respect, the particular article ought to set it respectfully forth, with its whole procession of attractions and probabilities. But the edifice of mud ought

* State permission for publication, subject to conditions.

to be overthrown and an unprofitable heap of dust scattered to the wind, by references to articles in which solid principles serve as base for the opposite truths. This way of undeceiving men operates promptly on minds of the right stamp, and it operates infallibly and without any troublesome consequences, secretly and without disturbance, on minds of every description."

And d'Alembert, in a letter to Voltaire, wrote : " Our fanatics feel the blows, though they are sorely puzzled to know from which side they come."

An example of the wrapping up of revolutionary content in disarming externals is given later (p. 48). In addition to all the above reasons which contributed to emasculate the *Encyclopedia*, there were further crude mutilations of articles by the printer Le Breton himself, who feared the consequences of printing the more dangerous pieces.

For all these reasons the *Encyclopedia* does not give the clearest picture of the revolutionary thinking of the period. This is found in the books printed secretly or abroad (e.g., Helvétius, d'Holbach). Much of Diderot's best work was not printed during his life-time but circulated in manuscript copies among his friends and the subscribers to Grimm's manuscript *Literary Correspondence*.

In spite of all the shortcomings imposed by the conditions under which it was produced, the *Encyclopedia* remains a monument to Diderot's organizational ability and energy, and his foresight with regard to its objective showed deep social consciousness. Diderot's articles contributed to the *Encyclopedia* fill four volumes of the collected edition of his works.

The most brilliantly imaginative and creative of Diderot's writings, however, are to be found in the other sixteen volumes of the collected works, which contain the pieces written without fear of the censor. For the convenience of description this work may be divided into several groups, although it is truer of Diderot than of many other writers of such capacity and many-sidedness, that all the elements, scientific, philosophical, literary, artistic and critical, are fused harmoniously in all his work.

He left about four volumes of criticism, principally on painting, with some on sculpture and music. His criticisms of the Salons of 1759 to 1771, are famous and practically founded art-criticism. He wrote critical essays on dramatic and literary theory, such as the *Reflexions on Terence,* the *Eulogy of Richardson,* the *Paradox of the Comedian,* and a treatise on *Dramatic Poesy.*

To support his severe criticism of the artificiality of the contemporary French theatre, he wrote several plays of naturalist flavour. The rule of his taste and of his art was that it should be natural, living. The plays are the least good part of his work.

His extraordinary realistic novel *La Religieuse* and the satirical *Jacques the Fatalist* outwardly modelled on *Tristram Shandy* are well known by name, if not by their content.

The Indiscreet Toys (Les Bijoux Indiscrets) was described by Carlyle as " the beastliest of all past, present and future dull novels " and he recommended " the next mortal creature, even a Reviewer, to bathe in running water, put on a change of raiment, and be unclean until the even." Morley could not bring himself to name its title, and dismissed " this tale as the lees of Diderot's strong, careless, sensualized understanding," . . . " the vein of defilement." (Morley. *op. cit.,* I, 75.) *The Indiscreet Toys,* although in form a frivolous " gallant " novel of the type of the younger Crébillon, is much more than merely that. It contains satirical criticisms of the abuses and morals of the Court and its satellite society, of religious prejudices and corrupt personalities, veiled by its setting in a fabulous Eastern country. The chapters we have selected (see p. 35) clearly show that Diderot put serious content of high order even in a romance of " gallantry " written chiefly to obtain money for his mistress. He himself entitled the brilliant allegorical Chapter XXXII. " *Perhaps the best and the least read in this book,*" and was evidently fully conscious of its value. It is an interesting index of his philosophic development that at this early stage, 1748, when he was thirty-five, he looked to the development of natural science, to practice, as the critic of all philosophies (see p. 42). The chapters from *The Indiscreet Toys* printed here adequately neutralize Carlyle's and Morley's hysterical criticism.

Diderot's introduction of profound content under a gay form is typical of the whole of his writing ; he has expressed this attitude in a letter to Sophie Volland (see p. 331). A fairly large volume of Diderot's correspondence is preserved (*Œuvres Complètes*, Vols. XVIII, XIX, XX) the most remarkable part of it being the series of letters to Sophie Volland. [*Lettres à Sophie Volland*, edited by André Babelon, (1931) contains newly discovered letters, not included in the *Œuvres Complètes* of Assézat and Tourneux, which bring the total to 187].

The letters, covering the period 1759–1774, are one of the masterpieces of French, if not of all, epistolary literature. In Sophie Volland, Diderot found someone to whom he could reveal every side of his manifold nature. " My Sophie is both man and woman when she pleases," he wrote, and into his letters to her went everything that was in his head, "narrating the incidents of the day, telling what he was thinking about or projecting, repeating current scandal or sometimes a not quite decent story, flashing instinctively into wise or witty reflection ; always with a swift, almost unconscious pen, forgetting now and again what he had already said." (Havelock Ellis. *The New Spirit*, p. 49.)

The last and most important group of work is that comprising the more directly philosophical and scientific writings, although, as already mentioned, the scope of these is extremely wide and embraces moral, social, sexual, philosophical and scientific problems, not treated didactically, but extremely freely in a typically spontaneous manner. Diderot's favourite and characteristic form was a dialogue between two or three people. He was a brilliant talker and this is clearly reflected in the profusion and rapid succession of ideas that are introduced into these pieces, and in the tremendous *élan* with which they are carried forward.

Probably the most remarkable are the *Conversation between d'Alembert and Diderot* with the complementary *D'Alembert's Dream* and the *Conclusion* (p. 49 *et seq.*), and *Rameau's Nephew* (p. 235). Here in small compass is expressed the quintessence of Diderot's genius. Diderot himself said that the d'Alembert group of dialogues were the only writings of his own, together with a mathematical memoir, with which he was content.

The writings chosen for this selection are taken principally from the group of philosophical and scientific writings, and need not therefore be described ; they speak eloquently for themselves in a way that Diderot has known best how to use, clothing profound thought in brilliant dialogue.

iii. THE DEVELOPMENT OF DIDEROT'S PHILOSOPHY

Diderot nowhere expounded his philosophic ideas formally, nor sought to embody them in a system ; this would have been entirely contrary to his character and to his mode of working. Consequently the understanding of his philosophic position must be built up from passages, phrases, and comments scattered prodigally throughout his writings. This task has barely been begun by modern dialectical materialists, who are the real heirs of Diderot in philosophy. The following brief sketch of Diderot's philosophic evolution is based on the study by I. K. Luppol (1936), and will serve to connect the earlier writings of Diderot with the maturer work which is reproduced here.

The *Encyclopedia* article on philosophy (appearing in 1757) might have been expected to give an opportunity for a formal definition and exposition of Diderot's conceptions.

But what is found there, however, is only the then current Wolffian metaphysical view and classification of philosophy. The conclusions which Diderot is known from other work to have reached during the previous twelve years are not given. Luppol (*op. cit.*) concludes that the *Encyclopedia* article must be considered simply as intended to show the average contemporary view of philosophy in mid-eighteenth century, and not in the least to represent Diderot's personal view.

Furthermore, the necessity to avoid police interference, which led to much dissimulation, as already described, must be remembered. Any clear-cut statement of Diderot's views as they were in 1757, must have led to suppression, as proved by the condemnation of the relatively mild *Philosophic Thoughts* in 1746. An article on " Philosophy " would have been the obvious place for a censor to look for " dangerous writing " ; hence only the most ordinary material was put there.

Diderot elaborated his philosophy fragmentarily through a number of years, in a series of writings, basing himself eventually on the early materialists (Epicurus, Lucretius) and the facts of contemporary science, but only after a process of criticism of religious and philosophical doctrines.

The evolution of his ideas begins with the adaptation and translation of Shaftesbury's *Inquiry Concerning Virtue* ; Diderot's adaptation appeared in 1745. In his preface, Diderot proposed to show that virtue was related to the knowledge of God and that the earthly happiness of man was inseparable from virtue. What Diderot found uncomfortable about religion was, however, the fanaticism to which it gave rise. He felt that " religion . . . practised with enlightened zeal could not fail to encourage moral virtues." Barbarous fanatics only knew the ghost of religion.

" All the efforts of unbelief were less to be feared than this Inquisition. Unbelief combats the proofs of religion ; this Inquisition seeks to destroy them. . . . Recall the history of our civil disturbances and you will see one half of the nation batheing, out of piety, in the blood

21

of the other half, and violating the most primitive feelings of humanity in order to uphold the cause of God ; as if it were necessary to cease to be human in order to show one's self *religious* ! " (Introduction to " Essay on Merit and Virtue," *Œuvres Complètes*, I, p. 10.)

The religious events of his time precipitated Diderot's rupture with Catholicism. He was disgusted much more by the fanaticism of bigots, princes and servants of the Church, than he was repelled by the lack of faith of the unbelievers.

" It was necessary to free belief in God from the prejudices with which the fanatics were overwhelming it, and to put it in agreement with the science of man, to infuse it with the spirit of tolerance." (Luppol. *op. cit.*, p. 117.)

In 1745 Diderot still retained a belief in most of the Christian dogmas, but suspended judgment with regard to revelation, wishing to obtain direct proof of it. Thus he was then a *theist*, believing in the existence of God, the reality of moral good and evil, the immortality of the soul, the idea of recompense and future punishment ; he was not yet a *deist*, a term introduced by Shaftesbury to distinguish from theists those who denied revelation while accepting the other dogmas of the theists.

Diderot used the idea of *relative*, as against absolute good and evil, thus renouncing orthodox Christian conceptions on this matter. He closely united particular interest, the personal happiness of each individual, to the happiness of all. Virtue is the search for happiness by contributing to the happiness of others ; vice is the opposite attitude and has evil as a result. This was Shaftesbury's view and was accepted by Diderot in 1745. At the same time Diderot recognized that atheists were not malefactors. He saw acknowledged atheists living honest lives without expectation of recompenses or punishment in an after-life to keep them to the straight and narrow path, which he at first had thought could be pursued only with the aid of a belief in God—" there is no virtue without a belief in God."

Life itself, in the persons of these atheists, showed Diderot that virtue, which he founded on religious faith, could be self-sufficient ; virtue could do without the support of religious belief ; an atheist could be virtuous. This was a great advance, and the next stage is represented by the *Philosophic Thoughts* (1746) in which the clear break with orthodox Christianity was made.

The *Thoughts* were intentionally fragmentary and disconnected ; on the whole they are a series of reflections in which on the one hand, deist, and on the other, atheist arguments are put forward. Diderot was still concerned with theological questions ; the questions of religion were the most pressing to him at that time, and this was the field in which the social question, the pre-revolutionary ideological struggle, was discussed in its most open form.

In the *Thoughts* Diderot passed beyond the theism of the *Essay.*

" Why demand of me that I should believe that there are three persons in God, as firmly as I believe that the sum of the three angles of a triangle is equal to two right angles ? Every proof must produce in one a certitude proportional to its degree of strength ; and the action of geometrical, of moral and of physical demonstrations on my mind must differ or the distinction is frivolous. . . ." (*Philosophic Thoughts,* § 58.)

Miracles were not proofs to a man who could talk like this about the Trinity.

" What is God ? is a question which children are asked and which philosophers find great difficulty in answering. One knows at what age a child ought to learn reading, singing, dancing, latin, geometry. Only in religious matters is their capacity not consulted ; they can no sooner hear but they are asked : What is God ? It is at the same time, and from the same lips, that they learn that there are fairies, ghosts, ogres and a God." (*Philosophic Thoughts,* § 25.)

In the *Philosophic Thoughts* Diderot was working slowly forward to solve the religious and philosophic questions, giving attention to the arguments of each trend of opinion, concluding nothing hurriedly, but observing, reflecting, and testing each conclusion. He maintained as yet no one point of view, and was neither Christian, deist nor atheist. He was at a transitional stage, not a sceptic who ends by doubting, but an inquirer who begins by doubting and investigates to get knowledge ; a truly scientific investigator. He recognized that atheism was the most powerful rival of deism. Atheism used arguments of a physical and cosmological kind, and against these the deists usually brought forward moral arguments. But Diderot found it necessary to introduce arguments of physical and cosmological type also to support the deist position—evidence of " design " in nature, and the authority of Newton and other learned men who had " found satisfying proofs of the existence of a sovereign, intelligent Being " (*Philosophic Thoughts*, § 18) in the amazing complexity and organization of nature. The teleological " proof " of the existence of God was abandoned by Diderot when he later studied chemistry, physiology and mechanics ; the element of wonder, incomprehension, dissolved before the investigations of science and the knowledge and understanding which later scientific developments brought (see *On the Interpretation of Nature*, p. 43).

The *Promenade of the Sceptic, or The Garden-Walks* appeared in 1747. The action takes place in a vast garden, and the people in the various garden-walks represent different theological and philosophical schools.

In the Thorn Walk, pious people wandered, clothed in white, with their eyes bandaged. Although thus blinded they are forbidden to tear or soil their garments (sin) ; in bad cases soap is sold to them (absolution). In the Chestnut Walk are the various schools of philosophers, the principal discussion concerning the existence of a God ; how to represent Him if there is one, and why not do without one? This is the most interesting section of the work; the allegory of the Thorn Walk, and the Flower Walk (pleasure seekers) is dull beside it. The importance Diderot attached to these discussions is indicated by this phrase in the preliminary discourse: " If you impose upon me silence about religion and government, I shall have nothing to talk about." Diderot was still investigating in the *Promenade* with, on the whole, a further movement from deism towards atheism. There are no Christians in the Chestnut Walk; he refused them the title of philosopher, to him an honourable one.

Diderot gave most attention to the deists and atheists; those were the most formidable protagonists whose philosophy merited the most careful attention. He now used the cosmological argument against the idea of God, putting it this time in the atheists' hands. " If matter is eternal, if motion has so disposed it and originally impressed on it all the different forms which we see that it preserves, what need have I of your prince?" . . . " So long as the structure and organization (*économie*) of our organs persist, we think; we rave when this changes. When it is destroyed, what becomes of the soul? " The arguments which were opposed to these were of physico-teleological type, the deists speaking of " universal order," the stars and the hands which must have lighted them.

The atheist answers: " We have before us a vast unknown machine about which observations have been made which prove the regularity of its movements, according to some, and its irregularity and disorder, according to the feeling of others. Ignorant people who have only examined one cogwheel of it, of which they understood hardly a few teeth, make conjectures about their interlocking with a hundred thousand other cogs of which they are ignorant of the motions and actions; and in conclusion, like artisans, they put on the work the name of its author." . . . " A worm and an ant instal themselves comfortably in a great rubbish heap, made of soil and fragments of stone from a ruined building. What would you think of these insects, if, reasoning your way, they became enraptured with the intelligence of a gardener who had placed all these materials in that way for their convenience".

The deist opposed teleology to causality ; not wishing to admit necessity he appealed to liberty. 'The closer investigation of nature, as with the miscroscope revealing the structure of the internal organs of a silk-worm, was put forward as further evidence for the existence of God. " What conclusion could be drawn from the anatomy of the human body and from the knowledge of other natural phenomena ? " Nothing, except that matter is organized, was the reply of the atheist. In substance this answer went unrefuted ; and the discussion is summed up : perhaps the atheist is right, but probability remains with the deist.

The following phase in Diderot's philosophic development is marked by the *Letter on the Blind, for the Use of Those who See* (1749). In this the questions discussed covered a wider field than in the previous writings ; the theory of knowledge, cosmogony and the philosophy of nature were included in its scope. Diderot showed now that his previous inquiries had allowed him to reach a definite materialism, and the philosophy of his subsequent writings was largely a development of germinal ideas to be found in the *Letter on the Blind*. Apart from the intrinsic interest of his discussion of blindness in relation to the way in which lack of sight affected the understanding of the surrounding environment, and the ability to think in the abstract, etc. in which field Diderot made interesting original observations, the most important aspect of the *Letter* is that which develops the philosophical problems.

The fictitious conversation attributed to Saunderson (a famous blind mathematician of Cambridge) allowed Diderot to express his views on the relativity of moral and metaphysical notions. The blind cannot understand how such importance is attributed to visual perception. People who can see are moved when they see a suffering animal, yet take no note of the insects they crush underfoot. Some parts of the body may be exposed to view, but not others.

Blind Saunderson, dying, is made to advance the views of the atheist in the *Promenade of a Sceptic*. He recognizes only what he can feel ; to believe in God he must be able to touch him ; man can believe in God when he has visible palpable, concrete evidence. Indirect evidence from the beauty and perfection of nature are insufficient ; they carry no weight in the face of ugliness and blindness.

The minister of religion who visits Saunderson on his death-bed, discusses with him the possibility of the existence of God, citing the marvels of nature as evidence for a divine intelligence. Saunderson answers him :

" Ah, sir, leave out all about that beautiful spectacle, which was never made for me. I have been condemned to pass my life in darkness ; and you cite these prodigies which I do not understand, and which only have weight with you and those who see like you. If you want me to believe in God, you must let me touch him."

The minister directs Saunderson's attention to the divine origin which he should find by manual examination of the admirable mechanism of his own organs, Saunderson answers :

". . . But if the animal organism is as perfect as you say, and as I should like to believe . . . what has it in common with a sovereign intelligent being ? If it amazes you, perhaps that is because you are in the habit of treating as a miracle everything that appears to be beyond your own capacity. I have so often been an object of admiration for you, that I have a poor opinion of what surprises you. I have drawn here from all parts of England people who cannot conceive how I could do geometry ; you must agree that these people had no very clear ideas about the possibilities of things. If a phenomenon is in our opinion

beyond the power of man, we say at once : ' It is God's handiwork ' ;
our vanity is content with nothing less. Why cannot we put into our
discussion a little less pride and a little more philosophy ? If nature
offers us a difficult knot to unravel, let us leave it for what it is ; do not
let us introduce, in order to untie it, the hand of a Being who then at
once becomes an even more difficult knot to untie than the first one.
Ask an Indian why the world stays suspended in space, and he will tell
you that it is carried on the back of an elephant . . . and the elephant
on a tortoise. And what supports the tortoise ? . . . You pity the
Indian ; and yet it might be said to you, as to him : Mr. Holmes,
my friend, confess your ignorance and spare me your elephant and your
tortoise."

The minister falls back upon the authority of Newton,
Clarke and Leibnitz, who had been impressed with the
marvels of nature and were satisfied with this as evidence
for an Intelligent Being as their author. Saunderson replies :

" I see nothing ; I admit, however, an admirable order in everything ; but I trust you not to expect anything more of me. I grant it
you about the present state of the universe, in order to get from you, in
return, the liberty of thinking what I like about its ancient and primitive
state, about which you are no less blind than I. You have no evidence
to oppose me here, your eyes are of no use to you. You may imagine,
if you wish, that that order which impressed you has always existed.
But leave me free to think it has done no such thing, and that if we went
back to the birth of things and of time, and perceived matter in motion
and chaos becoming unravelled, we should encounter a multitude of
shapeless beings instead of a few highly organized beings. If I have
no objections to offer you about the present condition of things, I can at
least question you about their past condition. I can ask you, for example,
who told you, Leibnitz, Clarke and Newton, that at the first moment of
the formation of animals, some were not without heads, others without
feet ? I can maintain to you, that these had no stomachs, those no intestines ; that some to whom a stomach, palate and teeth seemed to
promise continued existence, came to an end through some defect of
heart or lungs ; that monsters annihilated one another in succession ;
that all the defective (*vicieuses*) combinations of matter have disappeared,
and that there have only survived those in which the organization
(*méchanisme*) did not involve any important contradiction (*contradiction*),*
and which could subsist by themselves and perpetuate themselves. On

* See *Elements of Physiology*, p. 134.

this hypothesis, if the first man had had a blocked larynx, had lacked suitable food, had had defective organs of generation, had not found a mate, or had propagated with another species, Mr. Holmes, what would have become of our human race ? It would have remained enfolded in the general depuration (*dépuration*) of the universe ; and that arrogant being who calls himself man, dissolved and scattered among the molecules of matter, would perhaps have remained for ever among the number of possibilities.

" If there had never been any shapeless creatures, you would not have failed to claim that none will ever appear and that I am plunging into fantastic hypothesis ; but the order is not yet so perfect that monstrous productions do not appear from time to time. . . . I conjecture then, that, in the beginning, when matter in fermentation was hatching out the universe, blind creatures like myself were very common. But why should I not believe about worlds what I believe about animals ? How many worlds, mutilated and imperfect, were perhaps dispersed, reformed and are dispersing again at every moment in distant space, which I cannot touch and you cannot see, but where motion continues, and will continue, to combine masses of matter until they shall have attained some arrangement in which they can persist. O philosophers, transport yourselves with me to the confines of the universe, beyond where I can touch and where you can see organized beings ; move over that new ocean, and seek among its irregular movements some trace of that intelligent Being whose wisdom so astounds you here ! But what is the good of taking you out of your element ? What is this world ? A complex whole subject to revolutions which all indicate a continual tendency to destruction ; a swift succession of beings which follow each other, thrust forward and disappear ; a transient symmetry ; a momentary order. I reproached you just now with estimating the perfection of things by your own capacity ; and I might accuse you here of measuring its duration by the length of your own days. You judge the continuous existence of the world as an ephemeral insect might judge your existence. The world is eternal for you, as you are eternal for the being that lives only for an instant ; yet the insect is the more reasonable of the two. What prodigious succession of ephemeral generations attests your eternity ? What immense tradition ? Yet we shall all pass away without being able to assign the real extent we filled in space, nor the precise time that we shall have endured. Time, matter, space are perhaps only a point."

The passage just quoted is one of the earliest of Diderot's great flights of scientific imagination, hinting at a theory of biological and cosmological evolution. He returned to the subject again in the *Conversation between d'Alembert and Diderot* (p. 49), in *D'Alembert's Dream* (p. 64) and in the *Elements of Physiology* (p. 134); it always evoked his most eloquent and brilliant efforts.

So much for the earlier development of Diderot's materialism; the subsequent development of his philosophy is contained in the maturer writings which make up the bulk of the present selection.

IV. DIDEROT'S DIALECTIC

One aspect of Diderot as a thinker which has never been adequately acknowledged, much less studied, is the fact that *within* the field of natural science and the philosophy of nature, he was far in advance of his contemporaries in his recognition of the dialectical character of natural phenomena. Outside the field of natural science and of philosophy in the restricted sense, French writers of the Enlightenment produced masterpieces of dialectic. Rousseau's *Treatise on the Origin of Inequality among Men*, and Diderot's own *Rameau's Nephew* are high-water marks of this kind of writing. But Diderot alone was able in some measure to apply the same mode of thinking to the philosophy of nature, or rather, was able to observe this same mode of development in natural phenomena and to apply it in a speculative manner.

It has been usual in the past to class all the French materialists of this period as *mechanical* materialists, and this is admittedly true of the majority of them. But Diderot is an exception to this generalization; as will be seen, there are many instances, scattered through the writings in this volume, which show him surmounting this limited, mechanical, materialism when he is discussing natural phenomena.

Engels has shown why it was that the working scientists of this period should have been unable to pass beyond mechanical materialism. He pointed out that the primitive, naïve view of nature is of " an endless maze of relations and interactions " and that

" this intrinsically correct conception of the world was that of ancient Greek philosophy, and was first clearly formulated by Heraclitus : everything is and also is not, for everything is in *flux*, is constantly changing, constantly coming into being and constantly passing away. But this conception, correctly as it covers the general character of the picture of phenomena as a whole is yet inadequate to explain the details of which this total picture is composed, and so long as we do not understand these, we also have no clear idea of the picture as a whole. In order to understand these details, we must detach them from their natural or historical connections, and examine each one separately, as to its nature, its special causes and effects, etc. This is primarily the task of natural science and historical research." (Engels, *Anti-Dühring*, p. 27. See also p. 335 of this book.)

When real natural science began to develop, in the second half of the fifteenth century, it was first necessary to collect facts, to analyse nature into its individual parts, to group and classify natural objects and their constituent parts, to systematize the accumulating knowledge; it was primarily a collecting science. The only possible way for the laboratory worker to investigate at that stage of development, was to analyse his materials, to discover the elements from which the more complex materials and processes were built up, to isolate portions and to study phenomena piecemeal, and while at rest. This method of study was necessarily imposed by the limitations of the technique that was then available in the laboratories. This static method of investigation, historically inevitable, left as a legacy

" . . . the habit of observing natural objects and natural processes in their isolation, detached from the whole vast interconnection of things ; and therefore not in their motion, but in their repose ; not as essentially changing, but as fixed constants ; not in their life but in their death. And when, as was the case with Bacon and Locke, this way of looking at things was transferred from natural science to philosophy, it produced the specific limitations of the last [eighteenth—Ed.] century, the metaphysical mode of thought." (Engels. *Anti-Dühring*, pp. 27–8. See the note on p. 336 of this book.)

This, then, was the background of the French mechanical materialists such as Lamettrie in his *Man-Machine*, d'Holbach in the physics section of his *System of Nature*, Cabanis and others. Along the same lines Büchner, Vogt and Moleschott later developed their mechanical materialism in the nineteenth century. Thus it can be understood that in the investigation of particular limited fields in natural science, there was a two-fold compulsion to remain mechanical materialists, namely the heritage of the metaphysical mode of thought and the practical limitations of laboratory technique and the stage of development of science. The latter factor necessarily kept practical investigations, especially in the biological fields, at the stage of analysis, of simplification, of dissection. In the historical circumstances, therefore, it was almost inevitable that these French materialists should have been and have remained *mechanical* materialists.

Diderot, on the other hand, was able to surmount these limitations and that to a surprising degree. In part this may have been because he was not an experimental investigator in a particular field, and was therefore not tied down by the limitations of experimental technique. With his encyclopædic mind, embracing wide fields of science, he was able to survey various special fields, to observe their interconnections, and, viewing natural processes dynamically, to recognize their dialectical character, in contrast to the laboratory workers who had, initially, to isolate and to observe phenomena, not in motion, but at rest. Furthermore, he was a natural dialectic thinker, and was thus able to think in this way when handling scientific material, as well as in the field of social criticism as in *Rameau's Nephew*.

For these reasons, Diderot was able to take a longer view and to produce the brilliant speculative hypotheses which contain in embryo the evolutionary transformist ideas of Lamarcke and Darwin. Diderot criticized the rigidity of the static, arbitrary classifications of the systematists with their " fury " for " modelling existing things after conceptions " instead of " re-shaping conceptions to existing things." This is particularly clearly shown in the *Interpretation of Nature* (see p. 46). Diderot's criticism is entirely parallel with Engels's remarks that " Nature is the test of dialectics " and that " it is no longer a question anywhere of inventing interconnections out of our brains but of discovering them in the facts."

The most clear-cut example showing Diderot's distinction from the mechanical materialists is in the section on Animals in the *Elements of Physiology* (see p. 135), where he remarks : " What idiotic things can be said following this one supposition " that " the animal is a hydraulic machine." He then gives an expansion of his criticism entirely along dialectical materialist lines. An analogous passage from the *Dialectics and Nature* of Engels is given in the Notes (see p. 349, section V, note 4).

Other examples of dialectic thinking and the recognition of dialectic processes in nature abound in the *Conversation between d'Alembert and Diderot* and *D'Alembert's Dream* to which references are made in the Notes. Similarly there is the passage in the *Supplement to Bougainville's " Voyage,"* on the mutability of human vows in the face of a constantly changing nature.

Diderot's recognition of the dialectical character of natural phenomena is derived from the naïve dialectics of the early Greek philosophers ; it is not a conscious analysis of the forms of dialectic development. This was to come, and fourteen years before Diderot's death the man had already been born—namely Hegel—who was to develop conscious dialectics in its widest and most general form, although upon an idealist basis. But for Diderot the recognition of the dialectics of nature was that of a scientist on whom the facts of science, the facts of life itself, thrust themselves, " making evident the dialectical character of natural events " to a mind not rendered unreceptive by the heritage of a metaphysical philosophy, but avid to receive it.

Diderot is the outstanding example for his epoch of this process by which natural science is forced to recognize the dialectical character of nature, a process which Engels has described for the natural science of his own time in the preface to *Anti-Dühring*. Not until the work of Marx and Engels was conscious dialectics applied to the materialist conception of nature and history. Only since their work has *consciously* dialectical natural science been possible. Diderot marks the transitional stage in the development of natural science towards the conscious recognition of the dialectic of nature. He is the first materialist who began to burst through the restrictions of mechanical, metaphysical materialism.

J. K.

I

From

THE INDISCREET TOYS

From Chapter XXIX. Mirzoza's Metaphysics. *The Souls.*

"HAVE the philosophers of Monoémugi, who have supervised the education of your Highness, never discussed the nature of the soul ? "

" Oh, very often," answered Mangogul ; " but all their systems have only ended by giving me very uncertain notions ; and without some feeling within oneself which seems to me to suggest that it is something different from matter, either I should have denied the existence of it, or I should have confused it with, or mistaken it for, the body. Do you undertake to unravel this chaos for us ? "

" I am far from being able to do that," replied Mirzoza ; " and I confess that I am no clearer about it, than are your pedagogues. The only difference there is between them and myself, is that I assume the existence of a substance different from matter, while they hold it to be proved. But this substance, if it exists, must be hidden somewhere. Now, haven't they uttered many extravagant things about that ? "

" No," said Mangogul, " all agreed pretty well that it resides in the head ; and this notion has seemed to me to be probable. It is the head which thinks, imagines, reflects, judges, disposes, orders ; and it is commonly said of a man who doesn't think, that he has no brains, or that he's lost his head."

" There," replied the Sultana. " Now see to what your long studies and all your philosophy is reduced : to assuming

35

something and then supporting it by everyday phrases. What would you say to your geographical expert, Prince, if he had put the east at the west, or the north at the south, when he presented the map of your State to your Highness ?"

"That's too gross a blunder," answered Mangogul ; "no geographer has ever committed one like that."

"That may be," continued the favourite, "and in that case your philosophers have been clumsier than the clumsiest geographer can ever be. They had no vast empire to survey, there was no question of fixing the boundaries of the four quarters of the earth ; it was only a question of examining into themselves, and noting the true site of their souls. Nevertheless they have put the east at the west, or the north at the south. They have pronounced that the soul resides in the head, while the greater part of mankind dies without its ever having inhabited that site, but having had its first residence in the feet."

"In the feet !" interrupted the Sultan ; "that's the most extraordinary idea I've ever heard."

"Yes, in the feet," continued Mirzoza. "And this idea, which appears so foolish to you, only needs to be developed somewhat more deeply to become reasonable, quite contrary to all those notions which one admits as true, but which one recognizes as false as soon as one begins to investigate them. Your Highness agreed with me, just now, that the existence in us of a soul was based only on the evidence which it gave of itself within us ; and I am going to demonstrate to you that all imaginable tests concur in placing the soul in the situation I have assigned to it."

"That's what we are waiting for," said Mangogul.

"I don't ask for mercy," she continued, "and I invite you all to propose your difficulties to me. I say, then, that the soul has its first dwelling in the feet ; it's there that it begins to exist, and it is from there that it advances through the whole body. It is to experience that I shall turn for this fact ; and I am, perhaps, now going to put forward the

fundamentals of an experimental metaphysics. We have all
experienced how in infancy the drowsy soul remains for
whole months in a state of torpor. Then the eyes are open
without seeing, the mouth without speaking and the ears
without hearing. It is elsewhere that the soul tries to
expand and to awake ; it is in other members that it
exercises its first functions—it is with its feet that a child
announces its formation. Its body, its head and its arms are
stilled in the womb of its mother ; but its feet stretch out
and move, and manifest its existence, and perhaps its needs.
When it is at the point of birth, what of the body, head and
arms ? They would never get out of their prison if they
were not aided by the feet. It is the feet which play the
principal role and which thrust the rest of the body before
them. Such is the order of nature. And when some other
member takes control, and the head, for example, takes the
place of the feet, everything goes wrong ; and then God
knows what happens sometimes to the mother and to the
child. The child is born, but it is still the feet which make
the principal movements. If one tries to restrain them it
is never without some opposition on their part. The head
is a lump with which one does as one likes ; but the feet
feel, shake off the restraint and seem jealous of the liberty
that one tries to take from them. When the child can
hold himself upright, the feet make a thousand efforts to
bring him into motion, they set everything into action ;
they control the other members, and the obedient hands
help him to lean against the walls, and are held out to
prevent falls and to help the motion of the feet."

" What do all the thoughts of the child revolve round,
and what are its pleasures, when it is firm on its legs and it
has acquired the habit of moving them ? It wants to exercise its limbs, to move about, to run, jump, leap. This
activity pleases us, and is an indication for us, of cleverness,
and we prophesy that a child will be stupid when we see it
lazy and dejected. If you want to make a four-year-old

miserable, make it sit still for a quarter of an hour, or keep it imprisoned between four chairs. Ill humour and vexations will seize it ; thus it is not only the limbs that you deprive of exercise, but its soul which you also hold captive."

" The soul remains in the feet till the age of two or three ; it lives in the legs at four ; it reaches the knees and thighs at fifteen. Then one loves dancing, fighting, running and other violent exercises of the body. That is the dominating passion of all young people, and even the obsession of some. What ! The soul can not reside in the places where it almost solely manifests itself, and where it experiences its most agreeable sensations ? But if its dwelling-place varies during childhood and youth, why shouldn't it vary during the whole of life ? "[1]

*   *   *   *   *

Chapter XXXII.   Perhaps the best and the least read in this story.

The Dream of Mangogul

or

A Journey in the Land of Hypotheses

" AH-E-OU ! " said Mangogul, yawning and rubbing his eyes, " I've got a headache. Don't ever let anyone speak about philosophy with me again ; it's unhealthy. Yesterday I went to bed with my head full of deep notions, and instead of sleeping like a sultan, my brain went on working more than those of my ministers would work in a year. You laugh ; but to convince you that I'm not exaggerating, and to get revenge for the wretched night all your reasonings have caused me, you're going to endure the whole of my dream."

" I was beginning to drowse, and my imagination to take

flight, when I saw a strange animal bounding beside me. It had the head of an eagle, the feet of a griffon, the body of a horse and the tail of a lion. I seized it, in spite of its gambols, and, holding its mane, leapt on its back. It at once stretched out long wings from its sides, and I felt myself carried through the air with incredible speed. Our flight had been long when I saw a building suspended in the void of space, as by enchantment. It was huge. I shall not say that it had no foundations, because it rested on nothing. Its columns, which were only half a foot thick, rose out of sight and upheld vaulted ceilings, so high that they could only be seen thanks to openings to the sky with which they were symmetrically pierced. It was at the entry to this edifice that my mount stopped. I hesitated to dismount at first, for I felt it less hazardous to fly on my hippogriff, than to walk under this dizzy portico. However, encouraged by the sight of a multitude of people who were walking there, and by a remarkable calm which reigned on all their faces, I dismounted, went forward, plunged into the crowd and observed the people who composed it."

" They were old men, either puffy or thin, not stout, feeble and all deformed. One had too small a head, another's arms were too short. Here was one who lacked a trunk, another legs. Most of them had no feet at all, and hobbled only with crutches. A breath of wind would make them fall, and they stayed on the ground till it pleased some newcomer to lift them up. In spite of all these defects, they appeared quite pleasing at first glance. They had in their looks something interesting and bold. They were almost naked, for their whole clothing consisted of a little rag of cloth which did not cover a hundredth part of the body. I continued, pushing through the crowd, and at last got to the foot of a rostrum for which a large spider's web served as canopy. For the rest, its boldness was in keeping with the remainder of the building. It appeared to be poised on the point of a needle and to maintain itself there in equilibrium. I trembled a hundred times for the person who occupied it. This was an old man with a long beard, as shrivelled and naked as any of his disciples. Into a bowl full of a subtle fluid he dipped a pipe which he put to his lips, and blew bubbles to the crowd who were surrounding him and who were busy at lifting them up to the skies."*

" Where am I, I asked myself, confused by this childishness. What does this old fellow mean, blowing his bubbles, and all these decrepit children, occupied in trying to make them fly ? Who'll explain all this to me ? "

" The little pieces of cloth which they wore struck me again, and I had observed that the bigger the piece was, the less those who wore them were interested in the bubbles. This singular observation encouraged me to accost the one who appeared to be the least undressed."

" I noticed one of them whose shoulders were half covered with pieces of cloth joined with such art that the eye could not see the seams. He was going to and fro in the crowd, taking no notice of those about him. I thought that he had an affable manner, with a smile on his lips, a noble carriage and a gentle look, and I went straight to him."

" ' Who are you ? Where am I ? And who are all these people ? ' I asked without beating about the bush."

' I am Plato,' he answered. ' You are in the Land of Hypotheses, and these people are makers of systems.'

' But how comes it that the divine Plato should find himself here ; what is he doing among these lunatics ? . . .'

' I am making recruits,' he told me. ' Far away from this portico, I have a small sanctuary, to which I lead those who have turned away from the making of systems.'

' What do you give them to do ? '

' To know man, to practise virtue and to sacrifice to the Graces. . . .'

---

* There is a pun here in the French : " *qui travaillent à les porter jusqu'aux nues*," literally, carrying them up to the clouds, figuratively, " praising to the skies."

' Those are splendid occupations. But what do all these little rags and tatters signify, which make you look more like beggars than philosophers ? '

' Ah ! What a question you are asking me now,' he said sighing ; ' and what memories you recall to me ! This temple was once the temple of philosophy. Alas ! How it has changed. The living Socrates once walked in this place. . . .'

' What ! ' I said, interrupting him. ' Did Socrates have a pipe too, and did he blow bubbles ? '

' No, indeed no,' answered Plato. ' It was not for that, that he deserved of the Gods the name of the wisest of men ; it was in developing the brain and in moulding the heart that he occupied himself as long as he lived. The secret died with him. Socrates died, and the great days of philosophy were gone. These bits of cloth, which these makers of systems do themselves the honour of wearing, are fragments of his robe. His eyes were hardly closed when those who aspired to the title of philosopher flung themselves on his robe and tore it to shreds.'

' I understand,' I replied. ' And these fragments have served as passport for them and their posterity. . . .'

' Who will bring these fragments together once more,' continued Plato, ' and restore for us the robe of Socrates ?'

" He was just making this pathetic exclamation, when I saw in the distance a child walking towards us, slowly but surely. He had a small head and slender body ; his arms were frail and his legs short ; but all his limbs were growing and lengthening even as he came towards us. With each successive increase in size, he appeared to me to take on a hundred different forms ; I saw him turn a telescope towards the sky, and estimate with the aid of a pendulum the velocity of a falling body,[2] measure the weight of the atmosphere with the help of a tube full of mercury,[3] and, prism in hand, decompose light.[4] "

" He had become by then of colossal stature ; his head

touched the skies, his feet were lost in the abyss and his arms stretched from pole to pole. In his right hand he brandished a torch, whose light spread far through space, lighted the depths of waters, and penetrated into the bowels of the earth."

' Who is this giant coming towards us ? ' I asked Plato.

' Know that it is Experiment,' he answered ; ' his very self.'

" He had hardly answered, when I saw Experiment drawing very near, and the columns of the portico of Hypotheses trembling, its airy vaultings fading, and its pavement opening under our feet."

' We must fly,' said Plato ; ' this edifice can only last a few moments longer.' With these words he went ; I followed him. The colossus arrived, struck the portico, it collapsed with a terrible crash, and I woke up."

" Ah ! prince," said Mirzoza, " you do well to dream. I should have been very glad for you to have passed a good night ; but now that I know your dream, I should have been very sorry if you had not had it."

"Madame," said Mangogul to her, "I have known nights better employed than this one in dreaming ; and if I had been the master of my journey, there is every prospect that, not in the least hoping to find you in the Land of Hypotheses, I should have turned my footsteps in other directions. I should not have the headache at all which is afflicting me now ; or at least I should have something to console myself for it."

" Prince," answered Mirzoza, " we must hope that it will be nothing much, and that one or two experiments with your ring will relieve you of it."

" We must see," said Mangogul.

The conversation between the Sultan and Mirzoza lasted some moments longer ; and he did not leave her until nearly eleven o'clock, to do what we shall see in the next chapter.

(1748)

42

II

From

ON THE

INTERPRETATION

OF

NATURE

Quae sunt in luce tuemur
*E tenebris.**
Lucretius, *De Rerum Natura,* Book VI.

*   *   *   *   *

VII

So long as things are only in our understanding, they are
our opinions ; these are notions which can be true or false,
granted or denied. They take on consistency only by being
related to externally existing things. This connection is
made either by an uninterrupted chain of reasoning, which
is connected at one end with observation and at the other
with experiment ; or by a series of experiments dispersed
at intervals along the chain of reasoning, like weights along
a thread suspended by its two ends. Without these weights
the thread would be the sport of the slightest motion of the air.

VIII

One may compare ideas which have no foundation in
nature, to those forests of the North whose trees have no
roots. It needs only a breath of wind, only a small fact,
to overturn a whole forest of trees and of ideas.

IX

Men are disturbed to feel how severe are the laws of the
investigation of truth, and how limited is the number of

* Out of our darkness we see the things that are in the light.

43

our means. Everything is reduced to a return from the senses to reflection, and from reflection to the senses : to turn into oneself and to turn outwards again, ceaselessly; it is the labour of the bee. Much country has been covered in vain, if a load of wax is not brought back to the hive. A useless accumulation of wax has been made if it is not known how to make a comb of it.

X

But, unfortunately, it is easier and quicker to consult oneself than to consult nature. Also, reason is inclined to dwell within itself, and instinct to spread outward. Ceaselessly instinct goes, observing, tasting, touching, listening and there would be perhaps more experimental physics to be learnt by studying animals than by following a course of lectures by a professor. There is no deception in their behaviour. They proceed to their ends without caring about what surrounds them ; if they surprise us, it is not in the least their intention. Astonishment is the first effect of some great phenomenon : it is the task of philosophy to dissipate this. In a course of experimental philosophy, it is a question of sending the student away more enlightened and not more puzzled. To pride oneself about the phenomena of nature, as if one were the author of them oneself, is to imitate the stupidity of that editor of the *Essais*, who could not hear the name of Montaigne without blushing. A great lesson which there is often occasion to give, is the confession of one's insufficiency. Is it not better to gain the confidence of others by the sincerity of a " I know nothing about it," than to babble words and excite pity for oneself, by trying to explain everything ? He who freely admits that he does not know the things of which he is ignorant, disposes me to believe that what he undertakes to make me admit is correct.

XI

Astonishment often comes from supposing several marvels where there is only one ; from imagining in nature as many particular acts as there are phenomena, while perhaps it has ever produced but a single act. It seems, even, that if it had been under the necessity of producing several acts, the different results of these acts would have been isolated ; that there would have been collections of phenomena independent of one another, and that the general connection of things, of which philosophy supposes the continuity, would be broken at several places. The absolute independence of a single fact is incompatible with the idea of the whole ; and without the idea of the whole, no more philosophy.

*   *   *   *   *

XIV

I represent to myself the vast body of science as a large area strewn with dark places and with illuminated places. Our labours should have as their aim, either to extend the limits of the lighted places, or to multiply the number of centres of illumination. The latter is for the creative genius ; the other for the wisdom which improves, develops, amplifies.

XV

We have three principal means : the observation of nature, thought and experiment. Observation collects the facts, thought combines them, and experiment verifies the result of the combination. The observation of nature must be assiduous, the thinking must be profound and the experiment must be exact. One rarely sees these methods combined. And creative geniuses are not common.

*   *   *   *   *

XXIII

We have distinguished two kinds of philosophy, the experimental and that based on reasoning. The former has its eyes bandaged, walks always feeling its way, grasps whatever falls into its hands and finds precious things in the end. The other gathers these precious things, and tries to make a torch of them ; but this pretended torch has up to the present served it less well than the gropings of its rival, and this must be so. Experiment multiplies its actions infinitely, it is ceaselessly in action, it is busy seeking phenomena all the time that reasoning uses in seeking analogies. Experimental philosophy knows neither what will come nor will not come out of its labours; but it works on without relaxing. The philosophy based on reasoning, on the contrary, weighs possibilities, makes a pronouncement and stops short. It boldly said : " light cannot be decomposed " : experimental philosophy heard, and held its tongue in its presence for whole centuries ; then suddenly it produced the prism, and said, " light can be decomposed."

* * * * *

XLVIII

When following a wrong road, the faster one walks the more one goes astray. And how to retrace one's steps, when an immense distance has been covered ? Exhaustion does not allow it ; vanity opposes it without one's knowing it ; the stubbornness of principles spreads over everything a prestige which veils real objects. One no longer sees them as they are, but as it would be convenient that they might be. Instead of reshaping conceptions to existing things it seems that one makes a point of modelling existing things after conceptions. Among all philosophers, there is none in whom this fury is more evidently dominant than in the systematists. As soon as a systematist has put man at the head of the quadrupeds in his system, he no longer sees him in nature except as an animal with four feet. In vain the sublime reason with which he is endowed cries out against the denomination *animal*, and his structure contradicts that of *quadruped*; in vain has nature turned his looks towards the sky; the requirements of the system bow his body to earth. According to it, reason is only a more perfect instinct; it seriously believes that it is only by lack of habit that man loses the use of his legs, when it presumes to transform his hands into two feet.

XLIX

But this is a too peculiar thing in the dialectic of some systematists, not to give a sample of it.

Man, said Linnæus, is neither a mineral nor a plant; he is therefore an animal. He has not a single foot; therefore he is not a worm. He is not an insect since he has no *antennæ*. He has no fins, therefore he is not a fish. He is not a bird, since he has no feathers. What is man then? He was the mouth of a quadruped. He has four feet, the two in front to serve him for touching, the rear two, for walking. He is therefore a quadruped. "It is true," continues the systematist, "that as the result of my principles of natural history, I have never known how to distinguish man from ape; for there are some apes who have less hair than some men: these apes walk on two feet and use their hands and feet like men. Besides, speech is not a distinctive character for me; according to my method, I allow only distinctions which depend on number, shape, proportion and situation." Therefore your method is bad, says logic. "Therefore man is an animal with four feet," says the naturalist.

*　　*　　*　　*　　*

LVIII

Questions

Just as in the animal and vegetable kingdoms, an individual begins, so to speak, grows, subsists, decays and passes away, could it not be the same with whole species ? If faith did not teach us that the animals came from the Creator's hand as we see them now ; and if it were permitted to have any doubt about their beginning and their end, would not the philosopher, left free to speculate, suspect that animality had from all eternity its particular elements scattered in and mingled with the mass of matter ; that it has happened to these elements to reunite, because it was possible for this to be done ; that the embryo formed from these elements had passed through an infinity of different organizations and developments ; that it had had in succession, motion, sensitiveness, ideas, thought, reflection, consciousness, feelings, passions, signs, gestures, sounds, articulated sounds, a language, laws, science and arts ; that millions of years had passed between each of these developments ; that it has perhaps still other developments to undergo, and other increases to take on, which are unknown to us ; that it has had or will have a stationary condition ; that it changes or will change itself from this condition by an eternal decay, during which its faculties will go from it even as they had entered it ; that it will disappear for ever from nature, or rather it will continue to exist in it, but in a form, and with faculties, quite different from those observed in it at this moment of time. Religion spares us many errors and much labour. If it had not enlightened us on the origin of the world and on the universal system of beings, how many different hypotheses should we not have been tempted to take for the secret of nature ? These hypotheses being all equally false, they would have appeared to us almost all equally probable.[1] . . .

(1754.) *Œuvres Complètes.* Vol. II, pp. 9–62.

III

CONVERSATION
BETWEEN
D'ALEMBERT AND DIDEROT[1]

d'Alembert : I confess that a Being[2] who exists somewhere and yet corresponds to no point in space, a Being who, lacking extension, yet occupies space ; who is present in his entirety in every part of that space, who is essentially different from matter and yet is one with matter, who follows its motion, and moves it, without himself being in motion, who acts on matter and yet is subject to all its vicissitudes, a Being about whom I can form no idea ; a Being of so contradictory a nature, is an hypothesis difficult to accept. But other problems arise if we reject it ; for if this faculty of sensation,[3] which you propose as substitute, is a general and essential quality of matter, then stone must be sensitive.

Diderot : Why not ?

d'Alembert : It's hard to believe.

Diderot : Yes, for him who cuts, chisels, and crushes it, and does not hear it cry out.

d'Alembert : I'd like you to tell me what difference there is, according to you, between a man and a statue, between marble and flesh.

Diderot : Not much. Flesh can be made from marble, and marble from flesh.

d'Alembert : But one is not the other.

Diderot : In the same way that what you call animate force is not the same as inanimate force.[4]

d'Alembert : I don't follow you.

Diderot : I'll explain. The transference of a body from one place to another is not itself motion, it is the

49

consequence of motion. Motion exists equally in the body displaced and in the body that remains stationary.

d'Alembert : That's a new way of looking at things.

Diderot : True none the less. Take away the obstacle that prevents the displacement of a stationary body, and it will be transferred. Suddenly rarefy the air that surrounds the trunk of this huge oak, and the water contained in it, suddenly expanding, will burst it into a hundred thousand fragments. I say the same of your own body.

d'Alembert : That may be so. But what relation is there between motion and the faculty of sensation ? Do you, by any chance, distinguish between an active and an inactive sensitiveness, as between animate and inanimate force ? An animate force which is revealed by displacement, an inanimate force which manifests itself by pressure ; an active sensitiveness which would be characterized by a certain recognizable behaviour in the animal and perhaps in the plant, while your inactive sensitiveness only makes itself known when it changes over to the active state ?

Diderot : Precisely ; just as you say.

d'Alembert : So, then, the statue merely has inactive sensitiveness ; and man, animals, perhaps even plants, are endowed with active sensitiveness.

Diderot : There is undoubtedly that difference between the marble block and living tissue ; but you can well imagine that's not the only one.

d'Alembert : Of course. Whatever likeness there may be in outward form between a man and a statue, there is no similarity in their internal organization. The chisel of the cleverest sculptor cannot make even an epidermis. But there is a very simple way of transforming an inanimate force into an animate one—the experiment is repeated a hundred times a day before our eyes ; whereas I don't quite see how a body can be made to pass from the state of inactive to that of active sensitiveness.

Diderot: Because you don't want to see it. It is just as common a phenomenon.

d'Alembert: And what is this common phenomenon, if you please?

Diderot: I'll tell you, since you want to be put to shame; it occurs every time you eat.

d'Alembert: Every time I eat!

Diderot: Yes, for what do you do when you eat? You remove obstacles that prevented the food from possessing active sensitiveness. You assimilate it, you turn it into flesh, you make it animal, you give it the faculty of sensation; and, what you do to this foodstuff, I can do, when I please, to marble.

d'Alembert: And how?

Diderot: How? I shall make it edible.

d'Alembert: Make marble edible? That doesn't seem easy to me.

Diderot: It's my business to show you the process. I take the statue you see there, I put it in a mortar, then with great blows from a pestle . . .

d'Alembert: Careful, please; that's Falconet's masterpiece! If it were only by Huez or some one like that. . . .[5]

Diderot: Falconet won't mind; the statue is paid for, and Falconet cares little for present respect and not at all for that of posterity.

d'Alembert: Go on then, crush it to powder.

Diderot: When the block of marble is reduced to impalpable powder, I mix it with humus or leaf-mould; I knead them well together; I water the mixture, I let it decompose for a year or two or a hundred, time doesn't matter to me. When the whole has turned into a more or less homogeneous substance, into humus, do you know what I do?

d'Alembert: I'm sure you don't eat humus.

Diderot: No; but there is a means of connection, of assimilation, a link, between the humus and myself, a *latus* as the chemist would say.

d'Alembert : And that is plant life ?

Diderot : Quite right, I sow peas, beans, cabbages, and other vegetables ; these plants feed on the soil and I feed on the plants.[6]

d'Alembert : Whether it's true or false, I like this passage from marble into humus, from humus to the vegetable kingdom, from the vegetable to the animal kingdom, to flesh.

Diderot : So, then, I make flesh, or soul as my daughter said, an actively sensitive substance ;[7] and if I do not thus solve the problem you set me, at any rate I get pretty near solving it ; for you will admit that a piece of marble is much further removed from a being that can feel, than a being that can feel is from a being that can think.

d'Alembert : I agree. But nevertheless the feeling being is not yet the thinking being.

Diderot : Before going one step further let me tell you the history of one of the greatest geometricians in Europe. What was this wonderful creature to begin with ? Nothing.

d'Alembert : What, nothing ? Nothing comes from nothing.

Diderot : You take my words too literally. I mean to say that, before his mother, the beautiful and wicked Madame de Tencin, had reached the age of puberty, and before the adolescence of the soldier La Touche, the molecules which were to form the first rudiments of our geometrician were scattered throughout the frail young bodies of these two, filtering through with the lymph, circulating with the blood, till at last they reached the vessels whence they were destined to unite, the germ cells of his father and mother. The precious germ, then, is formed ; now according to the common belief, it is brought through the Fallopian tubes to the womb, it is attached to the womb by a long cord ; it grows gradually and develops into a foetus ; now comes the moment for it to leave the dark prison ; it is born, abandoned on the steps of Saint-Jean-le-Rond, whence it receives its name ; now, taken from the foundlings' home, it is put to the breast of good Madame Rousseau, the glazier's wife ; it is given suck, it grows in body and mind, becomes a man of letters, an engineer, a geometrician.[8] How was all this done ? Just through eating and other purely mechanical operations. Here, in four words you have the general formula : Eat, digest, distil *in vasi licito, et fiat homo secundum artem.** And to expound before the Academy the process of the formation of a man or an animal, one need employ only material agents, the successive results of which would be an inert being, a feeling being, a thinking being, a being solving the problem of the precession of the equinoxes, a sublime being, a marvellous being, a being growing old, fading away, dying, dissolved and given back to the soil.

d'Alembert : You don't believe, then, in pre-existent germs ?

Diderot : No.

d'Alembert : Ah, how glad I am of that !

Diderot : Such a theory is against reason and experiment ; against experiment, since you would seek in vain for these germs in the egg or in most animals before a certain age ; against reason, since, although the mind may conceive of matter as infinitely divisible, it is not so in nature, and it is unreasonable to imagine an elephant wholly formed within an atom, and within that elephant another wholly formed, and so on to infinity.

d'Alembert : But without these pre-existent germs, how can we account for the first generation of animals ?

Diderot : If you're worried by the question " which came first, the hen or the egg ",[9] it's because you suppose that animals were originally the same as they are now. What madness ! We can no more tell what they were originally than what they will become. The tiny worm, wriggling in the mud, may be in process of developing into a large

* . . . . . into the appropriate vessels and in this way let man be made.

53

animal ; the huge animal, that terrifies us by its size, is perhaps on the way to becoming a worm, is perhaps a particular and transient production of this planet.[10]

d'Alembert : What's that you are saying ?

Diderot : I was saying to you . . . But it'll take us away from our original discussion.

d'Alembert : What does that matter ? We can get back to it or not, as we please.

Diderot : Will you allow me to skip ahead a few million years in time ?

d'Alembert : Why not ? Time is nothing for nature.

Diderot : Will you consent to my extinguishing our sun ?

d'Alembert : The more readily, since it will not be the first to have gone out.

Diderot : Once the sun has been extinguished what will be the result ? Plants will perish, animals will perish, the earth will become desolate and silent. Light up that star once more, and you immediately restore the necessary cause whereby an infinite number of new species will be generated, among which I cannot swear whether, in the course of centuries, the plants and animals we know to-day will or will not be reproduced.

d'Alembert : And why should the same scattered elements coming together again not give the same results ?

Diderot : Because everything is connected in nature, and if you imagine a new phenomenon or bring back a moment of the past, you are creating a new world.[11]

d'Alembert : Anyone who thinks deeply cannot deny that. But, to come back to man, since the general order of things required his existence ; remember, you left me where the feeling being is about to become the thinking being.

Diderot : I remember.

d'Alembert : Frankly, I'd be very grateful if you would get me over that transition ; I'm eager to begin thinking.

Diderot : Even if I should not accomplish it, what effect could that have against a sequence of incontrovertible facts?

d'Alembert : None, unless we stopped short there.

Diderot : And in order to go further, would it be permissible for us to invent an agent whose attributes should be self-contradictory, a meaningless and unintelligible word ?

d'Alembert : No.

Diderot : Can you tell me what constitutes the existence of a perceiving being, for that being itself ?

d'Alembert : The consciousness of continued identity from the first moment of reflection to the present.

Diderot : And on what is this consciousness based ?

d'Alembert : On the memory of its actions.

Diderot : And without this memory ?

d'Alembert : Without this memory it would have no identity, since, realizing its existence only at the instant of receiving an impression, it would have no life-story. Its life would be an interrupted series of sensations with nothing to connect them.

Diderot : Very good. And what is this memory ? Whence does it spring ?

d'Alembert : From a certain organization, which develops, grows weaker, and is sometimes lost entirely.

Diderot : Then, if a being that can feel, and that possesses this organization that gives rise to memory, connects up the impressions it receives, forms through this connection a story which is that of its life, and so acquires consciousness of its identity, it can then deny, affirm, conclude and think.

d'Alembert : So it appears to me ; there is only one more difficulty.

Diderot : You are wrong ; there are many more.

d'Alembert : But one chief one ; that is, it seems to me that we can only think of one thing at a time, and that to form even a simple proposition, let alone those vast chains of reasoning that embrace in their course thousands of ideas, one would need to have at least two things present—the object, which seems to remain in the mind's eye while

55

that mind considers the quality which it is to attribute or to deny to that object.

Diderot : I think that is so ; that has made me sometimes compare the fibres of our organs to sensitive vibrating strings which vibrate and resound long after they have been plucked. It is this vibration, this kind of inevitable resonance, which holds the object present, while the mind is busied about the quality that belongs to that object. But vibrating strings have yet another property, that of making other strings vibrate ; and that is how the first idea recalls a second, the two of them a third, these three a fourth and so on, so that there is no limit to the ideas awakened and interconnected in the mind of the philosopher, as he meditates and hearkens to himself amid silence and darkness. This instrument makes surprising leaps, and an idea once aroused may sometimes set vibrating an harmonic at an inconceivable distance. If this phenomenon may be observed between resonant strings that are lifeless and separate, why should it not occur between points that are alive and connected, between fibres that are continuous and sensitive ?

d'Alembert : Even if it's not true, that is at least very ingenious. But I am inclined to think that you are, without realizing it, slipping into a difficulty that you wished to avoid.

Diderot : What is that ?

d'Alembert : You are opposed to making a distinction between the two substances.[12]

Diderot : I don't deny it.

d'Alembert : And if you look closer, you'll see that you are making of the philosopher's mind a being distinct from the instrument, a musician, as it were, who listens to the vibrating strings and decides as to their harmony or dissonance.

Diderot : I may have laid myself open to this objection, but you might not have made it if you had considered the difference between the instrument philosopher and the instrument harpsichord.[13] The philosopher is an instrument that has the faculty of sensation ; he is, at the same time, both the musician and the instrument. As he can feel, he is immediately conscious of the sound he gives forth ; as he is an animal, he retains the memory of it. This faculty of the organism, connecting up the sounds within him, produces and preserves the melody there. Just suppose that your harpsichord has the power to feel and to remember, and tell me if it will not know and repeat of its own accord the airs that you have played on its keys. We are instruments endowed with feeling and memory ; our senses are so many keys that are struck by surrounding nature, and that often strike themselves. This is all, in my opinion, that happens in a harpsichord which is organized like you or me. An impression is created by some cause either within or outside the instrument, a sensation is aroused by this impression, a sensation that persists, since you cannot imagine it arising and dying instantaneously ; another impression follows, which equally has its cause either within or outside the animal, a second sensation, and voices to indicate them by natural or conventional sounds.

d'Alembert : I understand. So then, if this harpsichord were not only sensitive and animate but were further endowed with the faculty of feeding and reproducing itself, it would live and breed of itself, or with its female, little harpsichords, also living and vibrating.

Diderot : Undoubtedly. In your opinion, what, other than this, is a chaffinch, a nightingale, a musician or a man ? And what other difference do you find between a bird and a bird-organ ?* Do you see this egg ? With this you can overthrow all the schools of theology, all the churches of the earth. What is this egg ? An unperceiving mass, before the germ is introduced into it ; and after the germ is

* Mechanical musical-box to teach a canary tunes.

57

introduced, what is it then ? still only an unperceiving mass, for this germ itself is only a crude inert fluid. How will this mass develop into a different organization, to sensitiveness, to life ? By means of heat. And what will produce the heat ? Motion. What will be the successive effects of this motion ? Instead of answering me, sit down and let's watch them from moment to moment. First there's a dot that quivers, a little thread that grows longer and takes on colour ; tissue is formed ; a beak, tiny wings, eyes, feet appear ; a yellowish material unwinds and produces intestines ; it is an animal. This animal moves, struggles, cries out ; I hear its cries through the shell ; it becomes covered with down ; it sees. The weight of its head, shaking about, brings its beak constantly up against the inner wall of its prison ; now the wall is broken ; it comes out, it walks about, flies, grows angry, runs away, comes near again, complains, suffers, loves, desires, enjoys ; it has the same affections as yourself, it performs the same actions. Are you going to assert with Descartes that it is a purely imitative machine ?[14] Little children will laugh at you, and philosophers will retort that if this be a machine then you, too, are a machine. If you admit that between the animal and yourself the difference is merely one of organization, you will be showing good sense and reason, you will be honest ; but from this there will be drawn the conclusion that refutes you ; namely that, from inert matter, organized in a certain way, and impregnated with other inert matter, and given heat and motion, there results the faculty of sensation, life, memory, consciousness, passion and thought. You have only two courses left to take : either to imagine within the inert mass of the egg a hidden element that awaited the egg's development before revealing its presence, or to assume that this invisible element crept in through the shell at a definite moment in the development. But what is this element ? Did it occupy space or did it not ? How did it come, or did it escape without moving ? What was it doing there or elsewhere? Was it created at the instant it was needed? Was it already in existence? Was it waiting for a home? If it was homogeneous it was material; if heterogeneous, one cannot account for its previous inertia nor its activity in the developed animal. Just listen to yourself, and you will be sorry for yourself; you will perceive that, in order to avoid making a simple supposition that explains everything, namely the faculty of sensation as a general property of matter or a product of its organization, you are giving up common sense and plunging headlong into an abyss of mysteries, contradictions and absurdities.[15]

d'Alembert : A supposition! It pleases you to say so. But suppose this quality is in its essence incompatible with matter?

Diderot : And how do you know that the faculty of sensation is essentially incompatible with matter, you who do not know the essence of anything, either of matter or of sensation? Do you understand the nature of motion any better, how it comes to exist in a body, and its transmission from one to another?

d'Alembert : Without understanding the nature of sensation or that of matter, I can see that the faculty of sensation is a simple quality, entire, indivisible, and incompatible with a subject or substratum which is divisible.

Diderot : Metaphysico-theological nonsense! What! don't you see that all the qualities, all the forms by which nature becomes perceptible to our senses, are essentially indivisible? You cannot have more or less impenetrability. There is half a round body, but there is not a half of roundness; you can have motion to a greater or less degree, but either there is motion or there is not. You cannot have half, or a third, or a quarter of a head, an ear, a finger, any more than half, a third, or a quarter of a thought. If in the universe no one particle is like another, in a particle no one point like another, acknowledge that the atom itself possesses an indivisible quality or form ; acknowledge that division is incompatible with the essence of forms, since it destroys them. Be a physicist, and acknowledge the produced character of an effect when you see it produced, even if you cannot explain all the steps that led from the cause to the effect. Be logical, and do not substitute for a cause which exists and which explains everything, another cause which cannot be comprehended, whose connection with the effect is even more difficult to grasp, which engenders an infinite number of difficulties and solves not one of them.

d' Alembert : But what if I give up this cause ?[16]

Diderot : There is only one substance in the universe, in man and in the animal. The bird-organ is made of wood, man of flesh. The bird is of flesh, the musician of flesh differently organized ; but both of them have the same origin, the same formation, the same functions and the same end.

d' Alembert : And how is the convention of sounds established between your two harpsichords ?

Diderot : Since an animal is a perceiving instrument, resembling any other in all respects, having the same structure, being strung with the same chords, stimulated in the same way by joy, pain, hunger, thirst, colic, wonder, terror, it is impossible that at the Pole and at the Equator it should utter different sounds. And so you will find that interjections are about the same in all languages, living and dead. The origin of conventional sounds must be ascribed to need and to proximity. The instrument endowed with the faculty of sensation, or the animal, has discovered by experience that when it uttered a certain sound a certain result followed outside it, feeling instruments like itself or other animals drew nearer, went away, asked or offered things, hurt or caressed it. All these consequences became connected in its memory and in that of others with the utterance of these sounds ; and note that human intercourse consists only of sounds and actions. And, to appreciate the power of my system, notice further that it is subject to the same insurmountable difficulty that Berkeley[17] brought against the existence of bodies. There came a moment of madness when the feeling harpsichord thought that it was the only harpsichord in the world, and that the whole harmony of the universe resided in it.

d'Alembert : There's a lot to be said on all that.

Diderot : True.

d'Alembert : For instance, your system doesn't make it clear how we form syllogisms or draw inferences.

Diderot : We don't draw them ; they are all drawn by nature.[18] We only state the existence of connected phenomena, which are known to us practically, by experience, whose existence may be either necessary or contingent ; necessary in the case of mathematics, physics, and other exact sciences ; contingent in ethics, politics and other conjectural sciences.[19]

d'Alembert : Is the connection between phenomena less necessary in one case than in another ?

Diderot : No, but the cause undergoes too many particular vicissitudes which escape our observation, for us to be able to count with certainty upon the result that will ensue. Our certainty that a violent-tempered man will grow angry at an insult is not the same as our certainty that one body striking a smaller body will set it in motion.

d'Alembert : What about analogy ?

Diderot : Analogy, in the most complex cases, is only a rule of three working out in the feeling instrument. If a familiar natural phenomenon is followed by another familiar natural phenomenon, what will be the fourth phenomenon that will follow a third, either provided by nature or imagined in imitation of nature ? If the lance of an ordinary warrior is ten feet long, how long will the lance of Ajax be ? If I can throw a stone weighing four pounds, Diomedes must be able to shift a large block of rock. The strides of gods and the leaps of their horses will correspond to the imagined proportion between gods and men. You have here a fourth chord in harmony with and proportional to three others ; and the animal awaits its resonance, which always occurs within itself, though not always in nature. The poet doesn't mind about that, it doesn't affect his kind of truth. But it is otherwise with the philosopher ; he must proceed to examine nature[20] which often shows him a phenomenon quite different from what he had supposed, and then he perceives that he had been seduced by an analogy.[21]

d'Alembert : Farewell, my friend, good evening and good night to you.

Diderot : You're joking : but you will dream on your pillow about this conversation, and if it doesn't take on substance there, so much the worse for you ; for you will be obliged to adopt far more absurd hypotheses.

d'Alembert : You're wrong there ; I shall go to bed a sceptic, and a sceptic I shall arise.

Diderot : Sceptic ! Is there such a thing as a sceptic ?

d'Alembert : That's a good one ! Are you going to tell me, now, that I'm no sceptic ? Who should know about that better than I ?

Diderot : Wait a moment.

d'Alembert : Hurry up, for I'm anxious to get to sleep.

Diderot : I'll be brief. Do you believe there is a single debated question, on which a man can halt with a strictly equal measure of reason *for* and *against* ?

d'Alembert : No, that would be like Buridan's ass.[22]

Diderot : In that case, there's no such being as the sceptic, since, apart from mathematical questions which admit of no uncertainty, there is for and against in all questions. The scales, then, are never even, and it is impossible that they should not hang more heavily on the side that seems to us to have most probability.

d'Alembert : But probability appears to me on the right hand in the morning, on the left in the afternoon.

Diderot : That is to say, you are dogmatic *for* in the morning and dogmatic *against* in the afternoon.

d'Alembert : And in the evening, when I recall this rapid change in my judgments, I believe neither the morning's nor the afternoon's.

Diderot : That is to say, you don't remember which preponderated of the two opinions between which you wavered ; that this preponderance appears to you too slight to settle your feelings definitely, and that you decide to cease worrying over such problematic subjects, to leave the discussion of them to others and to contest them no further.

d'Alembert : That may be so.

Diderot : But if someone drew you aside, and asked you in a friendly way to tell him honestly, which of the two alternatives seemed to you to present fewer difficulties, would you really be at a loss to answer, and would you realize Buridan's ass in your own person ?

d'Alembert : I think not.

Diderot : Come, my friend, if you think over it well, you will find that, in everything, our true feeling is not that about which we have never vacillated, but that to which we have most constantly returned.

d'Alembert : I believe you're right.

Diderot : And so do I. Good night, my friend, and remember that " dust thou art, to dust thou shalt return."

d'Alembert : That is sad.

Diderot : And yet necessary. Grant man, I don't say immortality, but merely a double span of life, and you'll see what will happen.

d'Alembert : And what do you expect to happen ? . . . But what do I care ? Let happen what may. I want to sleep, so good night to you.

D'ALEMBERT'S DREAM [1]

The Speakers : *d'Alembert, Mademoiselle de l'Espinasse and Doctor Bordeu.*

Bordeu : Well ! What's been happening now ? Is he ill ?

Mlle. de l'Espinasse : I'm afraid. so ; he had the most restless night.

Bordeu : Is he awake ?

Mlle. de l'Espinasse : Not yet.

Bordeu (after going up to d'Alembert's bed and feeling his pulse and his skin) : It'll be nothing.

Mlle. de l'Espinasse : You think so ?

Bordeu : I'm sure of it. His pulse is good . . . somewhat weak . . . his skin moist . . . his breathing easy.

Mlle. de l'Espinasse : Is there anything to be done for him ?

Bordeu : Nothing.

Mlle. de l'Espinasse : So much the better, for he hates medicines.

Bordeu : And so do I. What did he eat for supper ?

Mlle. de l'Espinasse : He wouldn't take anything. I don't know where he had been spending the evening, but he seemed worried when he came back.

Bordeu : Just a slight touch of fever that won't have any ill effects.

Mlle. de l'Espinasse : When he got home, he put on his dressing-gown and nightcap and flung himself into his arm-chair, where he dozed.

Bordeu : Sleep is good anywhere, but he would have been better in bed.

Mlle. de l'Espinasse : He was angry with Antoine for telling him so ; he had to be worried for half an hour to get him to bed.

Bordeu : That happens to me every day, although I'm in good health.

Mlle. de l'Espinasse : When he was in bed, instead of resting as usual, for he sleeps like a child, he began to toss and turn, to stretch out his arms, throw off his covers and talk aloud.

Bordeu : And what was he talking about ? Geometry ?

Mlle de l'Espinasse : No ; it really sounded like delirium. To begin with, a lot of nonsense about vibrating strings and sensitive fibres. It seemed so crazy to me that I resolved not to leave him alone all night, and not knowing what else to do I drew up a little table to the foot of his bed, and began to write down all I could make out of his ramblings.

Bordeu : A good notion, and typical of you. Can I have a look at it ?

Mlle de l'Espinasse : Surely ; but I'll stake my life you won't understand a thing.

Bordeu : Perhaps I may.

Mlle. de l'Espinasse : Are you ready, Doctor ?

Bordeu : Yes.

Mlle. de l'Espinasse : Listen. " A living point. . . . No, I'm wrong. First nothing, then a living point. . . . To this living point is applied another, and yet another ; and the result of these successive increments is a being that has unity, for I cannot doubt my own unity. . . ." As he said this, he felt himself all over. " But how did this unity come to be ? " Oh, my friend, I said to him, what does that matter to you ? Go to sleep. . . . He was silent for a moment, but began again as if speaking to someone : " I tell you, philosopher, I can understand an aggregate or tissue of tiny sensitive beings, but not an animal ! . . . a whole ! a system, an individual, having consciousness of its unity ! I can't accept that, no, I can't accept it. . . ." Doctor, can you make anything of it ?

Bordeu : A great deal.

Mlle. de l'Espinasse : Well, you're lucky. . . . " Perhaps my difficulty comes from a mistaken idea."

Bordeu : Are you speaking yourself ?

Mlle. de l'Espinasse : No, that's the dreamer. I'll go on.
. . . He added, apostrophizing himself : " Take care,
friend d'Alembert, you are assuming only contiguity where
there exists continuity . . . yes, he's clever enough to tell
me that. . . . And how is this continuity formed ? That
won't offer any difficulty to him. . . . As one drop of
mercury coalesces with another drop of mercury, so one
living and sensitive particle coalesces with another living
and sensitive particle. . . .[2] First there were two drops,
after the contact there is only one. . . . Before assimilation
there were two particles, afterwards there was only one . . .
sensitiveness becomes a common property of the common
mass. . . . And indeed why not ? I may imagine the
animal fibre divided up into as many sections as I please,
but that fibre will be continuous, will be a whole, yes, a
whole. . . . Continuity arises from the contact of two
perfectly homogeneous particles ; and this constitutes the
most complete union, cohesion, combination, identity that
can be imagined . . . yes, philosopher, if these particles
are elementary and simple ; but what if they are aggregates,
what if they are compound ? . . . They will combine none
the less, and in consequence become united, continuous . . .
And then there is continual action and reaction. . . . It is
certain that contact between two living particles is quite
different from contiguity between two inert masses. . . .
Let that pass ; it might be possible to start a quarrel with
you on that point ; but I don't care to do so, I don't like
carping. . . . Let's go back to where we were. A thread
of purest gold, I remember, was one comparison he used ;
a homogeneous network between the particles of which
others thrust themselves and form, it may be, another
unified network, a tissue of sensitive matter ; contact
involving assimilation ; sensitiveness, active in one case,
inert in another, which is communicated like motion, not
to mention that, as he very well put it, there must be a
difference between the contact of two sensitive particles

and the contact of two that are not sensitive ; and wherein
can that difference lie ? . . . a continual action and reaction
. . . and this action and reaction having a particular
character. . . . Everything then, concurs to produce a sort
of unity which exists only in the animal. . . . Well ! if
that's not truth it's very like it. . . ."[3] Doctor, you're
laughing ; can you see any sense in this ?

Bordeu : A great deal.

Mlle. de l'Espinasse : Then he's not mad ?

Bordeu : By no means.

Mlle. de l'Espinasse : After this preamble he began to cry :
" Mademoiselle de l'Espinasse ! Mademoiselle de l'Espinasse ! " " What do you want ? " " Have you sometimes
seen a swarm of bees escaping from their hive ? . . . The
world, or the general mass of matter, is the hive. . . .
Have you seen them go and form, at the end of the branch
of a tree, a long cluster of little winged animals, all clinging
to one another by their feet ? . . . This cluster is a being,
an individual, an animal of sorts. . . . But such clusters
should all be alike. Yes, if he accepted only a single
homogeneous matter. . . . Have you seen them ? " " Yes,
I've seen them." " You've seen them ? " " Yes, my friend,
I tell you, yes." " If one of these bees should take a fancy
to nip, in some way, the next bee it's attached to, what do
you think will happen ? Tell me." " I don't know." " Go
on, tell me. . . . You don't know then, but the philosopher
knows well enough. If you ever see him—and you may or
may not see him, for he promised me—he will tell you
that this bee will nip the next ; that, throughout the
cluster, there will be aroused as many sensations as there
are little animals ; that the whole will be disturbed, will
stir, will change its position and its shape ; that a noise
will arise, little cries, and that anyone who had never seen
a similar cluster in formation would be inclined to take it
for an animal with five or six hundred heads and a thousand
or twelve hundred wings. . . ." Well, Doctor ?

Bordeu : Well, do you know, that's a very fine dream, and you were quite right to take it down.

Mlle. de l'Espinasse : Are you dreaming too ?

Bordeu : So far from it, that I'd almost undertake to tell you how it goes on.

Mlle. de l'Espinasse : I defy you to.

Bordeu : You defy me ?

Mlle. de l'Espinasse : Yes.

Bordeu : And if I get it right ?

Mlle. de l'Espinasse : If you get it right I promise . . . I promise . . . to take you for the greatest madman on earth.

Bordeu : Look at your paper and listen to me. " A man who took this cluster to be an animal would be wrong." But, Mademoiselle, I presume he went on addressing you. " Would you like him to judge more sanely ? Would you like to transform the cluster of bees into one single animal ? Modify a little the feet by which they cling together ; make them continuous instead of contiguous. Between this new condition of the cluster and the former, there is certainly a marked difference ; and what can that difference be, if not that now it is a whole, a single animal, whereas before it was a collection of animals ? . . . All our organs. . . ."

Mlle. de l'Espinasse : All our organs !

Bordeu : To one who has practised medicine and made a few observations . . .

Mlle. de l'Espinasse : Next ?

Bordeu : Next ? . . . " Are just separate animals held together by the law of continuity in a general sympathy, unity and identity."

Mlle. de l'Espinasse : I'm dumbfounded ! You've got it almost word for word. Now I can proclaim to all the world that there's no difference between a waking doctor and a dreaming philosopher.

Bordeu : That was already suspected. Is that the whole of it ?

Mlle. de l'Espinasse : Oh no, not nearly. After your, or his, ravings, he said : " Mademoiselle ? " " Yes, my friend ? " " Come here . . . nearer, nearer. . . . I want you to do something." "What is it ? " " Take this cluster, here it is, you're sure it's there ? now, let's make an experiment." " What experiment ? " " Take your scissors : do they cut well ? " " Perfectly. " " Go up gently, very gently, and separate these bees, but be careful not to divide them through the middle of the body ; cut just where they're joined on to one another by the feet. Don't be afraid. You may hurt them a little, but you won't kill them. . . . Very good, you're as skilful as a fairy. . . . Do you see how they fly apart on every side ? They fly one by one, in twos, in threes. What a lot of them there are ! If you've understood me . . . you're sure you've understood me ? " " Quite sure." " Now suppose . . . suppose . . ." On my word, Doctor, I understood so little of what I was writing, he was speaking so softly, this part of my paper is so much scribbled over, that I can't read it.

Bordeu : I'll fill in the gaps, if you like.

Mlle. de l'Espinasse : If you can.

Bordeu : Nothing easier. " Suppose these bees to be so tiny, that their organisms always escaped the coarse blade of your scissors : you could go on dividing as much as you pleased, without killing one of them, and this whole, composed of imperceptible bees, would really be a polypus that you could destroy only by crushing. The difference between the cluster of continuous bees and the cluster of contiguous bees is precisely that existing between ordinary animals like ourselves or the fishes on the one hand and worms, serpents and polypous animals ; moreover the whole of this theory undergoes further modifications." . . . (*Here Mlle. de l'Espinasse gets up suddenly and pulls the bell-cord.*) Gently, gently Mademoiselle, you will wake him, and he needs rest.

Mlle. de l'Espinasse : I'm so bewildered I never thought of

69

that. (*To the servant who enters*) Which of you went to the doctor's ?

Servant : I did, Mademoiselle.

Mlle. de l'Espinasse : How long ago ?

Servant : I've not been back an hour.

Mlle. de l'Espinasse : Did you take anything there ?

Servant : Nothing.

Mlle. de l'Espinasse : No paper ?

Servant : None.

Mlle. de l'Espinasse : All right, you may go . . . I can't get over it ! Look here, Doctor, I suspected one of them of letting you see my scribble.

Bordeu : I assure you that's not so.

Mlle. de l'Espinasse : Now that I've discovered your gift, you'll be a great help to me socially. His dream talk didn't end there.

Bordeu : All the better.

Mlle. de l'Espinasse : You see nothing to worry about in that ?

Bordeu : Nothing at all.

Mlle. de l'Espinasse : He went on . . . " Well, then, philosopher, do you imagine polypi of every sort, even human polypi ? . . . But nature shows us none."

Bordeu : He did not know of the two girls who were joined together by their heads, shoulders, backs, buttocks and thighs, who lived thus joined together to the age of twenty-two, and died within a few minutes of each other. Then what did he say ? . . .

Mlle. de l'Espinasse : The sort of things you hear only in a madhouse. He said : " It has happened or else it will happen. And who knows the state of things on other planets ? "

Bordeu : Perhaps there's no need to go so far.

Mlle. de l'Espinasse : " On Jupiter or on Saturn, human polypi ! Males splitting up into males, females into females, it's an amusing notion. . . ." Thereupon he burst into fits of laughter that were quite terrifying. "Man splitting up into an infinite number of atomic men, that can be wrapped between sheets of paper like insects' eggs, that spin their cocoons, remain as chrysalides for a certain time, then break through their cocoons and escape like butterflies, a society of men formed and a whole province peopled out of the fragments of a single man, it's quite delightful to imagine. . . ." And then he burst out laughing again. "If, somewhere or other, man splits up into an infinite number of human animalcules, death must be less dreaded ; the loss of a man is so easily repaired that it ought to cause very little grief."

Bordeu : This extravagant hypothesis is almost the true story of all the species of animals which exist now and which are to come. If man does not split up into an infinite number of men, at any rate he splits up into an infinite number of animalcules, whose metamorphoses and whose future and final organization cannot be foreseen. Who knows if this is not the nursery of a second generation of beings, separated from this generation by an inconceivable interval of centuries and successive developments ?

Mlle. de l'Espinasse : What are you muttering away there, Doctor ?

Bordeu : Nothing, nothing, I was just dreaming on my own account. Go on reading, Mademoiselle.

Mlle. de l'Espinasse : " Everything considered, however, I prefer our way of renewing the population," he added. . . . " Philosopher, you who know what happens here, there and everywhere, tell me, doesn't the dissolution of different parts produce men of different characters ? The brain, the heart, the chest, the feet, the hands, the testicles. . . . Oh ! how this simplifies morality ! . . . A man born, a woman brought forth." . . . Doctor, you'll allow me to pass over this . . . " A warm chamber, lined with little packets, on each packet a label : *warriors, magistrates, philo-*

71

sophers, poets, packet of *courtiers,* packet of *whores,* packet of *kings.*"

Bordeu : This is very merry and very mad. This is a dream indeed, and a vision that calls up certain strange phenomena to my mind.

Mlle. de l'Espinasse : Then he began to mutter something or other about grains, strips of flesh put to macerate in water, different and successive races of creatures that he beheld being born and passing away. With his right hand he had imitated the tube of a microscope, and with his left, I think, the mouth of a vessel. He was looking into this vessel through the tube and saying : " Voltaire can make fun of it as much as he likes, but the ' Eel-man '[4] is right ; I believe my eyes ; I can see them ; what a lot there are! how they come and go, how they wriggle ! " The vessel in which he perceived so many short-lived generations, he compared to the Universe : he saw the history of the world in a drop of water. This idea seemed a tremendous one to him ; it appeared to fit in perfectly with sound philosophy, which studies great bodies in little ones. He said : " In Needham's[4] drop of water, everything occurs and passes away in the twinkling of an eye. In the world, the same phenomenon lasts a little longer ; but what is our duration compared with the eternity of time ? Less than the drop I have taken up on the point of a needle compared with the limitless space that surrounds me. An unbounded series of animalcules in the fermenting atom, the same unbounded series of animalcules in this other atom[5] that is called the Earth. Who knows what races of animals have preceded us ? Who know what races of animals will come after ours ? Everything changes and everything passes away, only the whole endures. The world is for ever beginning and ending ; each instant is its first and its last ; it never has had, it never will have, other beginning or end.[6] In this vast ocean of matter, not one molecule is like another, no molecule is for one moment

like itself. *Rerum novus nascitur ordo** is eternally inscribed
upon it." . . . Then he added with a sigh : " O the vanity
of our thoughts ! O the poverty of fame and of all our
labours ! O wretchedness ! O the brief scope of our understanding ! Nothing is solid save drinking, eating, living,
loving and sleeping. . . . Mademoiselle de l'Espinasse,
where are you ? " "Here I am. . . ." Then his face flushed.
I wanted to feel his pulse, but I did not know where he had
hidden his hand. He appeared to undergo a convulsive
movement. His mouth was half-open, his breathing
hurried : he heaved a deep sigh, then a weaker and still
deeper sigh ; he turned his head over on his pillow and fell
asleep. I looked at him attentively, and was much moved
without knowing why ; my heart was throbbing, and it
wasn't from fear. After a few minutes, I saw a slight smile
flit across his lips ; he whispered : " On a planet where
men multiplied after the fashion of fishes, where the spawn
of a man in contact with a woman's spawn . . . then I'd
regret it less. . . . Nothing should be lost that might be
useful. Mademoiselle, if it could be collected, sealed in a
flask and sent very early to Needham." . . . Doctor don't
you call this madness ?

Bordeu : When he was near you, assuredly !

Mlle. de l'Espinasse : Near me, away from me, it's all the
same ; you don't know what you're talking about. I had
hoped that the rest of the night would be quiet.

Bordeu : Such is usually the result.

Mlle. de l'Espinasse : Not at all ; about two in the morning
he harked back to his drop of water, calling it a mi . . .
cro . . .

Bordeu : A microcosm.

Mlle. de l'Espinasse : That was the word he used. He was
admiring the wisdom of the ancient philosophers. He was
saying, or making his philosopher say, I don't know which :
" If when Epicurus[7] maintained that the earth contained

* A new order of things comes into being.

the germs of everything, and that the animal species was a product of fermentation, he had proposed to show an illustration on a small scale of what happened on a large scale at the beginning of all time, what would have been the answer ? . . . And you have such an illustration before your eyes, and it teaches you nothing. . . . Who knows whether fermentation and its products are exhausted ? Who knows what point we have reached in the succession of these generations of animals ? Who knows whether that deformed biped, a mere four feet high, who is still called a man in the region of the Pole and who would quickly lose the name by growing a little more deformed, does not represent a disappearing species ? Who knows if this is not the case with all species of animals ? Who knows whether everything is not tending to be reduced to one vast, inert, motionless sediment ? Who knows how long that inertia will endure ? Who knows what new race may spring up again from such a great agglomeration of sensitive and living points ? Why not one single animal ? What was the elephant originally ? Maybe the same huge animal that we know to-day, maybe an atom—both are equally possible ; you need assume only motion and the varied properties of matter. The elephant, that huge organized mass, a sudden product of fermentation ! Why not ? There is less difference between that great quadruped and its first matrix than between the tiny worm and the particle of flour whence it sprang ; but the worm is only a worm . . . that is, its smallness, by concealing its organization from you, takes away the element of wonder. . . . Life, sensitivity, therein lies the miracle ; and that miracle is one no longer. . . . When once I have seen inert matter attain the state of feeling, of sensitivity, there is nothing left that can astonish me. . . . What a comparison ! A small number of elements in a state of ferment in the hollow of my hand, and this immense reservoir of divers elements scattered through the bowels of the earth, over its

surface, on the bosom of the sea, in the void of the air ! . . .
And yet, since the same causes persist, why have their
effects ceased ? Why do we no longer see the bull pierce the
earth with his horn, press his hoofs against the soil, and
struggle to disengage his ponderous body from it ? . . .
Let the present race of existing creatures pass away ; leave
the great inert sediment to work for a few million centuries.
It may be that the renewal of species takes ten times longer
than their allotted span of life. Wait, and do not give a
hasty judgment on the great work of nature. You have two
great phenomena, the transition from the state of inertia
to the state of sensitivity, and spontaneous generation ;[8]
let these suffice you ; draw correct conclusions from them,
and in an order of things which allows no absolute degree
of greatness or smallness, permanence or transience, avoid
the sophistry of the ephemeral." . . . Doctor, what is this
sophistry of the ephemeral ?

Bordeu : That of a transient being who believes in the
immortality of things.

Mlle. de l'Espinasse : Fontenelle's rose, saying that within
the memory of a rose no gardener had been known to die ?

Bordeu : Precisely ; that is graceful and profound.

Mlle. de l'Espinasse : Why don't your philosophers express
themselves with the grace he does ? We should understand
them then.

Bordeu : Frankly, I do not know if that frivolous tone
suits serious subjects.

Mlle. de l'Espinasse : What do you call a serious subject ?

Bordeu : Why, the general sensitivity of matter, the
formation of the sentient being, its unity, the origin of
animals, their duration, and all the questions connected
with these.

Mlle. de l'Espinasse : Well, I call those crazy questions,
about which one may dream when one is asleep, but which
no man of sense will trouble about in his waking hours.

Bordeu : And why so, if you please ?

Mlle. de l'Espinasse : Because some are so obvious that it's useless to seek their explanation, others so obscure that they can't possibly be understood, and all completely useless.

Bordeu : Do you think it a matter of indifference, Mademoiselle, whether one denies or accepts the existence of a Supreme Intelligence.

Mlle. de l'Espinasse : No.

Bordeu : Do you think one can come to a decision about the Supreme Intelligence without knowing what opinion to hold as to the eternity of matter, its properties, the distinction between the two substances, the nature of man and the production of animals ?

Mlle. de l'Espinasse : No.

Bordeu : So, then, these questions are not as idle as you said they were.

Mlle. de l'Espinasse : But what does their importance matter to me, if I cannot solve them ?

Bordeu : And how can you do that if you won't examine them ? But may I ask you which are those problems which you find so plain that examination of them appears to you superfluous ?

Mlle. de l'Espinasse : The question of my unity, of my individual identity, for instance. Heavens, it seems to me there's no need of so much talk to tell me that I am myself, that I have always been myself and shall never be anybody else.

Bordeu : No doubt the fact is plain, but the reason for the fact is by no means so, especially on the hypothesis of those who only admit a single substance and who explain the formation of man, or animals in general, by a series of contacts between sensitive particles. Each sensitive particle had its individual identity before the contact ; but how did it lose it, and how from all these losses did there result the consciousness of a whole ?

Mlle. de l'Espinasse : It seems to me that contact, in itself, is enough. Here's an experiment I've made a hundred times . . . but wait, I must go and see what's happening behind those curtains . . . he's asleep. . . . When I lay my hand on my thigh, I can clearly feel at first that my hand is not my thigh, but some time after, when both are equally warm, I can no longer distinguish between them ; the limits of the two parts of my body become blended and make only one.

Bordeu : Yes, until one or the other receives a prick ; then the distinction reappears. So, then, there is something in you that knows whether it is your hand or your ¬high that has been pricked, and that something is not your foot, nor even your pricked hand—the hand suffers, but the other thing knows and does not suffer.

Mlle. de l'Espinasse : Why, I think it's my head.

Bordeu : Your whole head ?

Mlle. de l'Espinasse : No; look, Doctor, I shall explain myself by means of a comparison, since comparisons make up almost the whole argument for women and poets. Imagine a spider . . .

d'Alembert : Who's there ? . . . Is it you, Mademoiselle de l'Espinasse ?

Mlle. de l'Espinasse : Hush, hush. . . . (*Mlle. de l'Espinasse and the doctor are silent for some time, then Mlle. de l'Espinasse says softly*) : I think he's gone to sleep again.

Bordeu : No, I fancy I hear something.

Mlle. de l'Espinasse : You're right ; is he beginning to dream again ?

Bordeu : Let's listen.

d'Alembert : Why am I what I am ? because it was inevitable I should be. Here, yes, but elsewhere ? at the Pole, below the Equator, on Saturn ? If a distance of a few thousand leagues can alter my species, what will be the effect of an interval of many thousand times the world's diameter ? And if all is in perpetual flux, as the spectacle of the Universe everywhere shows me, what may not be produced here and elsewhere by the lapse and vicissitudes of several million centuries ? Who knows what the thinking and feeling being may be on Saturn ? . . . But do feeling and thought exist on Saturn ? . . . why not ? . . . Perhaps the feeling and thinking being on Saturn has more senses than I have ? If that is so, ah, how wretched is the Saturnian ! . . . The more senses, the more needs.

Bordeu : He is right : organs produce needs, and reciprocally, needs produce organs.

Mlle. de l'Espinasse : Doctor, are you raving too ?

Bordeu : But why not ? I have seen two stumps end by becoming two arms.

Mlle. de l'Espinasse : That's a lie.

Bordeu : True ; but, where the two arms were lacking, I have seen the shoulder-blades grow long, move together like pincers, and become two stumps.

Mlle. de l'Espinasse : That's nonsense.

Bordeu : It's a fact. Assume a long succession of armless generations, assume continual efforts, and you will see the two ends of this pincer stretch out, stretch further and further, cross at the back, come round in front, perhaps develop fingers at their ends, and make arms and hands once more. The original conformation degenerates or is perfected by necessity and by normal function. We walk so little, we work so little and we think so much, that I don't despair that man may end by being only a head.

Mlle. de l'Espinasse : A head ! a head ! that's not very much ; I hope that excessive love-making won't . . . But you're suggesting some very ridiculous ideas to me. . . .

Bordeu : Hush !

d'Alembert : So I am what I am, because I had to be so. Change the whole, and you will necessarily change me ; but the whole is constantly changing . . . man is merely a common product, the monster an uncommon product ; both equally natural, equally necessary, equally part of the universal and general order of things. . . . And what is astonishing about that ? . . . All creatures intermingle with

each other, consequently all species . . . everything is in
perpetual flux. . . . Every animal is more or less man ;
every mineral is more or less plant ; every plant more or
less animal. There is nothing precise in nature . . . Father
Castel's ribbon.[9] Yes, Father Castel, it's your ribbon and
nothing more. Everything is more or less one thing or
another, more or less earth, more or less water, more or less
air, more or less fire ; everything belongs more or less to
one kingdom or another . . . therefore nothing is of the
essence of a particular being. . . . No, surely, since there
is no quality of which no being has a share . . . and that it
is the greater or less degree of this quality that makes us
attribute it to one being to the exclusion of another. . . .
And you talk of individuals, poor philosophers ! stop
thinking of individuals ; answer me. Is there in nature
one atom that strictly resembles another atom ? . . . No.
. . . Don't you agree that everything is connected in
nature, and that it is impossible that there should be a
missing link in the chain ? Then what do you mean by
your individuals ? There aren't any, no, there aren't any.
. . . There is only one great individual, that is the whole.
In that whole, as in a machine or some animal, you may
give a certain name to a certain part, but if you call this
part of the whole an individual you are making as great a
mistake as if you called the wing of a bird, or a feather on
that wing, an individual . . .[10] And you talk of essences,
poor philosophers ! leave your essences out of it. Consider
the general mass, or if your imagination is too feeble to
embrace that, consider your first origin and your latter
end. . . . O Architas ! you who measured the globe,
what are you ? a handful of ashes. . . . What is a being ?
The sum of a certain number of tendencies. . . . Can I be
anything other than a tendency ? . . . no, I am moving
towards an end. And species ? Species are only tendencies
towards a common end which is peculiar to them. . . .
And life ? . . . Life, a succession of actions and reactions.[11]

. . . Living, I act and react as a mass . . . dead, I act and react in the form of molecules. . . . Then I do not die ? . . . No, no doubt, I don't die in that sense, neither I myself nor anything else. . . . Birth, life, decay, are merely changes of form. . . . And what does the form matter ? Each form has the happiness and misfortune which pertain to it. . . . From the elephant to the flea, from the flea to the sensitive living atom, the origin of all, there is no point in nature but suffers and enjoys.

Mlle. de l'Espinasse : He says nothing more.

Bordeu : No. That was a fine flight he made ; that was very lofty philosophy : only theoretical at the moment, yet I believe that the more progress is made in human knowledge, the more will its truth be confirmed.

Mlle. de l'Espinasse : And where had we got to meanwhile ?

Bordeu : Really, I don't remember ; he suggested so many phenomena to my mind while I was listening to him !

Mlle. de l'Espinasse : Wait, wait . . . I'd got as far as my spider.

Bordeu : Yes, yes.

Mlle. de l'Espinasse : Come here, Doctor. Imagine a spider in the centre of its web. Shake one thread, and you will see the watchful creature run up. Well ! How if the thread that the insect draws out of its intestines, and draws back thither when it pleases, were a sensitive part of itself ?

Bordeu : I understand you. You imagine inside yourself, somewhere, in some corner of your head, in that part for instance that is called the *meninges*, one or several points to which are referred back all the sensations aroused along the threads.

Mlle. de l'Espinasse : Exactly.

Bordeu : Your idea is perfectly correct ; but don't you see that it comes to much the same thing as a certain cluster of bees ?

Mlle. de l'Espinasse : Why, so it does ; I've been speaking prose without knowing it.

Bordeu : And very good prose too, as you will see. Anyone who knows man only in the form he appears in at birth, has not the slightest idea what he is really like. His head, his feet, his hands, all his limbs, all his viscera, all his organs, his nose, his eyes, his ears, his heart, his lungs, his intestines, his muscles, his bones, his nerves, his membranes, are, properly speaking, only the gross developments of a network that forms itself, increases, extends, throws out a multitude of imperceptible threads.[12]

Mlle. de l'Espinasse : That's my web ; and the point whence all these threads originate is my spider.

Bordeu : Perfect.

Mlle. de l'Espinasse : Where are the threads ? Where is the spider placed ?

Bordeu : The threads are everywhere ; there is no point on the surface of your body which their ends do not reach ; and the spider has its seat in the part of your head that I have mentioned, the *meninges*, the slightest touch on which would make the whole organism fall into torpor.

Mlle. de l'Espinasse : But if an atom sets one of the threads of the web quivering, the spider is alarmed and disturbed, runs away or comes hurrying up. At the centre it learns all that is happening in any part of the huge chamber over which it has spun its web. Why can I not know what is happening in my chamber, the world, since I am a group of sensitive points, pressing on everything and subject to impressions from everything ?

Bordeu : Because impressions grow weaker in proportion to the distance whence they come.

Mlle. de l'Espinasse : If the lightest blow is struck at the end of a long beam, I hear that blow, if I have my ear placed to the other end. If this beam stood touching the Earth with one end and Sirius with the other, the same effect would be produced. Why, since everything is connected, contiguous, so that this beam exists in reality, do I not hear what is happening in the vast space that surrounds me, especially if I listen attentively ?

Bordeu : And who has told you that you don't hear it, more or less ? But the distance is so great, the impression is so weak and interrupted by so many others crossing its path ; you are surrounded and deafened by such violent and diverse noises ; the reason being that, between Saturn and you there are only contiguous bodies, whereas there should be continuity.

Mlle. de l'Espinasse : It's a great pity.

Bordeu : True, for then you would be God. Through your identity with all the beings in nature, you would know all that happens ; through your memory, you would know all that has happened.

Mlle. de l'Espinasse : And all that is going to happen ?

Bordeu : You would form, about the future, conjectures that were likely but liable to error. It's just as if you sought to guess what is going to happen inside yourself, at the tip of your foot or your hand.

Mlle. de l'Espinasse : And who has told you that this world has not also got its " *meninges,*" that there is not, dwelling in some corner of space, a large or a small spider whose threads reach out to everything ?

Bordeu : No one ; and still less, whether it has ever existed or ever will exist.

Mlle. de l'Espinasse : Could a God of that sort . . .

Bordeu : The only sort that is conceivable . . .

Mlle. de l'Espinasse : . . . have existed, or come into existence and pass away ?

Bordeu : No doubt ; but since he would be a material part of the material universe, subject to vicissitudes, he would grow old and die.

Mlle. de l'Espinasse : But now another extravagant idea comes into my mind.

Bordeu : I'll excuse you from telling it, I know what it is.

Mlle. de l'Espinasse : Well then, what is it ?

Bordeu : You picture intelligence combined with highly energetic portions of matter, and the possibility of every imaginable sort of prodigy. Others have thought like you.

Mlle. de l'Espinasse : You have guessed my thought, and I think none the better of you for it. You must have a remarkable tendency towards madness.

Bordeu : Granted. But what is there terrifying about that idea ? There would be an epidemic of good and evil geniuses ; the most constant laws of nature would be interrupted by natural agents ; our physical science would become more difficult thereby, but there wouldn't be any miracles.

Mlle. de l'Espinasse : Truly, one must be very circumspect about what one affirms and what one denies.

Bordeu : To be sure, anyone who described to you a phenomenon of this sort would seem a mighty liar. But let us leave all these imaginary beings, not excepting your spider with its infinite network ; let's get back to your own being and its formation.

Mlle. de l'Espinasse : I'm willing.

d'Alembert : Mademoiselle, you are with someone ; who is that talking to you ?

Mlle. de l'Espinasse : It's the doctor.

d'Alembert : Good morning, Doctor ; what are you doing here so early ?

Bordeu : You shall hear later : go to sleep now.

d'Alembert : I certainly need to. I do not think I ever passed a more restless night than this one. Don't go away before I am up.

Bordeu : No. . . . I'll wager, Mademoiselle, that you have assumed that you were at twelve years old a woman half your present size, at four years a woman half as small again, as a fœtus a tiny woman, in your mother's ovaries a very tiny woman, and that you have always been a woman in the same shape as to-day, so that only your successive increases in size have made all the difference between yourself at your origin and yourself as you are to-day.

Mlle. de l'Espinasse : I admit it.

Bordeu :[13] And yet nothing is further from the truth than this idea. At first you were nothing at all. You began as an imperceptible speck, formed from still smaller molecules scattered through the blood and lymph of your father and mother ; that speck became a loose thread, then a bundle of threads [a]. Up till then, not the slightest trace of your own agreeable form ; your eyes, those fine eyes, were no more like eyes than the tip of an anemone's feeler is like an anemone. Each of the fibres in the bundle of threads was transformed solely by nutrition and according to its conformation, into a particular organ ; exception being made of those organs in which the fibres of the bundle are metamorphosed, and to which they give birth [b]. The bundle is a purely sensitive system [c] ; if it continued under that form, it would be susceptible to all those impressions that affect simple sensitivity, such as cold and heat, softness and harshness. These impressions, experienced successively, varied amongst themselves and each varying in intensity, might perhaps produce memory, self-consciousness, a very limited form of reason. But this pure and simple sensitivity, this sense of touch, is differentiated through the organs that arise from each separate fibre [d] ; one fibre, forming an ear, gives rise to a kind of touch that we call noise or sound ; another forming the palate, gives rise to a second kind of touch that we call taste ; a third, forming the nose and its inner lining, gives rise to a third kind of touch that we call smell ; a fourth, forming an eye, gives rise to a fourth kind of touch that we call colour.

Mlle. de l'Espinasse : But, if I've understood you aright, those who deny the possibility of a sixth sense, a real hermaphrodite, are very stupid. Who has told them that nature could not form a bundle with a peculiar fibre which would give rise to an organ unknown to us ? [e]

Bordeu : Or with the two fibres that characterize the two sexes ? [f] You are right ; it's a pleasure to talk with you ; not only do you follow what is said to you, but you draw from it conclusions that astonish me by their soundness.

Mlle. de l'Espinasse : Doctor, you're saying that to encourage me.

Bordeu : No, on my word, I'm saying what I really think.

Mlle. de l'Espinasse : I can quite well see the purpose of some of the fibres in the bundle ; but what becomes of the others ?

Bordeu : And do you think any other woman but yourself would have thought of that question ?

Mlle. de l'Espinasse : Certainly.

Bordeu : You're not vain. The rest of the fibres [g] go to form as many different kinds of touch as there are different organs and parts of the body.

Mlle. de l'Espinasse : And what are they called ? I never heard speak of them.

Bordeu : They have no name.

Mlle. de l'Espinasse : Why not ?

Bordeu : Because there is less difference between the sensations excited through their means, than there is between the sensations excited by means of the other organs.

Mlle. de l'Espinasse : In all seriousness, do you believe that the foot, the hand, the thighs, the belly, the stomach, the chest, the lungs, the heart, have their own particular sensations ?

Bordeu : I do believe so. If I dared, I would ask you if, among those sensations that are not named . . .

Mlle. de l'Espinasse : I understand you. No. That one is quite unique of its kind, the more's the pity. But what reason have you for assuming this multiplicity of sensations, more painful than pleasant, which you are pleased to bestow on us ?

Bordeu : The reason ? That we distinguish them to a considerable extent. If this infinite variety of touch did not exist we should know that we experienced pleasure or pain but we should not know where they arose. We should need the aid of sight. It would no longer be a question of sensation, but of experiment and observation.

Mlle. de l'Espinasse : Then, if I should say my finger hurt, and I were asked why I declared it was my finger that hurt, I should be obliged to say, not that I felt it hurt, but that I felt pain and that I saw my finger was injured.

Bordeu : That's it. Come and let me kiss you.

Mlle. de l'Espinasse : With pleasure.

d'Alembert : Well done, Doctor, you are kissing Mademoiselle.

Bordeu : I have thought over this problem a great deal, and it seems to me that the direction and the place whence the shock arises would not be enough to determine the judgment immediately passed by the centre of the bundle.

Mlle. de l'Espinasse : I don't know about that.

Bordeu : I appreciate your doubt. It is so common to take natural qualities for acquired habits almost as old as ourselves.

Mlle. de l'Espinasse : And reciprocally too.

Bordeu : Be that as it may, you see that in a question that concerns the first formation of the animal, you are starting too late if you observe and consider only the fully formed animal ; that you need to go back to its first rudiments, and that it is therefore desirable to strip off your existing organization, and to go back to a moment when you were merely a soft, filamentous, shapeless, worm-like substance, more analogous to the bulb or root of a plant than to an animal.

Mlle. de l'Espinasse : If it were the custom to go naked in the streets I should be neither the first nor the last to conform to it. So, do what you like with me, as long as I learn something. You told me that every fibre in the bundle formed a particular organ ; what proof have you that this is so ?

Bordeu : Do in your mind what nature sometimes does actually ; deprive the bundle of one of its fibres, for instance of the fibre which should form the eyes ; what do you think will happen ?

Mlle. de l'Espinasse : Perhaps the animal will have no eyes.

Bordeu : Or one single one in the middle of its forehead.

Mlle. de l'Espinasse : It would be a Cyclops.

Bordeu : Yes, a Cyclops.

Mlle. de l'Espinasse : The Cyclops, then, may not be a purely fabulous creature ?

Bordeu : So far from it, that I can show you one whenever you like.

Mlle. de l'Espinasse : And who knows the cause of this peculiarity ?

Bordeu : The man who has dissected the monster and found that it has only one optic nerve. Do mentally what nature sometimes does actually ; suppress the fibre of the bundle which should form the ear, the animal will have no ears, or only one, and the anatomist will find on dissection neither the olfactory nerves nor the auditory nerves, or will find only one of these. Go on suppressing the fibres, and the animal will lack a head, feet, hands ; it will last but a short time, but it will have lived.[14]

Mlle. de l'Espinasse : And are there examples of this ?

Bordeu : Assuredly. And that's not all. Duplicate some of the fibres of the bundle, and the animal will have two heads, four eyes, four ears, three testicles, three feet, four arms, six fingers on each hand. Disturb the fibres of the bundle, and the organs will be out of place ; the head will be in the middle of the chest, the lungs will be on the left the heart on the right. Stick two fibres together, and the organs will be fused together ; the arms will cling to the body, the thighs, legs and feet will be joined up, and you will have every conceivable sort of monster.

Mlle. de l'Espinasse : But it seems to me that so complex a system as an animal, an organism which is born from a speck, from a seething fluid, perhaps from two fluids mingled haphazard, since one hardly knows what one's doing on these occasions; an organism which advances towards perfection by an infinite number of successive developments; an organism the regular or irregular structure of which depends on a bundle of thin, loose, flexible fibres, a sort of skein in which the slightest fibre cannot be broken, snapped, displaced or removed without distressing consequences for the whole, such an organism should become even more frequently tangled up in the place of its formation than do my silks on my bobbin.[14]

Bordeu : And in fact, the organism does suffer much more than people think. There is not enough dissection done, and ideas about its formation are very far from the truth.

Mlle. de l'Espinasse : Are there striking examples of these peculiar deformities at origin, other than hunchbacks and cripples, whose misshapen state might be attributed to some hereditary defect ?

Bordeu : There are countless examples, and quite recently there died at the hospital of la Charité in Paris, at the age of twenty-five, following an inflammation of the lungs, a carpenter called Jean-Baptiste Macé, native of Troyes, who had the internal viscera of the chest and the abdomen transposed, the heart on the right, whereas you have it on the left ; the liver on the left ; the stomach, the spleen, the pancreas on the right hypochondrium ; the *vena porta* to the liver on the left side, instead as it should be to the liver on the right ; a similar transposition of the alimentary canal ; the kidneys, back to back against the *vertebræ* or the loins, were in the shape of a horseshoe. And now let them talk about final causes !

Mlle. de l'Espinasse : It's very odd.

Bordeu : If Jean-Baptiste Macé had married and had children . . .

Mlle. de l'Espinasse : Well, Doctor, these children ? . . .

Bordeu : Would be formed in the normal way ; but some one of their children's children, after a hundred years or so, since these irregularities make leaps, will revert to the extraordinary conformation of his ancestor.

Mlle. de l'Espinasse : And what causes these leaps ?

Bordeu : Who knows ? It takes two to make a child, as you know. It may be that one of the agents counteracts the other's defect, and that the faulty network only reappears when the descendant of the monstrous breed is dominant and controls the formation of the network. The bundle of fibres constitutes the original primary difference between all species of animals. The varieties in the form of the bundle of each species constitute the monstrous varieties within that species.[15]

(After a long silence, Mlle. de l'Espinasse emerged from her reverie and awoke the doctor from his by the following question) :

Mlle. de l'Espinasse : I have just had a very mad idea.

Bordeu : What's that ?

Mlle. de l'Espinasse : Man may be merely a monstrous form of woman, or woman a monstrous form of man.

Bordeu : You would have had that idea much sooner, if you had known that a woman has all a man's organs, and that the only difference between them is that between a bag hanging down outside, and an inverted bag inside ; that a female fœtus looks deceptively like a male fœtus ; that the part that causes this confusion is gradually effaced in the female fœtus, as the interior bag grows bigger ; that it is never obliterated to the point of losing its original form, but keeps this form on a small scale ; that it is liable to the same movements, that it, too, gives rise to the voluptuous impulse ; that it has its *glans*, its foreskin, and that on the tip of it there can be seen a point which appears to be the opening of a urinary canal that is now closed ; that there is in man, from the *anus* to the *scrotum*, a space called the *perineum*, and from the *scrotum* to the tip of the *penis*, a scar that looks like a sewn-up *vulva* ;

that women whose *clitoris* is over-developed grow beards ;
that eunuchs are beardless, while their thighs broaden,
their hips curve, their knees grow rounded, and that, by
losing the characteristic organization of one sex, they seem
to revert to the characteristic conformation of the other.
Those Arabs who have become castrated through continual
horseback-riding lose their beards, develop a high voice,
dress like women, ride with the women in the wagons,
squat to urinate, and assume female ways and customs. . . .
But we have wandered far from our objective. Let us get
back to our bundle of animated and living filaments.

d'Alembert : I think you are talking filth to Mlle. de
l'Espinasse.

Bordeu : When one talks about science one has to use
technical terms.

d'Alembert : You are right ; then they lose the train of
associated ideas that would make them indecent. Go on,
Doctor. You were saying to Mademoiselle that the womb
is only a *scrotum* turned inside out, during which process
the ovaries were ejected from the bag that contained them
and thrown right and left in the cavity of the body ; that
the *clitoris* is a tiny male member ; that this woman's
member gets gradually smaller as the womb or inverted
scrotum grows longer, and that . . .

Mlle. de l'Espinasse : Yes, yes, be quiet and don't interrupt
us.

Bordeu : You see, Mademoiselle, that, when we examine
our sensations in general, which are all merely a differentiated sense of touch, we must neglect the successive forms
assumed by the network, and consider only the network
itself.

Mlle. de l'Espinasse : Every filament of the sensitive network can be hurt or stimulated along its whole length.
Pleasure or pain is here or there, in one spot or another
along the prolonged legs of my spider, for I always come
back to my spider ; that spider is the common origin of all

the legs and their prolongations, and refers the pain or the pleasure to such and such a place without feeling it.

Bordeu : It is the constant and unvarying communication of all impressions to this common origin which constitutes the unity of the animal.

Mlle. de l'Espinasse : It is the recollection of all these successive impressions which makes up, for each animal, the story of its life and of its individual being.

Bordeu : While memory, and the process of comparison, which inevitably result from all these impressions, form thought and reasoning power.

Mlle de l'Espinasse : And where does this process of comparison take place ?

Bordeu : At the origin of the network.

Mlle. de l'Espinasse : And this network ? . . .

Bordeu : Has, at its origin, no sense peculiarly its own ; it does not see, hear, or suffer. It is produced and nourished ; it emanates from a soft, insensitive, inert substance, that serves it as a pillow, seated on which it listens, judges and decides.

Mlle. de l'Espinasse : It feels no pain ?

Bordeu : No ; the slightest pressure cuts short its power to judge and the whole animal falls into a death-like condition. Remove the pressure, and the judge resumes its functions, and the animal lives again.

Mlle. de l'Espinasse : And how do you know this ? Has a man ever been made to die and live again at will ?

Bordeu : Yes.

Mlle. de l'Espinasse : And how was that ?

Bordeu : I will tell you ; it is a curious fact. La Peyronie, whom you may have known, was summoned to a patient who had received a violent blow on the head. This patient felt a throbbing there. The surgeon had no doubt that an abscess had formed in the brain, and that there was not a moment to lose. He shaved the patient's head and trepanned him. The point of the instrument fell exactly in the centre of the abscess. The pus was formed; he emptied it out; he cleaned the abscess with a syringe. When he drove the injection into the abscess, the sick man closed his eyes; his limbs remained inactive, motionless, without the slightest sign of life; when the injection was pumped out again, and the origin of the bundle relieved of the weight and pressure of the injected fluid, the sick man opened his eyes again, moved, spoke, felt, was reborn and lived.

Mlle. de l'Espinasse : That is very odd; and did the patient recover?

Bordeu : He recovered; and when he was well, he could reflect, think, reason, he had the same wit, the same good sense, the same acuteness, though lacking a considerable portion of his brain.

Mlle. de l'Espinasse : This judge of yours is a most extraordinary creature.

Bordeu : He, too, makes mistakes at times; he is subject to errors due to habit; one feels pain in a limb which one no longer has. You can deceive him when you wish; cross two of your fingers over each other, touch a little ball, and the judge will declare that there are two.

Mlle. de l'Espinasse : That's because he is like all the judges in the world, and needs experience, without which he would mistake the feeling of ice for that of fire.

Bordeu : He goes further than that; he may attribute an almost infinite volume to an individual, or else concentrate him almost to a point.

Mlle. de l'Espinasse : I don't understand.

Bordeu : What limits your real extension, the true sphere of your faculty of sensation?

Mlle. de l'Espinasse : My sight and my sense of touch.

Bordeu : By day; but what limits it at night, in darkness, especially when you are thinking of something abstract, and even by day, when your mind is preoccupied?

Mlle. de l'Espinasse : Nothing does. I exist as it were

within a single point ; I almost cease to be material, I feel nothing but my thought : I am no longer conscious of place or movement, body, distance or space : the universe is abolished for me, and I am as nothing to it.

Bordeu : That is the final term in the concentration of your being ; but its imaginary expansion can be limitless. When the true limit of your sensitiveness is exceeded, either by condensing yourself within yourself or by extending beyond yourself, there is no knowing what may result.

Mlle. de l'Espinasse : Doctor, you are right. It has often seemed to me in dreams . . .

Bordeu : And to sick people during an attack of gout. . . .

Mlle. de l'Espinasse : That I was becoming vast . . .

Bordeu : That their feet touched the canopy of their bed.

Mlle. de l'Espinasse : That my arms and legs were stretching out to infinity, that the rest of my body was growing in proportion ; that the Enceladus of legend was a pigmy to me, that Ovid's Amphitriton, whose long arms made a huge girdle round the Earth, was but a dwarf by my side, and that I scaled the heavens and embraced the two hemispheres.

Bordeu : Very fine. And I have known a woman who experienced the same phenomenon in the opposite sense.

Mlle. de l'Espinasse : What ! did she grow smaller by degrees and shrink within herself ?

Bordeu : To the point of feeling herself as thin as a needle ; she could see, hear, reason and judge ; she was in mortal fear of losing herself, shuddered at the approach of the smallest objects and scarcely dared move from her place.

Mlle. de l'Espinasse : That is a peculiar dream, most unpleasant and inconvenient.

Bordeu : It was no dream, but one of the symptoms accompanying the cessation of the menstrual flow.

Mlle. de l'Espinasse : And did she remain long in the shape of a tiny imperceptible woman ?

Bordeu : For an hour or so, after which she would gradually regain her normal volume.

Mlle. de l'Espinasse : And what is the reason for these queer sensations ?

Bordeu : In their natural and quiet state, the fibres that make up the bundle have a certain degree of tension ; a customary tone and energy that limits the extent—real or imagined—of one's body. I say real or imagined, for this tension, this tone, this energy being variable, our body has not always the same volume.

Mlle. de l'Espinasse : Then, physically as well as morally, we are liable to fancy ourselves greater than we are ?

Bordeu : Cold makes us shrink, heat makes us expand, and an individual may go through life thinking himself smaller or bigger than he really is. If the bulk of the bundle should happen to undergo a violent irritation—if the fibres stand erect and their innumerable tips suddenly stretch out beyond their accustomed limits, then the head, the feet, the other members, every point over the surface of the body will be projected to an immense distance, and the individual will feel himself a giant. The contrary phenomenon will take place if a gradual insensitiveness, apathy and inertia take hold of the tips of the fibres and creep gradually towards the origin of the bundle.

Mlle. de l'Espinasse : I can imagine that such expansion could never be measured, and I can also imagine that this insensitiveness, apathy and inertia of the tips of the fibres, this numbness, having progressed a certain distance, might be checked and halted. . . .

Bordeu : As happened to La Condamine ; then the person feels as if he had balloons under his feet.[16]

Mlle. de l'Espinasse : He exists beyond the limits of his sensitiveness, and if this apathy were to enfold him in every direction, he would appear as a tiny man living within a dead man.

Bordeu : From this you may conclude that the animal

which was to begin with a mere point, does not yet know whether he is anything more than that. But let us get back. . . .

Mlle. de l'Espinasse : To what ?

Bordeu : To La Peyronie's trepanning. . . . I fancy you have there what you asked for, an instance of a man living and dying alternately. . . . But there is a better one.

Mlle. de l'Espinasse : And what may that be ?

Bordeu : The fable of Castor and Pollux in real life ; two children, in whose case the life of one was immediately followed by the death of the other, and the life of the latter immediately followed by the death of the first.

Mlle. de l'Espinasse : Oh, that's a tall story. And how long did this go on ?

Bordeu : This existence lasted for two days, which they shared equally and alternately, so that each had for its portion one day of life and one of death.

Mlle. de l'Espinasse : I'm afraid, Doctor, that you are taking advantage of my credulity. Take care, for if you deceive me once I shall never trust you again.

Bordeu : Do you ever read the *Gazette de France* ?

Mlle. de l'Espinasse : Never, although it is the masterpiece of two clever men.

Bordeu : Borrow the issue of the fourth of this month, September, and you will see that at Rabastens, in the diocese of Albi, two girls were born back to back, joined by their lowest lumbar *vertebra*, their buttocks and the lower part of the trunk. One could not be held upright without the other's head being upside down. When laid down they were face to face ; their thighs were bent between their trunks, their legs in the air ; in the centre of the common circular line that connected them through their lower abdomens, the sexual organs could be discerned, and between the right thigh of one which corresponded to the left thigh of her sister, there was, in a hollow, a little *anus* through which the *meconium* flowed out.

Mlle. de l'Espinasse : What a peculiar species of creature !

Bordeu : They took some milk which was given them in a spoon. They lived for twelve hours as I have told you, one losing consciousness as the other regained it, one dying while the other lived. The first swoon of one and the first life of the other lasted four hours, the subsequent alternating swoons and returns to life were shorter ; they expired at the same instant. It was observed that their navels went in and stood out alternately ; that of the child who was unconscious was sucked in, while that of the child who was coming back to life stood out.

Mlle. de l'Espinasse : And what can you say about these alternations of life and death ?

Bordeu : Nothing significant perhaps ; but as one sees everything through the spectacles of one's pet theory, and I don't want to be an exception to that rule, I say, that it is the same phenomenon as that of the trepanned patient of La Peyronie's, duplicated in two beings joined together ; that the networks of these children were so thoroughly interconnected that they acted and reacted on one another ; when the origin of the network of one of them predominated, it affected the network of the other, who immediately lost consciousness ; the reverse happened if the latter's network were dominant in the common system. In the case of La Peyronie's patient, the pressure was from above downwards through the weight of a fluid ; in the case of the twins of Rabastens, it was from below upwards, through traction of a certain number of the fibres of the network ; a conjecture which is borne out by the alternating movements of the two navels, a movement outwards in the child that was reviving, a movement inwards in the one which was dying.

Mlle. de l'Espinasse : And there we have two souls linked together.

Bordeu : One animal with the rudiments of twofold senses and twofold consciousness.

Mlle. de l'Espinasse : And yet able to enjoy only one at a time ; but who knows what might have happened if that animal had lived ?

Bordeu : What sort of communication might have been set up between the two brains, by the common experience of every instant of life, the strongest bond of habit imaginable ?

Mlle. de l'Espinasse : Double senses, a double memory, a double imagination, a double power of concentration, one half of a creature observing, reading, meditating while its other half is resting ; the latter taking up the same functions when its companion is weary, life doubled for a double being.

Bordeu : It is possible ; and since nature, in the course of time, brings about all that is possible, she will form some such strange composite being.

Mlle. de l'Espinasse : What poor creatures we should be, compared with such a being !

Bordeu : But why ? A single mind is subject to so many uncertainties, contradictions and absurdities that I cannot imagine what a double mind might not produce. . . . But it is half-past ten, and I can hear a patient calling me all the way from the outskirts of the town.

Mlle. de l'Espinasse : Would he be in great danger if you did not see him ?

Bordeu : Less, perhaps, than if I did. If nature does not do her business without me, we shall find it hard to do it together, and I shall certainly not succeed without her.

Mlle. de l'Espinasse : Stay here then.

d'Alembert : Doctor, one word more and then I send you to your patient. Through all the changes I have undergone in the course of my existence, perhaps not having now a single one of the molecules which formed me at birth, how have I maintained my identity for others and for myself ?

Bordeu : You told us yourself in your dream.

d'Alembert : Have I been dreaming ?

Mlle. de l'Espinasse : All night long, and it sounded so like delirium that I sent for the doctor this morning.

d'Alembert : And all because a certain spider's legs were moving of their own accord, kept the spider on the watch, and made the animal talk. And what did the animal say?

Bordeu : That it was through memory that he maintained his identity for others and for himself ; and, let me add, through the slowness of the changes. If you had passed in the twinkling of an eye from youth to decay, you would have been thrown into the world as at the first moment of birth ; you would not have been yourself in your own eyes, nor in those of others ; while they would not have been themselves in your eyes. All connecting links would have been destroyed ; all that makes up the history of your life for me, all that makes up the history of my life for you, thrown into confusion. How could you have known that this man, leaning on a stick, his eyes grown dim, dragging himself along with difficulty, and even more unlike himself inwardly than outwardly, was the same who, the day before, walked so lightly, lifted heavy burdens, gave himself up to the deepest meditations, the pleasantest and the most strenuous forms of exercise ? You would not have understood your own works, you would not have recognized yourself nor any one else, and no one would have recognized you ; all the world's scene would have changed. Consider that there was less difference between yourself at birth and yourself in youth, than there would be between yourself as a young man and yourself grown suddenly decrepit. Consider that, although your birth was linked to your youth by an unbroken series of sensations, yet the first three years of your life form no part of your life-story. Then what would the days of your youth have meant to you if nothing linked them to the period of your decay ? D'Alembert grown old would not have the slightest recollection of d'Alembert young.

Mlle. de l'Espinasse : In the cluster of bees, not one would have had time to take on the spirit of the whole.

d'Alembert : What's that you're saying ?

Mlle. de l'Espinasse : I am saying that the monastic spirit is preserved, because the monastery repeoples itself gradually, and when a new monk enters it he finds a hundred old ones, who induce him to think and feel as they do. When one bee goes, its place in the cluster is taken by another that rapidly adapts itself.

d'Alembert : Come, you are crazy with your talk of monks, bees, clusters and convents.

Bordeu : Not as crazy as you might think. Although the animal has only one consciousness, it has an infinite number of wills ; each organ has its own.

d'Alembert : What do you mean by that ?

Bordeu : I mean that the stomach desires food, while the palate will have none of it ; that the difference between the whole animal on one hand and the stomach and palate on the other is that the animal knows what it wants, while the stomach and palate want without knowing it ; and the palate and the stomach are related like man to brute. The bees lose individual consciousness and retain their appetites and wills. The fibre is a simple animal, man a complex animal ; but we will keep this text for another time. It does not take so great an event as decay to take away self-consciousness from man. A dying man receives the sacraments with the deepest piety, confesses his sins, asks forgiveness of his wife, embraces his children, summons his friends, speaks to his physician, gives orders to his servants ; he dictates his last wishes, sets his affairs in order, and all this with complete sanity and presence of mind ; he recovers, he is convalescent, and he has not the slightest idea of what he has said and done during his illness. That interval, though sometimes a very long one, has disappeared from his life. There are even instances of persons resuming the conversations or the actions which the sudden attack of illness had interrupted.

d'Alembert : I remember that during a public debate, a

college pedant, inflated with learning, was worsted by a Capuchin monk whom he had despised. He, worsted! and by whom? by a Capuchin! and on what topic? on the contingent future! on that science of cause and effect which he had studied all his life! And in what circumstances? before a numerous assembly! before his pupils! Behold him disgraced. He worried his head over these things so much that he fell into a lethargy that deprived him of all the learning he had acquired.

Mlle. de l'Espinasse : But that was a blessing.

d'Alembert : Why, yes, you're right. He kept his natural senses, but he forgot everything. He was taught afresh to speak and read, and he died just as he was beginning to spell tolerably well. This man was not devoid of gifts; it seems, even, that he had a certain eloquence.

Mlle. de l'Espinasse : Since the doctor has heard your story, he must hear mine too. A young man of eighteen or twenty whose name I forget . . .

Bordeu : He was a M. de Schullemberg, of Winterthur; he was only fifteen or sixteen.

Mlle. de l'Espinasse : This young man had a fall, and suffered a violent shock to his head.

Bordeu : What do you call a violent shock? He fell from the top of a barn; his skull was fractured, and he remained unconscious for six weeks.

Mlle. de l'Espinasse : Be that as it may, do you know what was the sequel to this accident? The same as in your pedant's case; he forgot all he knew; he went back to his infancy; he had a second childhood, and one which lasted. He was timid and cowardly; he played with toys. If he had been naughty and was scolded, he would go and hide in a corner; he asked leave to pay a big or little " visit." He was taught to read and write; but I was forgetting to tell you that he had to learn to walk again. He became a man once more, and a clever man, and he has left a work on natural history.

Bordeu : It is a set of engravings, the plates for M. Zulyer's studies of insects according to the system of Linnæus. I knew about this already : it occured in the canton of Zurich in Switzerland, and there are many more instances like it. Disturb the origin of the bundle and you change the whole animal ; it seems as if it existed there in its entirety, now dominating the branches, now dominated by them.

Mlle. de l'Espinasse : And the animal is either under a despot's rule or under anarchy.

Bordeu : A despot's rule is an apt description. The origin of the bundle commands and all the rest obeys. The animal is master of itself, *compos mentis.*

Mlle. de l'Espinasse : Under anarchy, when all the fibres of the network rise up against their ruler, and there is no longer any supreme authority.

Bordeu : Exactly. In strong fits of passion, in delirium, at times of imminent peril, if the master brings all his subjects' strength to bear in one direction, the weakest animal may display an incredible strength.

Mlle. de l'Espinasse : In the vapours, that variety of anarchy to which we women are peculiarly liable.

Bordeu : There you have the picture of a weak administration, in which everyone claims the supreme authority himself. I know only one way of recovering ; it is difficult, but infallible ; it is for the origin of the sensitive network, that part that constitutes the individual's identity, to have some powerful motive for regaining its authority.

Mlle. de l'Espinasse : And what happens then ?

Bordeu : It happens that it does indeed regain it, or else that the animal perishes. If I had time, I would tell you two curious facts in this connection.

Mlle. de l'Espinasse : But, Doctor, the time of your visit is past, and your patient doesn't expect you any longer.

Bordeu : One should only come here when one has nothing to do, for it's impossible to get away.

Mlle. de l'Espinasse : That burst of ill-temper is quite flattering ! But your stories ?

Bordeu : For to-day you'll have to be content with this one. A woman fell into the most alarming hysterical condition, following her confinement ; she was subject to uncontrolled fits of weeping and laughing, to chokings, convulsions, heavings of the bosom, gloomy silence, shrill cries, all the most frightful things. This went on for several years. She was passionately in love, and she thought she saw that her lover, weary of her illness, was beginning to drift away from her ; then she resolved to be cured or to die. A kind of civil war took place within her, in which now the master had the upper hand, now the subjects. If it happened that the action of the fibres of the network equalled the reaction of their origin, she would fall in a death-like trance ; she had to be carried on to her bed and would remain there for hours, motionless and almost lifeless ; at other times she suffered only lassitude, general weakness, an exhaustion that looked like being fatal. She persisted in this state of conflict for six months. The rebellion always began in the fibres of the network ; she would feel it coming. At the first symptom she would get up, run about, undertake the most violent forms of exercise ; she would run up and down the stairs, saw wood, dig the earth. The organ of her will, the origin of the bundle, stiffened its resistance ; she said to herself : victory or death. After an infinite number of triumphs and defeats, the ruler maintained the mastery, and the subjects became so submissive that, although this woman has experienced all sorts of domestic troubles and suffered various illnesses, no sign of the hysteria has reappeared.

Mlle. de l'Espinasse : She was brave, but I think I'd have done as much.

Bordeu : Because if you loved at all you would love deeply, and because you are strong.

Mlle. de l'Espinasse : I see. One is strong, if, through habit or through one's organization, the origin of the bundle dominates the fibres ; weak if, on the contrary, it is dominated by them.

Bordeu : There are many other conclusions to be drawn from this.

Mlle. de l'Espinasse : But tell us your other story, and you may draw them afterwards.

Bordeu : A young woman had been rather a wanton in her conduct. One day she resolved to put pleasure from her. Living alone, she became subject to melancholy and nervous depression. She sent for me. I advised her to dress like a peasant, to dig the earth all day long, sleep on straw, live on coarse bread. This way of life did not attract her. Then travel, I said. She went all round Europe, and regained health on the high road.

Mlle. de l'Espinasse : That's not what you should have said ! But never mind, let's hear your conclusions.

Bordeu : There would be no end to them.

Mlle. de l'Espinasse : All the better : say on.

Bordeu : I haven't the courage.

Mlle. de l'Espinasse : Why not ?

Bordeu : Because, at the present rate, we skim the surface of everything and go into nothing deeply.

Mlle. de l'Espinasse : What does that matter ? We are only chatting, we are not composing a thesis.

Bordeu : For instance, if the origin of the bundle summons all the strength of the whole to itself, if the entire system is, so to speak, moved in reverse, as I think happens to a man sunk in deep thought, to a fanatic who sees the heavens opened, to the savage who sings in the midst of flames, or in ecstatic trances, in voluntary or involuntary madness. . . .

Mlle. de l'Espinasse : Well ?

Bordeu : Well, the animal becomes immune to feeling, exists in a single point. I have not seen that priest of Calamus, spoken of by St. Augustine, who could abstract himself to the point of not feeling burning coals, I have not seen those savages who at the stake, laugh at their enemies, insult them and suggest for themselves more exquisite torments than those they are already suffering ; I have not seen in the arena those gladiators who, as they died, remembered the graceful attitudes they had learnt in the gymnasium ; but I believe all the facts, because I have seen, seen with my own eyes, an effort as extraordinary as any of these.

Mlle. de l'Espinasse : Doctor, tell it me. I am like children, I love marvellous stories, and when they are to the credit of the human race, I rarely question their truth.

Bordeu : There was in a small town in Champagne, Langres, a good curé called le or de Moni, steeped and imbued with the truth of religion. He had an attack of the stone, and had to be operated on. The day was fixed, the surgeon, his assistants, and myself went to his home ; he greeted us with serenity, undressed, lay down ; he would not allow himself to be strapped down ; " just put me in the right position " ; this was done. Then he asked for a great crucifix which stood at the foot of his bed ; it was given him, he clasped it in his arms, he pressed his lips to it. The operation was performed, he did not stir, uttered neither tears nor sighs, and was delivered of his stone without knowing it.

Mlle. de l'Espinasse : That is fine : and after that how can one doubt that he whose breast-bones were shattered with stones, saw the heavens open ?

Bordeu : Do you know what earache is like ?

Mlle. de l'Espinasse : No.

Bordeu : So much the better for you ; it is the cruellest pain of all.

Mlle. de l'Espinasse : Worse than toothache, which I do know, unfortunately ?

Bordeu : Incomparably worse. A philosopher, one of your friends, had been tortured by it for a fortnight, and one morning he said to his wife : " I haven't the courage to get through the day . . ." He thought that his only hope was to cheat the pain by artifice. Gradually he sunk himself so deep in some problem of metaphysics or geometry, that he forgot his ear. His food was served him, he ate without noticing it ; he reached his bedtime without having suffered. The horrible pain only seized him again when the intellectual conflict had ceased, but then it was with an unheard-of ferocity, either because weariness had actually aggravated the complaint or because weakness rendered it less bearable.

Mlle. de l'Espinasse : On emerging from such a condition one must indeed be exhausted with fatigue ; that is what happens sometimes to that man yonder.

Bordeu : It is dangerous, he should take care.

Mlle. de l'Espinasse : I am for ever telling him so, but he pays no heed.

Bordeu : The thing is beyond his control now, it has become his life, he will die of it.

Mlle. de l'Espinasse : That sentence frightens me.

Bordeu : What does this exhaustion, this weariness, prove ? That the fibres of the bundle have not lain idle and that throughout the whole system there was a violent tension towards a common centre.

Mlle. de l'Espinasse : And if this violent tension, this tendency, should persist, if it should become habitual ?

Bordeu : Then you have a nervous habit of the centre of the bundle ; the animal is mad, and almost hopelessly so.

Mlle. de l'Espinasse : And why ?

Bordeu : A nervous habit of the origin is not like a nervous habit of one of the fibres. The head can command the feet, but the feet cannot command the head ; the origin can command one of the fibres, but one of the fibres cannot command the origin.

Mlle. de l'Espinasse : And what is the difference, if you please ? Indeed, why cannot the whole of me think ? That's a question I should have thought of earlier.

Bordeu : Because consciousness resides only in one place.

Mlle. de l'Espinasse : That's easily said.

Bordeu : Because it can only reside in one place, in the common centre of all sensations, where memory is, where the process of comparison goes on. Each fibre responds only to a certain definite number of impressions, which follow one another separately, unconnected by memory. The origin responds to them all, registers them, retains the recollection or continuous sensation of them, and the animal, from the first moment it is formed, is forcibly led to refer itself thereto, to be concentrated there in its entirety, to exist there.

Mlle. de l'Espinasse : And if my finger could remember ?

Bordeu : Your finger would think.

Mlle. de l'Espinasse : And what is memory then ?

Bordeu : The property peculiar to the origin of the network, its specific property, just as sight is the property of the eye ; and it is no more surprising that memory does not dwell in the eye, than that sight does not dwell in the ear.

Mlle. de l'Espinasse : Doctor, you are evading rather than answering my questions.

Bordeu : I evade nothing, I tell you what I know, and I should know more if the organization of the origin of the network were as familiar to me as that of its fibres, if I had had the same opportunity of observing it. But, if I am weak about particular phenomena, I make up for it where general phenomena are concerned.

Mlle. de l'Espinasse : Sucl as . . . ?

Bordeu : Reason, judgment, imagination, madness, idiocy, ferocity, instinct.

Mlle. de l'Espinasse : I understand. All these qualities are only consequences of the relation, original or acquired by habit, between the origin of the bundle and its branches.

Bordeu : Exactly. Where the origin or trunk is too vigorous in relation to the branches, you have poets, artists, imaginative people, cowards, fanatics, madmen. Where it is too weak you get so-called brutes and savage beasts. Where the whole system is slack and soft, without energy, you get imbeciles ; where the whole system is energetic, harmonious, well-disciplined, you have sound thinkers, philosophers, sages.

Mlle. de l'Espinasse : And according to which branch is dominant, we have the different forms of instinct in animals and the different forms of genius in man ; the dog has its scent, the fish its hearing, the eagle its sight ; d'Alembert is a geometrician, Vaucanson a mechanical engineer, Grétry a musician, Voltaire a poet ; the varied effects of some one fibre in the bundle being stronger in them than any other, and stronger than the corresponding fibre in other beings of the same species.

Bordeu : And there is the tyranny of habit ; old men go on loving women, Voltaire goes on writing tragedies.

(*Here the doctor began to muse and Mlle. de l'Espinasse said to him*) :

Mlle. de l'Espinasse : Doctor, you are day-dreaming.

Bordeu : True.

Mlle. de l'Espinasse : What about ?

Bordeu : Voltaire.

Mlle. de l'Espinasse : Well ?

Bordeu : I was wondering what makes a great man.

Mlle. de l'Espinasse : And what is it ?

Bordeu : How sensibility . . .[17]

Mlle. de l'Espinasse : Sensibility ?

Bordeu : Or the extreme mobility of certain fibres of the network, is the dominant quality of second-rate people.

Mlle. de l'Espinasse : Oh ! Doctor, what blasphemy !

Bordeu : I was expecting that. But what is a being possessed of sensibility ? One abandoned to the mercy of his diaphragm ; should a pathetic phrase strike his ear, a strange phenomenon meet his eye, of a sudden an inward tumult is set up, all the fibres of the bundle are agitated, a shudder runs through his frame, he is seized with horror, his tears flow, sighs choke him, his voice breaks, and the origin of the bundle does not know what it is doing : farewell to self-control, reason, judgment, instinct and resourcefulness.

Mlle. de l'Espinasse : I recognize myself.

Bordeu : The great man, if he has been unlucky enough to receive such a disposition from nature, will ceaselessly strive to weaken it, to dominate it, to gain the mastery over his movements and to let the origin of the bundle retain all the power. Then he will have self-control in the midst of the greatest dangers, he will judge coldly, but sanely. Nothing that might further his desires, help towards his object, will escape him ; he will not be easily surprised ; at forty-five he will be a great king, a great minister, a great politician, a great artist, above all a great actor, a great philosopher, a great poet, a great musician, a great doctor ; he will rule over himself and all around him. He will have no fear of death, that fear which, in the Stoic's sublime phrase, the strong man grasps as a handle to lead the weak man where he wishes ; he will have broken that handle and will, at the same time, be delivered from every tyranny in the world. Men of sensibility and madmen are on the stage, he is in the stalls, he is the wise man.

Mlle. de l'Espinasse : God preserve me from the society of such a wise man !

Bordeu : It is for want of striving to be like him that you will experience violent griefs and joys in turn, that you will pass your whole life in laughter and tears, and never grow out of your childhood.

Mlle. de l'Espinasse : I'm resigned to that.

Bordeu : And do you hope it will make you happier ?

Mlle. de l'Espinasse : I cannot tell.

Bordeu : Mademoiselle, this quality, that is prized so highly, that leads to nothing great, almost always brings pain when exerted strongly, tedium when exerted mildly ; either one is bored or one is intoxicated. You yield yourself without restraint to the enjoyment of some delicious music, you let yourself be carried away by the charm of a pathetic scene ; you feel a tightening of the throat, the pleasure passes, and you retain only a sense of suffocation that persists all the evening.

Mlle. de l'Espinasse : But supposing I can enjoy the sublime music or the touching scenes only on these conditions ?

Bordeu : You are mistaken. I too can enjoy, I can admire, and I never suffer pain except from colic ; my pleasure is pure ; my criticism is the more severe thereby, my praise more precious and more deliberate. Is there such a thing as a bad tragedy for souls as easily moved as yours ? How often have you not blushed, on reading a play, to think of the ecstasy you experienced at the performance of it, and *vice versa* ?

Mlle. de l'Espinasse : Yes, it has happened to me.

Bordeu : Therefore it is not sentimentalists such as you, it is calm, cold persons like myself that have a right to say : " This is true, this is good, this is beautiful. . . ." Let us strengthen the origin of the network, that is the best thing we can possibly do. Do you know that life depends upon it ?

Mlle. de l'Espinasse : Life ? That's a serious matter, Doctor.

Bordeu : Yes, life. There is no one who has not, at some time or other, felt sick of living. A single incident may be enough to turn this feeling into an unconscious habit ; and then in spite of distractions, of varied amusements, of friends' advice and of one's own efforts, the fibres of the bundle persist in shaking the origin with fatal blows ; the wretched victim struggles in vain, the whole scene of the universe grows dark for him ; he walks escorted by a relentless band of gloomy thoughts, and ends by casting off the burden of himself.

Mlle. de l'Espinasse : Doctor, you frighten me.

d'Alembert (who has got up and is wearing a dressing-gown and night-cap) : And sleep, Doctor, what have you to say about that ? Sleep is a good thing.

Bordeu : Sleep, that state in which, either through exhaustion or through habit, the whole network slackens and stays motionless, where, as in sickness, each separate fibre of the network stirs, quivers, sends back to the common origin a swarm of sensations, often incongruous, disconnected, confused ; at other times so linked up, so consistent, so well-ordered that a waking man could not be more reasonable, more eloquent, more imaginative ; sometimes so powerful and so vivid that one remains in doubt, on waking, whether the thing didn't really happen. . . .

Mlle. de l'Espinasse : Well, what about sleep ?

Bordeu : It is a condition of the animal in which there is no more unity ; all harmony, all discipline ceases. The master is left to the mercy of the subjects, and the unbridled energy of his own activity. Should the optic fibre quiver, the origin of the network sees ; should the auditory fibre urge it, it hears. Action and reaction alone subsist between them ; which follows from the property of the centre, from the law of continuity and from habit. Should action begin by the voluptuous fibre, destined by nature for the pleasures of love and the propagation of the species, the effect of the reaction at the origin of the bundle will be to call up the image of the loved one. If, on the contrary, this image is first called up at the origin of the bundle, the result of the reaction will be a tension of the voluptuous fibre, effervescence and effusion of the seminal fluid.

d'Alembert : So there is an upward dream and a downward dream. I had one of those last night ; but which direction it took I couldn't say.

Bordeu : When one is awake, the network responds to the impressions of external objects. In sleep, all that it experiences springs from the exercise of its own sensitiveness. In dreams there is no distraction, hence their vividness ;[18]

they nearly always result from some irritation, some temporary disorder. The origin of the network is alternately active and passive, in an infinite number of ways ; hence its confusion. Sometimes, in dreams, concepts are as connected and distinct as when the animal is in direct contact with the natural scene. It is simply that the image of this scene has been called up afresh ; hence the realism of the dream, hence the impossibility of distinguishing it from the waking state ; there is no greater probability in favour of one of these states than of the other ; experiment alone will indicate the error.

Mlle. de l'Espinasse : And is experiment always possible ?

Bordeu : No.

Mlle. de l'Espinasse : If, in a dream, I see a friend that I have lost, see him as vividly as though he were still in existence ; if he speaks to me and I hear him ; if I touch him and he seems solid to my hands ; if on waking I feel my heart full of tender emotion and grief and my eyes overflowing with tears ; if my arms are still outstretched towards the spot where he appeared to me, what will convince me that I have not really seen, heard and touched him ?

Bordeu : The fact of his absence. But, if it is impossible to distinguish sleep from the waking state, who can judge its duration ? A quiet sleep is an unconscious interval between bed-time and rising-time ; a troubled sleep may seem to last for years. In the first case, at any rate, consciousness of one's identity ceases entirely. Can you tell me of one dream that has never been dreamt and never will be ?

Mlle. de l'Espinasse . Yes, to dream that one is somebody else.

d'Alembert : And in the second case, one is not only conscious of one's identity but also of one's will and of one's liberty. What are the will and liberty of a dreaming man ?

Bordeu : What are they ? The same as those of a waking man ; the latest impulse of desire and aversion, the last result of all that one has been from birth to the actual moment ; and I defy the subtlest mind to perceive the least difference between them.

d'Alembert : Do you think so ?

Bordeu : And it's *you* who ask me that ! You, who, absorbed in profound speculations, have passed two-thirds of your life dreaming with your eyes open and doing involuntary actions ; yes, far more involuntary than in your dream. In your dream, you commanded, you gave orders, you were obeyed ; you were displeased or satisfied, you found your will opposed, you encountered obstacles, you grew angry, you loved, hated, blamed, you came and went. During your meditations, hardly were your eyes open in the morning than, possessed anew by the idea that had been occupying you the night before, you would dress, sit at your table, ponder, draw figures, make calculations, eat your dinner, resume your calculations, sometimes getting up from the table to verify them ; you would speak to other people, give orders to your servants, eat your supper, go to bed and sleep, without having performed one voluntary action. You have been reduced to a single point ; you have acted, but you have not exerted your will. Does one exert will by instinct ? Will is always moved by some inward or outward stimulus, by some present impression or recollection of the past, or by some passion or project for the future. After this I need only say one word about freedom, that is, that the most recent action of each one of us is the necessary result of a single cause—oneself ; a highly complex cause, but a single one.

Mlle. de l'Espinasse : And necessary ?

Bordeu : Undoubtedly. Try to imagine any other action resulting, assuming that the being who acts is the same.

Mlle. de l'Espinasse : He is right. Since I act in a certain way, the person who could act differently is no longer me ;

and to declare that, at the moment I am doing or saying one thing, I might be saying or doing another, is to declare that I am myself and someone else. But, Doctor, what about vice and virtue ? Virtue, so holy a word in all languages, so sacred an idea to all nations !

Bordeu : We must change it for that of doing good, and its contrary for that of doing harm. One is born well or ill endowed by nature ; one is irresistibly carried away by the general torrent that brings one man to glory and another to disgrace.

Mlle. de l'Espinasse : What of self-esteem, and shame, and remorse ?

Bordeu : Childish reactions founded on the ignorance and vanity of a person who attributes to himself the praise and blame for a moment of time that necessarily had to be.

Mlle. de l'Espinasse : And rewards and punishments ?

Bordeu : Ways of correcting that person whom we call wicked, but who can be altered, and of encouraging the one we call good.

Mlle. de l'Espinasse : Isn't there something dangerous about this doctrine ?

Bordeu : Is it true or is it false ?

Mlle. de l'Espinasse : I believe it to be true.

Bordeu : That is to say, you think that falsehood has its advantages and truth its inconvenient aspects.

Mlle. de l'Espinasse : I think so.

Bordeu : And so do I ; but the advantages of falsehood are transient and those of truth are eternal ; the distressing results of truth, when they occur, disappear quickly, and those of a lie last as long as the lie. Examine the effects of falsehood in man's mind and in his conduct ; in his mind, either falsehood has become somehow or other mingled with truth, and then he is muddle-headed ; or else it is thoroughly and consistently united with falsehood, and then he is wrong-headed. Now, what conduct can you expect from a head that is either inconsistent in its reasoning or consistent in its errors ?

Mlle. de l'Espinasse : The latter vice, though less contemptible, is perhaps more dangerous than the former.

d'Alembert : Very good ; now all is reduced to a question of the faculty of sensation or feeling, memory, organic movements ; that suits me very well. But what about imagination ? And abstract ideas ?

Bordeu : Imagination. . . .

Mlle. de l'Espinasse : One moment, Doctor ; let us recapitulate. According to your principles, it seems to me that by a series of purely mechanical operations, I could reduce the greatest genius on earth to an unorganized mass of flesh, which would only retain the faculty of momentary sensation, and that this formless mass could then be brought back from the state of the most utter stupidity imaginable, to the condition of a man of genius. One of these two processes would consist in depriving the original skein of a certain number of its fibres, and thoroughly confusing the rest ; and the inverse process, in restoring to the skein the fibres one had removed, and then leaving the whole to a lucky development. For instance : I take away from Newton the two auditory fibres, and he has no more sense of sound ; the olfactory fibres, and he has no more sense of smell ; the optic fibres, and no more sense of colour ; the fibres that form the palate, and he loses his sense of taste ; I suppress or entangle the others, and there's an end to the organization of the brain, memory, judgment, desire, aversion, passion, will, self-consciousness, and behold an amorphous mass which has retained only life and sensitiveness.

Bordeu : Two qualities which are almost identical ; life pertains to the aggregate, sensitiveness to the elements.

Mlle. de l'Espinasse : I take up this mass again and I restore to it the olfactory fibres, and it can smell ; the auditory fibres, and it can hear ; the optic fibres, and it can

see ; the fibres of the palate, and it can taste. Disentangling
the rest of the skein, I allow the other fibres to develop,
and I behold the rebirth of memory, of the faculty of
comparison, of judgment, reason, desire, aversion, passion,
natural aptitude, talent, and I find my man of genius once
more, without the intervention of any heterogeneous or
unintelligible agent.

Bordeu : Excellent ; keep to that, all the rest is senseless
verbiage. . . . But what about abstract ideas, and imagination ? Imagination is the recollection of forms and colours.
The picture of a scene or an object inevitably tunes up the
sensitive instrument in a certain fashion : either it tunes
itself, or it is tuned up by some outside cause. Then it
vibrates within, or resounds externally ; it retraces in
silence the impressions it has received, or echoes them
abroad in sounds fixed by convention.

d'Alembert : But its recital exaggerates, omits certain
circumstances and adds others, distorts the fact or embel-
lishes it, and the sensitive instruments around it receive
impressions which assuredly correspond to those of the
instrument which is sounding, but not to the original thing
that took place.

Bordeu : True, the recital may be either historical or
poetical.

d'Alembert : But how does this poetry or falsehood find its
way into the recital ?

Bordeu : Because ideas awaken one another, and they
awaken one another because they have always been connected. Since you took the liberty of comparing an animal
to a harpsichord, you will surely allow me to compare the
poet's recital to a song.

d'Alembert : That is quite fair.

Bordeu : In any song there is a scale. This scale has its
intervals ; each of its notes has its harmonics, and these in
turn have their own harmonics. That is how modulations
are introduced into the melody, and how the song is

enriched and extended. The fact is a given theme that each musician feels in his own way.

Mlle. de l'Espinasse : But why confuse the question with this figurative style ? I should say that, since every one has his own eyes, every one sees and tells a thing differently. I should say that each idea awakens others and that, according to one's turn of mind and one's character, either one keeps to those ideas that strictly represent the fact, or one introduces ideas suggested by association ; I should say that there is a choice to be made among these ideas ; I should say that this one subject, treated thoroughly, would furnish a whole book.

d'Alembert : You are right ; but that won't prevent me from asking the doctor if he is convinced that a form that was not like anything else could not be engendered in the imagination and introduced into the recital.

Bordeu : I think that is the case. The wildest fantasy of this faculty is nothing more than the talent of those tricksters who, from the parts of several animals, compose a strange creature that was never seen in nature.

d'Alembert : And abstract ideas ?

Bordeu : They don't exist ; there are only habitual omissions, ellipses, that make propositions more general and speech swifter and more convenient. It is the symbols of speech that have given rise to the abstract sciences. A quality common to several beings engendered the terms ugliness and beauty. We first said one man, one horse, two animals ; then we said one, two, three, and the whole science of numbers was born.[19] It is impossible to conceive of an abstract word. It was observed that all bodies have three dimensions, length, breadth and depth ; each of these was studied, and hence arose all mathematical sciences. An abstraction is merely a symbol emptied of its idea. The idea has been excluded by separating the symbol from the physical object, and it is only when the symbol is attached once more to the physical object that science becomes a science of ideas again ; hence the need, so frequently felt both in conversation and in books, of having recourse to examples. When, after a long series of symbols, you ask for an example, you are only requiring the speaker to give body, shape, reality, to attach an idea to the series of sounds made by his speech, by connecting those sounds with sensations that have been experienced.

d'Alembert : Is this quite clear to you, Mademoiselle ?

Mlle. de l'Espinasse : Not exceedingly, but the doctor will explain.

Bordeu : You are good enough to say so ! No doubt there is some correction and much addition to be made to what I've said ; but it is half-past eleven, and at twelve I have a consultation at the Marais.

d'Alembert : Speech swifter and more convenient ! Doctor, does one ever understand ? Is one ever understood ?

Bordeu : Almost all conversations are like accounts already made up . . . where has my stick got to ? . . . one has no idea present in one's mind . . . and my hat ? . . . And for the simple reason that no man is exactly like another, we never understand precisely, we are never precisely understood ; it is always a case of more or less, in everything ; our speech always falls short of experience or goes beyond it. A great difference between man's judgments can be observed, an infinitely greater difference passes unobserved, and luckily can never be observed. . . . Good-bye, good-bye.

Mlle. de l'Espinasse : One word more, I implore you !

Bordeu : Quickly then.

Mlle. de l'Espinasse : Do you remember those leaps of which you spoke to me ?

Bordeu : Yes.

Mlle. de l'Espinasse : Do you think that fools and men of intelligence might have those leaps in their lineage ?

Bordeu : Why not ?

Mlle. de l'Espinasse : All the better for our great-nephews ; perhaps a second Henri IV will appear.

Bordeu : Perhaps he has already appeared.

Mlle. de l'Espinasse : Doctor, you must come and dine with us.

Bordeu : I'll do what I can, I don't promise : expect me when you see me.

Mlle. de l'Espinasse : We will wait for you till two o'clock.

Bordeu : So be it.

CONCLUSION OF THE CONVERSATION

The Speakers : *Mademoiselle de l'Espinasse and Doctor Bordeu.*

About two o'clock the doctor came back. D'Alembert had gone out to dine, and the doctor was alone with Mlle. de l'Espinasse. Dinner was served. They talked of indifferent matters until dessert ; but when the servants had retired, Mlle. de l'Espinasse said to the doctor : Come now, Doctor, drink a glass of malaga, and then you shall give me the answer to a question that has passed through my head a hundred times, and that I shouldn't dare put to anyone but you.

Bordeu : Excellent malaga, this. . . . What is your question ?

Mlle. de l'Espinasse : What do you think of the intermingling of species ?

Bordeu : Well, that is certainly a good question. I think that men have attributed great importance to the act of generation, and rightly so ; but I'm not satisfied with their laws, either civil or religious.

Mlle. de l'Espinasse : And what fault do you find with them ?

Bordeu : They have been made without justice, without purpose, and without any consideration for the nature of things or for the public good.

118

Mlle. de l'Espinasse : Try and explain.

Bordeu : I mean to. . . . But wait . . . (*he looks at his watch*). I've still a good hour to spare you ; I'll go quickly, and it will be long enough. We are alone, you're no prude, you won't fancy that I intend any lack of that respect I owe you ; and whatever may be your opinion of my ideas, I hope, on my side, that you won't conclude therefrom anything derogatory to my morals.

Mlle. de l'Espinasse : Of course not ; but I don't much like your opening.

Bordeu : In that case let's change the subject.

Mlle. de l'Espinasse : No, no, go on. One of your friends who was looking out for husbands for myself and my two sisters allotted a sylph to the younger, a great angel of the Annunciation to the elder and a disciple of Diogenes to me ; he knew us well, all three. Nevertheless, Doctor, a veil, just a slight veil.

Bordeu : That goes without saying, insofar as the subject and my profession allow of it.

Mlle. de l'Espinasse : It won't inconvenience you. . . . But here is your coffee . . . drink your coffee.

Bordeu (having drunk his coffee) : Your question has physical, moral and poetical aspects.

Mlle. de l'Espinasse : Poetical !

Bordeu : Surely ; the art of creating non-existent beings in imitation of those that exist is true poetry. This time then, instead of Hippocrates, you'll allow me to quote Horace. This poet, or maker, says somewhere : *Omne tulit punctum, qui miscuit utile dolci* ; the supreme merit lies in combining the pleasant with the useful. Perfection consists in reconciling these two qualities. The action that is both pleasant and useful must occupy the first place in the æsthetic hierarchy ; we cannot deny the second place to that which is useful ; the third will be for what is pleasant ; and to the lowest rank we must relegate the action that produces neither pleasure nor profit.

Mlle. de l'Espinasse : So far I can agree with you without blushing. But where is it going to lead us ?

Bordeu : You shall see. Mademoiselle, can you tell me what profit or what pleasure is derived from strict chastity and continence, either by the individual who practises them or by society ?

Mlle. de l'Espinasse : None, I declare.

Bordeu : Then, despite the magnificent praises lavished on them by fanaticism, despite the protection afforded them by civil laws, we will cross them out of the catalogue of virtues, and we will agree that there is nothing so childish, so ridiculous, so absurd, so harmful, so contemptible, nothing worse, except positive evil, than these two rare qualities.

Mlle. de l'Espinasse : I'll grant you that.

Bordeu : Take care, I warn you, you'll want to withdraw in a moment.

Mlle. de l'Espinasse : We never withdraw.

Bordeu : And what about solitary actions ?

Mlle. de l'Espinasse : Well ?

Bordeu : Well, they at least give pleasure to the individual, and either our principle is wrong or. . . .

Mlle. de l'Espinasse : What, Doctor ! . . .

Bordeu : Yes, Mademoiselle, yes, since on the one hand they are just as neutral, and on the other they are not so sterile. It is a need, and even if one were not urged by the need it is still a pleasant experience. I want people to be well, I absolutely insist on it, do you understand ? I am against all excess, but, in a state of society such as ours, there are a hundred reasonable considerations if there's one such as lack of fortune, the dread, for men, of a painful repentance, for women the dread of dishonour ; not to mention passionate temperament and the disastrous effect of strict continency, particularly on young people, which all drive a wretched creature that's consumed with languor and boredom, a poor devil who doesn't know where to get help, to relieve himself in the manner of the cynic. Would Cato, who said to a young man on the point of visiting a courtesan : " Courage, my son . . ." speak to him in the same way to-day ? If, on the contrary, he caught him in the act alone, would he not add : " That is better than corrupting the wife of another, or risking one's honour and one's health " ? What ! just because circumstances deprive me of the greatest happiness imaginable, that of mingling my senses with those of a partner chosen by my heart, my ecstasy with her ecstasy, my soul with her soul, and of reproducing myself in her and with her ; just because I cannot imprint upon my action the sacred stamp of utility, must I forbid myself the enjoyment of a necessary and delicious moment ? One is bled to relieve plethora ; and what matters the nature of the superabundant humour, its colour, and the way one gets rid of it ? It is just as superfluous in the one disturbance as in the other ; and if it were pumped back out of the vessels that contain it, distributed throughout the whole body, to find its way out by a longer, more painful and perilous way, would it be any the less wasted ? Nature allows nothing useless ; and how can I be held guilty for helping her, when she appeals for my assistance by the plainest of symptoms ? Let us never provoke her, but let us lend her a hand when the occasion demands it ; to refuse this, to remain idle, seems to me mere foolishness and a lost chance of pleasure. Live soberly, people may say to me, tire yourself out. I understand : I am to deprive myself of one pleasure : I am to inflict pain on myself to ward off another pleasure. A very happy notion !

Mlle. de l'Espinasse : Your doctrine isn't suitable to be preached to children.

Bordeu : Nor to anyone else. Nevertheless, will you allow me to suggest a possibility ? You have a daughter who is virtuous, too virtuous ; innocent, too innocent ; she has reached the age when the temperament develops. Her mind becomes bewildered, nature does not assist her ; you send for me. I see at once that all the symptoms that alarm you arise from the superabundance and retention of the seminal fluid ; I warn you that she is threatened with a kind of madness that is difficult to prevent and some- times impossible to cure ; I indicate the remedy. What will you do ?

Mlle. de l'Espinasse : To tell you the truth, I believe . . . but such cases don't occur.

Bordeu : That's where you are wrong ; they are not un- common, and they would be quite common if the loose- ness of our morals did not prevent it. . . . Be that as it may, to divulge such principles would mean trampling underfoot all decency, exposing oneself to the most odious suspicions and offending the dignity of society. . . . But you're absorbed by some thought.

Mlle. de l'Espinasse : Yes, I was wondering if I should ask you whether you had ever had to impart this secret to any mothers ?

Bordeu : Certainly.

Mlle. de l'Espinasse: And what course did these mothers take?

Bordeu : All, without exception, took the right course, the sensible course. . . . I would not take off my hat in the street to a man suspected of practising my doctrine ; it would be enough for me that he'd be called a vile wretch. But we are talking without witnesses and informally ; and I will say to you about my philosophy what Diogenes, stark naked, said to the young and bashful Athenian with whom he was preparing to wrestle : "My son, fear nothing, I am not so wicked as yonder man."

Mlle. de l'Espinasse : Doctor, I see where you are tending, and I wager . . .

Bordeu : I won't wager, you would win. Yes, Made- moiselle, such is my opinion.

Mlle. de l'Espinasse : What ! Whether one remains within the limits of one's own species, or passes beyond them ?

Bordeu : True.

Mlle. de l'Espinasse : You are monstrous !

Bordeu : Not I, but either nature or society. Listen, Mademoiselle, I don't let myself be imposed on by words, and I express myself all the more freely because my conscience is clear, and the purity of my morals beyond reproach on all sides. I will therefore ask you : of two actions both confined solely to pleasure, which can only bring enjoyment without profit, but of which one brings enjoyment to the agent alone, whereas in the other the enjoyment is shared by the agent and a fellow-creature, male or female, for the sex and even the use of sex do not affect the question, in favour of which will common sense declare itself ?

Mlle. de l'Espinasse : Such questions are too lofty for me.

Bordeu : Oh ! After having been a man for four minutes, now you're resuming mob-cap and petticoats, and becoming a woman again. Very good ; well ! you shall be treated as such. That is easily done. . . . We hear nothing nowadays about Madame du Barry. . . . You see, everything is settling down ; people thought the court would be turned upside down. The master acted like a sensible man ; " *omne tulit punctum* " ; he's kept the woman who gave him pleasure, and the minister who was useful to him. . . . But you are not listening to me. . . . Where have you got to ?

Mlle. de l'Espinasse : I'm thinking of those unions that seem to me wholly against nature.

Bordeu : Nothing that exists can be either against nature or outside nature. I don't except even voluntary chastity and continence, which would be the chief crimes against nature if one could sin against nature, and the chief crimes against the social laws in a country where actions were weighed in a balance other than that of fanaticism and prejudice.

Mlle. de l'Espinasse : I am back at your accursed syllogisms and I see no middle course, one has to deny or accept everything. . . . But see, Doctor, the most honest way and the quickest, is to jump over the mess and come back to my first question : What do you think of the intermingling of species ?

Bordeu : We don't need to jump to get there ; we were there already. Do you mean from the physical or the moral point of view ?

Mlle. de l'Espinasse : Physical, physical.

Bordeu : So much the better : the moral question came first and you've decided it. So then . . .

Mlle. de l'Espinasse : Agreed . . . no doubt it is a preliminary, but I wish . . . that you could separate cause from effect. Let us leave the horrid cause out of it.

Bordeu : You are asking me to begin at the end ; but, since you desire it, I will tell you that, thanks to our faint-heartedness, our aversions, our laws, our prejudices, very few experiments have been made. It is not known in which cases copulation would be wholly unfruitful, in which cases utility and pleasure would combine ; what sort of species might be expected from varied and continuous experimentation ; whether fauns are real or fabulous creatures ; whether we could not multiply races of mules in a hundred different ways, and whether those that we know are really sterile. But there's one odd fact which an infinite number of learned folk will swear to you is true, and which is false ; that is, that they have seen in the archduke's poultry-yard a vile rabbit acting as cock to twenty vile hens, who put up with him. They will add that they were shown chickens covered with hair, the product of this bestiality. You may take it from me that someone was making fun of them.

Mlle. de l'Espinasse : But what do you mean by continuous experimentation ?

Bordeu : I mean that the circulation of creatures is gradual, that their assimilation has to be prepared beforehand, and that, in order to succeed in such experiments, one ought to start a long way back and endeavour first to make animals more like one another by a similar diet.

Mlle. de l'Espinasse : You'll find it hard to bring a man to graze.

Bordeu : But not to drink goat's milk frequently, and one could easily bring the goat to feed on bread. I've chosen the goat for reasons peculiarly my own.

Mlle. de l'Espinasse : What are these reasons ?

Bordeu : You are very bold ! They are . . . well . . . they are, that we should thus produce a vigorous, swift, intelligent and indefatigable race of beings, of whom we could make excellent servants.

Mlle. de l'Espinasse : Very fine, Doctor ; I fancy already that I can see five or six great insolent goats'-feet behind the carriages of your duchesses, and it delights me.

Bordeu : And we should no longer degrade our brothers by subjecting them to functions unworthy of them and of ourselves.

Mlle. de l'Espinasse : Better still.

Bordeu : And that we should no longer reduce men in our colonies to be mere beasts of burden.

Mlle. de l'Espinasse : Quickly, quickly, Doctor, set to work and make these goats'-feet for us.

Bordeu : You have no scruples about allowing it ?

Mlle. de l'Espinasse : Stop, though, one has occurred to me ; your goats'-feet would be wildly licentious.

Bordeu : I can't guarantee they'd be highly moral.

Mlle. de l'Espinasse : There will be no more safety for honest women ; they will multiply unceasingly, and in the end we shall have either to destroy them or obey them. I don't want them any more, I don't want them any more. You had better keep quiet.

Bordeu (going away) : And the question of their baptism ?

Mlle. de l'Espinasse : Would cause a great to-do in the Sorbonne.

Bordeu : Have you seen in the King's garden, in a glass

cage, an orang-outang that looks like St. John preaching in the wilderness?

Mlle. de l'Espinasse : Yes, I've seen it.

Bordeu : Cardinal de Polignac said to it one day : " Speak, and I will baptize thee."

Mlle. de l'Espinasse : Good-bye then, Doctor ; don't forget us for centuries as you do, and remember sometimes that I love you to distraction. If people only knew what horrors you've been telling me !

Bordeu : I'm sure you'll keep silent about them.

Mlle. de l'Espinasse : Don't be too confident, I only listen for the pleasure of repeating things. But just one more word, and I'll never reopen the subject again.

Bordeu : What is it?

Mlle. de l'Espinasse : Whence come these abominable tastes ?

Bordeu : Everywhere from a weakness of the organism among young people and the mental corruption of the old; in Athens, from the attraction of beauty ; in Rome, from the scarcity of women; and in Paris, from the fear of the pox. Good-bye, good-bye.

(1769)

IV
PHILOSOPHIC PRINCIPLES
ON
MATTER AND MOTION

I DO not know in what sense philosophers have supposed that matter was equally indifferent to motion and to rest. What is quite certain is that all bodies gravitate one upon another ; that in this universe, everything is either in translation or *in nisu*,[1]* or else in translation and *in nisu* at one and the same time.

The supposition of philosophers perhaps resembles that of geometricians, who admit of points having no dimensions, of lines having no width or depth, of surfaces having no thickness ; or they may speak of the relative state of rest of one mass compared to that of another. Everything is in relative rest in a tempest-tossed ship. Nothing in it is in a state of absolute rest, not even the molecules which compose the ship itself, nor those which compose the bodies in the ship.

If they do not conceive of more tendency to rest than to motion in any body whatsoever, it is because they apparently regard matter as homogeneous ; because they abstract all the qualities which are essential to it ; because they consider it unalterable during the almost indivisible moment of their speculation ; because they reason about the relative state of rest of one aggregate compared to that of another aggregate ; because they forget that while they are reasoning about the indifference of a body to motion or to repose, the block of marble is proceeding towards its dissolution ; because they abolish by thought both the

* In a state of potential energy.

general motion which animates all bodies and their particular actions one upon another, which destroys them all ; because this indifference, although false in itself and only transitory, will not prove the laws of motion to be wrong.

A body, according to some philosophers, *is, in itself, without action and without force.* This is a terrible error, contrary to all sound physics and to all sound chemistry : a body in itself, by the nature of its essential qualities is full of action and of energy, whether one considers it molecule by molecule or whether one considers it in the mass. '

In order to represent motion to yourself, they add, *you must not only conceive of existing matter, but also of a force acting upon it.* That is not the case : the molecule[2] endowed with a quality proper to its own nature, is in itself an active force. It exercises its force upon another molecule, which in turn exercises its force upon the first one. All these paralogisms are related to the false supposition of homogeneous matter. You who so easily imagine matter in repose, can you imagine fire in repose ? Everything in nature has its own different form of action, like this mass of molecules which you call *fire*. In this mass which you call *fire*, each molecule has its own nature, its own action.

This is the real difference between rest and motion : absolute rest is an abstract concept which does not exist in nature, and motion is a quality as real as length, breadth, and depth. What does it matter to me what is going on in your head ? What does it matter to me whether you regard matter as homogeneous or heterogeneous ? What does it matter to me that, abstracting its qualities and only considering its existence, you see it in a state of rest ? What does it matter to me that, in consequence, you seek for an external cause to move it ? You can concern yourselves with geometry and metaphysics as much as you like ; but I, who am a physicist and a chemist, I, who consider bodies as they are in nature and not as they are in my head, I see them existing, differing, having properties and actions, and moving in the universe as they do in the laboratory, where a spark cannot be placed beside three particles made of saltpetre, carbon, and sulphur, without an explosion necessarily following.

Gravity is by no means a tendency to rest ; it is a tendency to local movement. Again, some say, *in order that matter should be moved an action, a force, is necessary.* Yes, a force either exterior to the molecule, or else inherent, essential, intimately a part of the molecule, constituting its nature as a fiery, watery, nitrous, alkaline or sulphurous molecule ; whatever this nature may be, energy results from it, action outside itself, action of other molecules on it.

Force which acts on the molecule exhausts itself ; force, which is a part of the molecule does not exhaust itself. It is immutable, eternal. These two kinds of forces can produce two kinds of *nisus* ; the first, a *nisus* which comes to an end ; the second, a never-ending *nisus*. Therefore, it is absurd to say that matter has a real resistance to motion.

The quantity of force in nature is constant, but the sum of the *nisus* and the sum of translations are variable. The greater the sum of the *nisus* the smaller the sum of translations ; and, reciprocally, the greater the sum of translations the smaller the sum of *nisus*. The burning of a town immediately increases the sum of translations by a prodigious amount.

One atom moves the world ; nothing is more true ; it is as true as the atom which is moved by the world : since the atom has its own force it cannot be without effect.

A physicist must never say *the body as a body* ; because that is not physics ; it is an abstraction which leads to nothing.

We must not confound action with mass. There can be a great mass and a slight action. There can be a small mass and a great action. One particle of air splits a block of steel. Four grains of powder are sufficient to divide a rock.

Yes, doubtless, when one compares a homogeneous

aggregate to another aggregate of the same homogeneous matter ; when one speaks of the action and reaction of these two aggregates, their relative energies are in direct propor-tion to their masses. But when heterogeneous aggregates or heterogeneous molecules are concerned, the laws are no longer the same. There are as many different laws as there are varieties of individual and characteristic force of each elementary and constituent molecule of the body.

A body resists horizontal motion. What does that mean ? We know very well that there is a general force common to all the molecules of the globe which we inhabit, a force which presses them in a certain direction, perpendicular, more or less, towards the surface of the globe ; but this general and common force is opposed by a hundred thousand others. A heated tube of glass makes gold leaf flutter about. A hurricane fills the air with dust ; heat turns water to steam, the steam carries with it molecules of salt ; while this mass of brass weighs on the earth, the air acts upon it, turns its initial surface into a metallic calx, begins the destruction of this body ; and what I say of masses is to be understood also of molecules. Each molecule must be considered as actually animated by three kinds of action ; the action of weight or gravity ; the action of its own force, proper to its nature of water, fire, air, or sulphur ; and the action of all the other molecules on it : and it may happen that these three actions are convergent or divergent. If they are convergent, then the molecule has the strongest action with which it can be endowed. To obtain an idea of this greatest possible action it would be necessary, so to speak, to make a host of absurd suppositions, to put a molecule in an entirely metaphysical situation.

In what sense can it be said that the greater the mass of a body, the more it resists motion ? It must not be thought that the greater its mass the weaker its pressure against an obstacle ; every street porter knows better than that ; it is only relative to a direction opposite to its pressure. In this direction it is certain that the greater its mass the more it resists movement. In the direction of gravity it is no less certain that its pressure or force, or tendency to motion increases in proportion to its mass. What does all this signify, then ? Nothing.

I am not in the least surprised to see a body fall any more than to see a flame rise upwards, any more than I am surprised to see water act in all directions, and weigh in accordance with its height and its base, so that with a moderate quantity of liquid I can make the strongest vessels break ; any more than I am surprised to see steam expanding under pressure break up the strongest bodies in Papin's machine or raise the heaviest bodies in a " fire-machine." But I fix my gaze on the general mass of bodies ; I see everything in action and reaction, everything destroying itself under one form, recomposing itself under another ; sublimations, dissolutions, combinations of all kinds, phenomena incompatible with the homogeneity of matter ; and therefore I conclude that matter is heterogeneous, that an infinity of divers elements exist in nature, that each of these elements, by its diversity, has its own particular force, innate, immutable, eternal, indestructible ; and that these forces contained in bodies have their action outside the bodies ; whence comes the motion, or rather the general fermentation of the universe.

What are those philosophers doing, whose errors and paralogisms I am refuting ? They are concerning themselves with one single and unique force, which is, perhaps, common to all the molecules of matter ; I say *perhaps,* for it would not surprise me at all if there were in nature certain molecules which, joined to others, would make the resulting combination lighter. Every day in the laboratory we make one inert body turn another inert body into a gas ; and those who, considering all action in the universe to be only that of gravity, thence conclude the indifference of matter to rest or to motion, or rather the tendency of matter to rest, believe that they have solved the question, whereas they have not even touched the fringes of it.

When one considers a body as more or less resistant, and not as heavy or tending to the centre of gravity, one already recognizes this body to have a force, an action, proper to itself and part of it ; but there are many other actions, among which some work in any direction while others have special directions.

The supposition of any being whatever placed outside the material universe is impossible. We must never make such suppositions, because one can never infer anything from them.

Everything that is said about the impossibility of an increase of motion or of speed is in direct opposition to the hypothesis of homogeneous matter. But how does that concern those who deduce the motion of matter from its heterogeneity ? The supposition of homogeneous matter indeed leads to other absurdities.

If a man is determined not to consider things as they are in his head, but rather as they are in the universe, he will be convinced, by the diversity of phenomena, of the diversity of elementary substances, of the diversity of actions and reactions, of the necessity of motion ; and once all these truths have been admitted, he will no longer say, " I see matter as existing, I see it first in repose," because he will feel that to speak thus is to make an abstraction from which nothing can be concluded. Existence does not entail either repose or motion ; but existence is not the only quality of bodies.

All physicists who suppose matter to be indifferent to motion and to rest have no clear ideas as to the nature of resistance. In order for them to be able to conclude something about resistance, it would be necessary for this quality to be exercised indistinguishably in all directions, and that its energy should be the same in all directions. Then it would be an intimate force, such as that of all molecules ; but in fact this resistance varies to the extent of the number of different directions in which the body may be pushed : it is greater vertically than horizontally.

The difference between weight and the force of inertia is that weight is not equally resistant in all directions, while the force of inertia, on the other hand is equally resistant in all directions.

And why does the force of inertia not have the effect of keeping the body in its state of rest and in its state of motion, according to the sole conception of resistance proportional to the quantity of matter ? The conception of pure resistance is equally applicable to rest and to motion ; to rest, when the body is in motion, and to motion when the body is at rest. Without this resistance, there could be no collision before motion, nor arrest after the collision, for the body would be nothing.

In the experiment of the ball suspended by a thread, weight is destroyed. The ball pulls the thread as much as the thread pulls the ball. Therefore the resistance of the body comes solely from the force of inertia.

If the thread pulled the ball more than the weight pulled it, the ball would rise. If the ball were more pulled by weight than by the thread, it would fall. . . .[3]

(1770)

V

From

ELEMENTS OF PHYSIOLOGY

BEINGS[1]

ONE must begin by classifying beings, from the inert molecule, if there is one, to the living molecule, to the microscopic animal, to the plant-animal, to the animal, to man.

Chain of Beings.

It is not necessary to believe that the chain of beings is interrupted by diversity of forms ; the form is often only a deceptive mask, and the link which would appear to be missing perhaps exists in a known being which the progress of comparative anatomy has not yet been able to assign to its true place. This method of classifying beings is very difficult and very slow, and can only be the fruit of the labours of a large number of naturalists. Let us wait and let us not hasten to form judgments.

Contradictory Beings.

These are those whose organization does not conform with the rest of the universe. Blind nature, which produces them, exterminates them ; she lets only those exist which can co-exist tolerably with the general order, which is vaunted by her panegyrists.

Existing Contradictory Beings.

Delicate chest and violent character, speedily passes away.
Melancholy and miserable, speedily passes away.

Active, ardent and penetrating mind, frail body, speedily
passes away.
She lets the misfits (*mécontents*)[2] endure but a little while.
The long life : strong constitution, lack of sensitiveness,
stupidity, wealth, moderate tastes, etc. . . .

Elements.

The elements in isolated molecules have none of the
properties of the mass.
Fire is without light and without heat.
Water, without moistness and without elasticity.
Air has nothing of what it presents to us.
That is why they do nothing in bodies in which they are
combined with other substances.

Duration, Extension.

In nature : duration, succession of actions.
Extension : co-existence of simultaneous actions.
In the understanding : duration resolves itself into motion ;
by abstraction, extension into rest.
But rest and motion are the rest and motion of a body.[3]

On Existence.

I cannot separate, even abstractly, place and duration from
existence. These two properties are therefore essential to
it. (P. 253–4.)

ANIMALS

The animal is a hydraulic machine. What idiotic things
can be said following this one supposition.
The laws of motion of hard bodies are unknown, for there
are no perfectly hard bodies.
The laws of motion of elastic bodies are no more certain,
for there is no perfectly elastic body.
The laws of motion of fluid bodies are quite uncertain,
and the laws of motion of bodies which are sensitive,

animated, organized, living, are not even outlined. Anyone who omits from the calculation of this last kind of motion, sensitiveness, irritability, life, spontaneity, does not know what he is doing.[4] A gross body acts on a sensitive, organized, animal body ; the latter has consciousness or a feeling of the impression and often of the site of the impression ; it is pleased or hurt ; it wishes or does not wish to move. (P. 262-3.)

* * * * *

The vegetable kingdom might well be and have been the first source of the animal kingdom, and have had its own source in the mineral kingdom ; and the latter have originated from universal heterogeneous matter. (P. 265.)

Animal functions.

Let someone teach me how the young swallow makes its nest, and I will explain all the actions which belong to inexperienced man, to animal man.

An observation which must not be neglected, is that from the mother to the infant, which during nine months is one with her, there pass dispositions, tastes, organic aptitudes, of which it is impossible for us thoroughly to know the whole strength. About this subject two absurd suppositions are commonly made ; then insoluble difficulties are deduced therefrom. One of these suppositions is that there might be on the surface of the earth a being, an animal, which might have been from time immemorial what it is now.

The other supposition is that there is no difference between the man who would come from the hand of a creator and the infant which comes from the womb of its mother. (P. 265.)

Animal and Machine.

What difference between a sensitive and living watch and a watch of gold, of iron, of silver and of copper ? If a soul were joined to the latter, what would it produce therein ?

If the union of a soul to a machine is impossible, let someone prove it to me.

If it is possible, let someone tell me what would be the effects of this union.

The peasant who sees a watch working, and who, not being able to understand the mechanism, puts a spirit into the hands, is neither more nor less foolish than our spiritualists. (P. 265–6.)

Sensitiveness. [5]

Quality proper to the animal which makes it aware of the relations between itself and all that environs it.

But all parts of the animal do not have this quality. There are only the nerves which may have it by themselves.

*   *   *   *   *

I should be tempted to believe that sensitiveness is nothing else but the motion of the animal substance, its corollary ; for if I introduce torpor into it, cessation of motion at one point, the sensitiveness disappears.

Sensitiveness is more powerful than the will.

The sensitiveness of matter is the life proper to organs.

The proof of this is evident in a skinned and headless viper, in fragments of the eel and other fish, in the adder cut up, in the separated and palpitating members of a body, in the contraction of a pricked heart.

I do not believe in the absolute lack of sensitiveness of any part whatever of an animal.

An intermediate non-sensitive organ between two sensitive and living organs would arrest sensation, and would become a foreign body in the system ; it would be like two animals joined by a rope.

What would a loom in the Lyons silk manufacture be, if the workman and the woman drawer made a sensitive whole with the warp and woof, the *sample** and the *gavassine*?*

---

* Two technical terms relating to parts of the silk-loom.

It would be an animal like the spider, which thinks, which wills, which nourishes itself, reproduces itself and weaves its web. (P. 267–8.)

On Sensitiveness and the Law of Continuity in the Animal Texture.

Without these two qualities the animal could not be one. Once you have supposed the sensitive molecule, you have the reason for an infinite number of different effects or sensations (*touchers*). There is the infinite variety of impacts (*chocs*) relative to the mass.

There is the infinite variety of impacts relative to the speed.

There is the infinite variety of a physical quality.

There is the infinite variety of combined effects, of a second, of a third of a multitude of physical qualities.

And all these infinites further combine with the infinite variety of organs and perhaps of parts of the animal.

What ! an oyster could experience all these sensations ?

Not all, but a sufficiently great number without counting those which are born within itself and which originate in the depths of its own organization.

But in all these sensations are not many indiscernible ? Many ; there remain, however, more of them than the most fertile language could distinguish. Language offers only some degrees of comparison for an effect which passes, by an uninterrupted succession, from the least appreciable quantity to its extreme intensity.

Take an animal, analyse it, take from it all its modifications one after another, and you will reduce it to a molecule which will have length, breadth, depth and sensitiveness.

Suppress the sensitiveness, and there will remain to you only the inert molecule.

But if you begin by removing the three dimensions, sensitiveness disappears.

Some day it will be demonstrated that sensitiveness or feeling is a sense common to all beings. There are already phenomena which suggest this. Then matter in general will have five or six essential properties, dead or living force, length, breadth, depth, impenetrability and sensitiveness.

I would have added attraction, if it were not perhaps a consequence of motion or of force. (P. 268–9).

ON MAN

A tolerably clever man began his book with these words : " *Man, like all animals, is composed of two distinct substances, the soul and the body. If anyone denies this proposition, it is not for him that I write.*"

I nearly shut the book. Oh! ridiculous writer, if I once admit these two distinct substances, you have nothing more to teach me. For you do not know what it is that you call soul, less still how they are united, nor how they act reciprocally on one another.

The Double Man, Animal and Man.

A musician is at the clavecin ; he is chatting with his neighbour, the conversation interests him, he forgets that he is playing a piece of concerted music with others ; however, his eyes, his ear and his fingers are not the less in accord with them because of it ; not a false note, not a misplaced harmony, not a rest forgotten, not the least fault in time, taste or measure. The conversation ceases, our musician returns to his part, loses his head and does not know where he has got to ; the man is troubled, the animal is disconcerted. If the distraction of the man had continued for a few more minutes, the animal would have played the piece to the end without the man having been aware of it.

There, then, are sensitive and living organs, coupled, in sympathy, either by habit or naturally, and concurring to the same end without the participation of the whole animal.

On the Perfectibility of Man.

The perfectibility of man results from the feebleness of his senses, of which not one predominates over the organ of reason. If he had the nose of the dog, he would always be smelling ; the eye of the eagle, he would never cease to look ; the ear of the mole, he would be a listening being.

Stupidity of Certain Defenders of Final Causes.

They say : *See Man,* etc.

What are they speaking of ? Is it real man or ideal man ?

It cannot be real man, for there is not on the whole surface of the earth a single perfectly constituted, perfectly healthy man.

The human species is therefore only a collection of individuals more or less deformed, more or less sick. Now, what praise can be drawn from that, in favour of the pretended Creator ? It is not about eulogy, but about an apology that it is necessary to think.

What I say about man, there is not a single animal, a single plant, a single mineral of which I might not say as much.

If the present whole is a necessary consequence of its previous state, there is nothing to be said. If one wants to make of it the masterpiece of an infinitely wise and all powerful Being, that is not common sense.

What are these extollers doing then ? They are felicitating Providence for what it has not done ; they are supposing that everything is good, while, relative to our ideas of perfection, everything is bad.

In order for a machine to give proof of a maker, does it need to be perfect ? Assuredly, if the maker is perfect. (P. 270–2.)

* * * * *

System acting backwards.

It is that nothing is more contrary to nature than habitual meditation or the condition of men of learning. Man is born to act ; the true motion of the system is not to draw itself back constantly from the extremities to the centre of the bundle, but to carry itself from the centre to the extremities of the fibres. All the servants are not made to remain inert ; then the three great functions are suspended : conservation, nutrition and propagation. The man of nature is made to think little and act much ; the man of science, on the contrary, thinks much and bestirs himself but little. It has been well remarked that there is in man an energy which solicits employment, but that which study gives is not the true one, since it concentrates it and is accompanied by forgetfulness of all animal things. (P. 273.)

*   *   *   *   *

Man has all the varieties of existence : inertia, sensitiveness, vegetable life, polypous life, animal life, human life.

*   *   *   *   *

There are certainly two quite distinct kinds of life, perhaps even three :
The life of the whole animal.
The life of each one of its organs.
The life of the molecule.[6]   (P. 275.)

MISCELLANEOUS

From the molecule to man, there is a chain of beings which pass from the state of living stupidity to the state of extreme intelligence. (P. 334.)

Organization determines functions and needs ; and sometimes needs react on the organization, and this influence can sometimes go so far as to produce organs, and always so as to modify them. (P. 336.)

*   *   *   *   *

Understanding.

What we understand the least is ourselves. The object, impression, representation, attention.

*   *   *   *   *

Imagination : faculty of seeing absent things again.

Memory varies with age. The brain hardens and memory is effaced.

One can live without any feeling. Example, an old man who experiences neither hunger nor thirst.

Musician who remains a musician after the loss of memory of the notes.

Memory is of signs, the imagination of objects. Memory makes learned men, imagination poets. (P. 346.)

Sensations.

The sensation and the volition which follows it are corporeal ; these are two functions of the brain. Volition precedes the action of the muscle fibres.

Sensation : a mode of existence of the soul which has the consciousness of it and which is produced in itself by its own activities or by some change excited in the nervous system. (P. 355.)

*   *   *   *   *

Pre-existing Germs.

I admit these germs, but having nothing in common with beings.

This is a production consequent on development. A production which did not exist and which began to exist, and of which the successive expansion forms a new being similar to the first.

An eye is made like an anemone. What is there in common between the off-set tubers of the anemone and the flower ?

142

A man is made like an eye is made. What is there in common between the molecule of the bark of a willow and the willow? Nothing. However, this molecule gives rise to a willow.

How? By an initial disposition which cannot, with the nutritive material, lead to any other effect.

This seems to me as simple as to blow into an empty bladder in order to make a round body.

If the comparison with a bladder shocks, this is because it is too simple, but it is none the less real and true.

The scattered molecules which ought to form the germ translate themselves there of necessity. Arrived there they form a seed. This seed has but one necessary development, namely a tree. And so with man. (P. 411.)

* * * * *

Monsters.

Why should not man and all the animals be kinds of monsters, only a little more lasting?

The monster is born and passes away. Nature exterminates the individual in less than a hundred years. Why should nature not exterminate the species in a longer period of time?

Sometimes the universe seems to me only an assemblage of monstrous beings.

What is a monster? A being whose continued existence is incompatible with the subsisting order.

But the general order changes ceaselessly; how can the duration of the species remain the same in the midst of these vicissitudes? There is only the molecule which remains eternal and unalterable.

The vices and virtues of the preceding order have led to the order which is and of which the vices and virtues will lead to the order which follows, without one's being able to say that the whole amends or deteriorates. To amend and to deteriorate are terms relative to the individuals of a species among themselves, or between different species. (P. 418-9.)

*　　*　　*　　*　　*

I do not know if it is not with morals as it is with medicine, which has begun to perfect itself only in proportion as the vices of man have made diseases more common, more complicated and more dangerous.

When national morals are pure, bodies are healthy and diseases simple.

The precepts of this delicate and lofty morality, the science of this subtle and profound medicine, are unknown, and no one has had the interest to seek them out.

Where will you find great doctors and great moralists? In the most populous and most dissolute societies, in the capitals of empires. (P. 427-8.)

MISCELLANEA

On Intolerance.

Is it not astonishing, to see those scribblers, whose writings are so full of visions, affecting to despise those in whom a just and firm spirit admits only what it can conceive clearly? Glance through the last pages of Needham. If one judges the clarity of their ideas by the manner in which they express themselves, how obscure their minds must be!

They assert that the existence of God is evident, yet Pascal explicitly says of God that one knows neither what He is nor if He is.

The existence of God is evident! And the man of genius is halted by a child's difficulty; and Leibnitz is obliged, in order to resolve it, to produce, with incredible efforts of the brain, a system which does not resolve the difficulty and which gives rise to a thousand others.

Final causes demonstrate it! And Bacon said that final

cause is a virgin consecrated to God, who gives birth to nothing and must be rejected.

And these miserable fanatics accuse atheists of bad morals—atheists whom they have never seen do an evil action amidst devout people soiled with every kind of crime. (P. 437-8.)

Organized Beings.

Each part of these beings has its pleasure and its pain. This extends perhaps to the sensitive and living molecules. (P. 439.)

Necessity.

Turns the goitres of certain peoples of the Alps into beauty and gives importance to the matins of monks. (P. 439.)

(1774–80).

(The page references are to *Œuvres Complètes*, Vol. IX.)

VI

SUPPLEMENT TO BOUGAINVILLE'S *VOYAGE*

or

Dialogue between A. and B.

ON THE DISADVANTAGE OF ATTACHING MORAL IDEAS TO CERTAIN PHYSICAL ACTIONS INCOMPATIBLE THEREWITH

> *At quanto meliora monet, pregnantiaque istis.*
> *Dives opis Natura suæ, tu si modo recte*
> *Dispensare velis, ac non fugienda petendis.*
> *Immiscere ! Tuo vitio rerumne labores,*
> *Nil referre putas ?**
>
> (Horat. Sat. lib I, Sat II line 73 et seq.)

I. *Judgment on Bougainville's* Voyage:

A. : That superb starry sky, under which we came back yesterday and which seemed to promise us glorious weather for to-day, hasn't kept its word.

B. : Why do you say that?

A. : The fog is so thick that we can't see the nearby trees.

B. : That is true ; but suppose the fog, which only stays in the lower part of the atmosphere because it is sufficiently charged with moisture, should fall to earth ?

A. : But suppose, on the contrary, it rises and gains the upper regions of the atmosphere, where the density is less, and it cannot become saturated, as the chemists say ?

---

* How much better, and how conflicting with all that, is the advice of Nature, beautiful giver of her wealth, if only you are ready to manage properly and not to confound things desirable with those undesirable ! Do you think that it does not matter, whether your troubles are due to your fault or to circumstances ?

146

B. : Well then, we must wait.

A. : And while waiting, what are you doing ?

B. : I'm reading.

A. : Still this *Voyage* of Bougainville's ?[1]

B. : Yes, still.

A. : I don't understand that man at all. The study of mathematics, which presupposes a sedentary life, occupied his youth ; then suddenly he changed from this retired and contemplative life to the active, hard, roving and unsettled life of an explorer.

B. : Not at all. The vessel is only a floating house, and if you regard the navigator, who crosses immense distances, as enclosed and motionless within his narrow surroundings, you will visualize him going round the world on a plank just as you and I explore the universe on your floor.

A. : Another apparently curious thing is the contradiction between the character of the man and of his enterprise. Bougainville has a taste for the amusements of society : he loves women, plays and good food ; he accepts the whirl of fashion with as good grace as he did the inconstancy of the element on which he has been tossed. He is amiable and gay : a true well-balanced Frenchman ; on the one hand, a treatise on the differential and integral calculus, on the other, a voyage round the world.

B. : He is like everybody else : he enjoys himself after toil, and applies himself to work after relaxation.

A. : What do you think of his *Voyage.*

B. : So far as I can judge from a fairly superficial reading, I should relate its value to three principal points : a better knowledge of our old earth and its inhabitants, greater security on the seas which he sailed, sounding with the lead, and greater accuracy in our maps and charts. Bougainville started with the necessary understanding and qualities for these ends : philosophy, courage and truthfulness ; a keen vision which seized everything and shortened the times of observation ; circumspection and patience ; the desire to see, to be enlightened and to learn ; a knowledge of the calculus, mechanics, geometry, astronomy, and a sufficient smattering of natural history.

A. : And his style ?

B. : Without affection ; its tone is practical, simple and clear, particularly if you understand the language of seamen.

A. : Was it a long voyage?

B. : I have traced it on this globe. You see the line of red dots ?

A. : Which starts from Nantes ?

B. : And runs to the Straits of Magellan, enters the Pacific Ocean, winds between these islands forming the immense archipelago which stretches from the Phillipines to New Holland, skirts Madagascar, the Cape of Good Hope, continues into the Atlantic, follows the African coast and rejoins itself where the navigators embarked.

A. : They had a hard time ?

B. : Every navigator exposes himself, and consents to expose himself, to the perils of air, fire, land and water. But, after having wandered whole months between sea and sky, between life and death, after having been lashed by storms, menaced with death from shipwreck, disease, lack of food and water, that one of these unfortunates should come, with his ship wrecked, to fall dying with exhaustion and wretchedness at the feet of a brazen monster who refuses assistance or who pitilessly makes him wait for the most urgent help, that is dreadful. . . .

A. : A crime worthy of heavy punishment.

B. : One of those calamities on which the explorer has not counted.

A. : And should not have to count. I believed that the European powers sent to govern their overseas possessions only honest souls, good men, people full of humanity and capable of compassion. . . .

B. : That is the last thing they care about !

A. : There are some queer things in that *Voyage* of Bougainville's.

B. : Many.

A. : Didn't he assert that wild animals approached men, and that birds came and perched on them, before they knew the danger of that familiarity ?

B. : Others had said it before him.

A. : How does he explain the existence of certain animals on islands separated from all the continents by enormous expanses of sea ? Who took the wolf, the fox, the dog, stag and snake there ?

B. : He explains nothing ; he only attests the fact.

A. : But how do you explain it ?

B. : Who knows the primitive history of our globe ? How many wide areas of land, now isolated, were once continuous ? The only phenomenon on which we could form some conjectures is the direction of the body of waters which separated them.

A. : How so ?

B. : By the general form of the erosion. Some day we will amuse ourselves with this research, if you agree. For the moment, do you see this island called the Lancers ? Anybody would ask, from the inspection of its position on the globe, who has put people on it ; what means of communication joined them to the rest of their species ; what happens about multiplication on an area no more than a league in diameter ?

A. : They kill and eat themselves, and perhaps therefrom arises a very old and very natural primary epoch of cannibalism, of island origin.

B. : Or multiplication is limited by some superstitious law ; the child is crushed in its mother's womb, trodden under the feet of a priestess.

A. : Or men are sacrificed under the knife of a priest ; or they have recourse to the castration of males. . . .

149

B. : Or to the infibulation of females. From all that, there result different cruel customs, both necessary and bizarre, whose cause is lost in the mists of antiquity, and which put philosophers to the torture to explain them. It is a fairly constant observation that supernatural and divine institutions strengthen and preserve themselves by being transformed, ultimately, into civil and national laws ; and that civil and national institutions become consecrated, and degenerate into supernatural and divine precepts.

A. : That is one of the most disastrous of vicious circles.

B. : One more link added to the chains which bind us.

A. : Wasn't he in Paraguay at the time of the expulsion of the Jesuits ?

B. : Yes.

A. : What did he say about it ?

B. : Less than he could have said ; but enough to teach us that these cruel Spartans in the black habit used their Indian slaves like the Lacedemonians did their helots. They condemned them to hard labour, sweated them, and left them no rights of property ; kept them under the opium of superstition ; exacted from them profound veneration ; strode among them, lash in hand, striking every one, irrespective of sex or age. Another hundred years and their expulsion would have become impossible, or the motive of a war between these monks and the sovereign whose authority they would have undermined little by little.

A. : And these Patagonians about whom Doctor Maty and La Condamine of the Academy have made so much fuss ?

B. : They are fine people, who come and embrace you, crying " Chaoua " ; strong, vigorous, hardly ever exceeding five feet six inches in height, with nothing enormous about them except their girth, the largeness of their heads and the thickness of their limbs. Born with a taste for the marvellous, which exaggerates everything around him, how could the man leave a just proportion to objects, when he has, so to speak, to justify the journey he has made and the difficulties he had in going so far to see them ?

A. : And what does he think of the savage?

B. : It seems that the cruel character which is sometimes found in him comes from his having to defend himself against wild beasts. He is innocent and gentle wherever nothing troubles his repose and security. Every war is born from the common claim to the same property. One civilized man has a common claim with another civilized man to the possession of a field of which each occupies one end ; and this field becomes the subject of dispute between them.

A. : And the tiger has a common claim, with the savage, to the possession of a forest ; that is the first of all claims and the oldest cause of wars. . . . Have you seen the Tahitian whom Bougainville took on board and brought to this country ?

B. : I've seen him ; he is named Aotourou. The first land he saw he took for the native land of the explorers. Either they had deceived him about the length of the voyage, or, naturally misled by the apparent short distance from the shore of the sea where he lived to where the sky seemed to limit it at the horizon, he was ignorant of the real extent of the earth. The idea of the communal enjoyment of women was so well established in his mind that he threw himself upon the first European woman he met and prepared very seriously to treat her with true Tahitian courtesy. He was bored among us. The Tahitian alphabet having no b, c, d, f, g, q, x, y, nor z, he could never learn to speak our language, which presented too many foreign articulations and new sounds for his inflexible organs of speech. He never ceased to sigh for his own country, and I am not surprised. Bougainville's *Voyage* is the only one which has given me a taste for any other country than my own. Until reading this I had thought that nowhere was there anything so good as at home, with the result that I believed the same for every inhabitant of the earth : a natural effect of the attraction of the soil, an attraction which holds for good things which one enjoys at home and which one has not the same certainty of finding elsewhere.

A. : What ! Don't you think that the Parisian is convinced that he might grow corn in the Roman Campagna[2] as in the fields of the Beauce ?[3]

B. : Indeed, no. Bougainville sent Aotourou back, after having provided for his expenses and ensured his return.

A. : Oh, Aotourou ! How glad you will be to see your father and mother again, and your brothers, sisters, lovers and fellow-countrymen ! What will you tell them about us ?

B. : Only a little, and that they won't believe.

A. : Why only a little ?

B. : Because he has understood only a few things, and because he will not find in his language any terms corresponding to those things which he has understood.

A. : And why won't they believe him ?

B. : Because after comparing their ways with ours, they would much rather take Aotourou for a liar, than believe us to be so mad.

A. : Really ?

B. : I don't doubt it. The life of a savage is simple, and our societies are such complex mechanisms. The Tahitian is at a primary stage in the development of the world, the European is at its old age. The interval separating us is greater than that between the new-born child and the decrepit old man. He understands nothing of our customs, our laws, or he sees in them only fetters disguised in a hundred ways ; fetters which can only excite indignation and hatred in a being for whom liberty is one of the most profound of feelings.

A. : Are you wanting to make a fable about Tahiti ?

B. : It is not a fable ; and you would have no doubt of the sincerity of Bougainville, if you knew the *Supplement* to his *Voyage*.

A. : Where is this *Supplement* to be found ?

B. : There on the table.

A. : Won't you entrust it to me ?

B. : No ; but we could run through it together if you agree.

A. : Certainly, I should like to do so. See, the fog is going now, and the blue sky is beginning to appear. It seems to be my lot always to be wrong with you, even in the smallest things ; I must be very good to forgive you such continual superiority !

B. : Hold on ! read. Let's skip this preamble which doesn't matter and go straight to the farewell of one of the island chiefs to our explorers. This will give you some idea of the eloquence of these people.

A. : How did Bougainville understand these farewells spoken in a language of which he was ignorant ?

B. : You will see. It is an old man speaking.

II. The Old Man's Farewell.

He was the father of a large family. At the arrival of the Europeans, he looked disdainfully at them, showing neither astonishment, fear nor curiosity. They accosted him. He turned his back on them, and withdrew into his hut. His silence and his anxiety revealed his thoughts only too well : he lamented within himself for the great days of his country, now eclipsed. At the departure of Bougainville, when the inhabitants ran in a crowd to the shore, clinging to his garments, embracing his companions and weeping, the old man came forward with a stern air and said :

" Weep, poor folk of Tahiti, weep ! Would that this were the arrival and not the departure of these ambitious and wicked men. One day you will know them better.

One day they will return, in one hand the piece of wood you now see attached to the belt of this one, and the other grasping the blade you now see hanging from the belt of another. And with these they will enslave you, murder you or subject you to their extravagances and vices. One day you will serve under them, as corrupted, as vile, as loathsome as themselves.

" But I console myself ; I am reaching the end of my journey ; I shall not live to see the calamity I foretell. Oh people of Tahiti ! Oh my friends ! You have a means to escape this tragic future ; but I would rather die than counsel it. Let them go their ways, let them live."

Then, addressing himself to Bougainville, he continued :

" And you, chief of these brigands who obey you, quickly take your vessel from our shores. We are innocent, we are happy ; and you can only spoil our happiness. We follow the pure instincts of nature ; and you have tried to wipe its impress from our souls. Here everything belongs to everybody. You have preached to us I know not what distinctions between " mine " and " thine." Our daughters and our wives are common to us all. You have shared this privilege with us ; and you have lighted passions in them before unknown. They have become maddened in your arms ; you have become ferocious in theirs. They have begun to hate each other ; you have slain each other for them, and they have returned to us stained with your blood.

" We are a free people ; and now you have planted in our country the title deeds of our future slavery. You are neither god nor demon ; who are you, then, to make slaves ? Orou ! You understand the language of these men, tell us all, as you have told me, what they have written on this sheet of metal : ' This country is ours.' This country yours ? And why ? Because you have walked thereon ? If a Tahitian landed one day on your shores, and scratched on one of your rocks or on the bark of your

trees : ' This country belongs to the people of Tahiti '—
what would you think ?

" You are the strongest ! And what of that ? When
someone took one of the contemptible trifles with which
your vessel is filled, you cried out and you were revenged.
Yet at the same time in the depths of your heart you plotted
the theft of a whole country ! You are not a slave ; you
would suffer death rather than be one ; yet you want to
enslave us. Do you think the Tahitian does not know
how to defend his liberty and to die ? The Tahitian you
want to seize like a wild animal is your brother. You are
both children of nature ; what right have you over him
that he has not over you ? When you came, did we rush
upon you, did we pillage your ship ? Did we seize you
and expose you to the arrows of our enemies ? Did we
yoke you with the animals for toil in our fields ? No.
We respected our own likeness in you. Leave us to our
ways ; they are wiser and more honest than yours. We
do not want to barter what you call our ignorance for your
useless civilization. Everything that is necessary and good
for us we possess. Do we deserve contempt, because we
have not known how to develop superfluous wants ? When
we hunger, we have enough to eat ; when we are cold we
have wherewith to clothe us. You have been in our huts ;
what is lacking there, in your opinion ? You may pursue
as far as you like what you call the comforts of life ; but
allow sensible people to stop, when they would only have
obtained imaginary good from the continuation of their painful efforts. If you persuade us to exceed the narrow limits
of our wants, when shall we ever finish toiling ? When
shall we enjoy ourselves ? We have reduced the sum of our
annual and daily labours to the least possible, because
nothing seems to us preferable to repose. Go to your
own country to agitate and torment yourself as much as
you like ; leave us in peace. Do not worry us with your
artificial needs nor with your imaginary virtues. Look

on these men ; see how upright, healthy and robust they are. Look on these women ; see how upright, healthy, fresh and beautiful they are. Take this bow ; it is my own. Call one, two, three or four of your friends to help you and try to bend it. I can bend it myself, alone. I till the soil. I climb mountains. I pierce the forest. I can run a league on the plains in less than an hour. Your young companions would be hard put to follow me, yet I am more than ninety years old.

" Woe unto this island ! Woe to these people of Tahiti and to all who will come after them, woe from the day you first visited us ! We should know only one disease ; that to which all men, animals and plants are subject— old age ; but you have brought us another ; you have infected our blood.

" It will perhaps be necessary to exterminate our daughters, wives, children, with our own hands ; all those who have approached your women ; those who have approached your men.

" Our fields shall be soaked with the foul blood which has passed from your veins into ours ; or else our children, condemned to nourish and perpetuate the evil which you have given to the fathers and mothers, will transmit it for ever to their descendants. Villains ! You will be the guilty ones ; guilty either of the ravages of disease that will follow the fatal embraces of your people, or of the murders which we shall commit to stop the spread of the poison.

" You speak of crimes ! Do you know any more enormous than your own ? What is your punishment for him who kills his neighbour ?—death by the sword ; what is your punishment for the coward who poisons ?—death by fire. Compare your crime to his ; tell us then, poisoner of whole peoples, what should be the torment you deserve ? But a short while ago, the young Tahitian girl yielded herself to the transports and embraces of the Tahitian youth ; waited impatiently until her mother, authorized by her having reached the age of marriage, should remove her veil and make naked her breast. She was proud to excite the desire and to attract the amorous glances of unknown men, of relatives, of her brother. Without dread and without shame, in our presence, in the midst of a circle of innocent Tahitians, to the sound of flutes, between the dances, she accepted the caresses of the one to whom her young heart and the secret voice of her senses urged her. The idea of crime and the peril of disease came with you. Our enjoyments, once so sweet, are now accompanied by remorse and terror. That man in black who stands near you listening to me, has spoken to our lads. I do not know what he has said to our girls. But our lads are hesitant ; our girls blush. Plunge if you will into the dark depths of the forest with the perverse companion of your pleasure ; but let the good and simple Tahitians reproduce themselves without shame, under the open sky, in the full light of day. What finer and more noble feeling could you put in place of that with which we have inspired them, and which animates them now ? They think that the moment to enrich the nation and the family with a new citizen is come, and they glory in it. They eat to live and to grow ; they grow in order to multiply and they find in it nothing vicious nor shameful.

"Listen to the continuation of your crimes. You had hardly come among our people than they became thieves. You had scarcely landed on our soil, than it reeked with blood. That Tahitian who ran to meet you, to receive you crying 'Taio ! friend, friend,' you slew. And why did you slay him ? . . . because he had been taken by the glitter of your little serpents' eggs. He gave you of his fruits ; he offered you his wife and daughter, he ceded you his hut ; yet you killed him for a handful of beads which he had taken without having asked. And the people ? At the noise of your murderous shot, terror seized them, and they fled to the mountains. But be assured that they would not

have waited long to descend again. Then you would all
have perished, but for me. Ah! why did I pacify them,
why did I hold them back, why do I still restrain them,
even now? I do not know; for you deserve no pity; for
you have a ferocious soul which will never feel it. You
have wandered, you and yours, everywhere in our island.
You have been respected; you have enjoyed all things;
you have found neither barrier nor refusal in your ways;
you have been invited within, you have sat, and all the
abundance of our country has been spread before you.
When you desired young girls, only excepting those who
had not yet the privilege of unveiling their faces and breasts,
their mothers have presented to you all the others, quite
naked. You have possessed the tender victim of the duties
of hospitality; flowers and leaves were heaped up for you
and her; musicians sounded their instruments; nothing
has spoiled the sweetness, nor hindered the freedom of your
caresses nor of hers. They have sung the anthem exhorting
you to be a man, and our child to be a woman, yielding and
voluptuous. They danced around your couch. And it was
when you came from the arms of this woman, after ex-
periencing on her breast the sweetest of all intoxications,
that you slew her brother, friend or father.

"You have done still worse. Look over there, see that
enclosure bristling with weapons. These arms which have
menaced only your enemies are now turned against our own
children. See these unhappy companions of our pleasures.
See their sadness, the grief of their fathers and the despair
of their mothers. They are those condemned to die, either
by our hands or by the diseases you have given them.

"Away now, unless your cruel eyes revel in the spectacle
of death. Go now, go; and may the guilty seas which
spared you on your voyage hither, absolve themselves and
avenge us, by engulfing you before you return.

"And you, oh people of Tahiti! Go into your huts, go,
all of you; and let these strangers as they leave hear only

the roar of the tide and see only the foam of its fury whitening a deserted shore."

He had scarcely finished before the crowd of people had disappeared. A vast silence reigned over the whole island, and only the keen whistling of the wind and the dull sound of the breakers along the shore could be heard. One might have said that the air and the sea, conscious of the voice of the aged man, were moved to obey him.

B. : Ah ! . . . well, what do you think of it ?

A. : This speech seems vehement to me ; but in spite of something abrupt and wild about it I seem to detect European ideas and turns of phrase.

B. : Remember that it's a translation from Tahitian into Spanish, then from Spanish into French. The old man had come, at night, to that Orou, whom he had called upon in his speech, and in whose home the use of the Spanish language had been preserved from time immemorial. Orou had written out the old man's harangue in Spanish ; and Bougainville had a copy of it in his hand while the old man was speaking.

A. : I see only too well why Bougainville has suppressed this fragment. But that's not all there is ; and my curiosity about the rest is not tepid.

B. : What follows will perhaps interest you less.

A. : That doesn't matter.

B. : It is a conversation between the almoner[4] of the expedition and an inhabitant of the island.

A. : With Orou ?

B. : Yes, Orou. When Bougainville's vessel neared Tahiti, a great number of dug-out canoes were launched on the water. In an instant his ship was surrounded by natives ; wherever he turned his eyes he saw demonstrations of surprise and goodwill. They threw provisions on board, held out their arms to him, tied on to the vessel and climbed its sides. They filled his launch. They shouted to the land, from which came answering cries, and the inhabitants of the island ran out. They all land ; they take possession of the members of the crew, whom they allot among themselves. Each takes his guest to his hut, the men with their arms round their waists, the women stroking their cheeks. Imagine yourself there ; be a witness in thought, of this spectacle of hospitality, and tell me your opinion of the human species.

A. : Very beautiful.

B. : But I should perhaps forget to tell you of a very strange event. This scene of goodwill and humanity was suddenly stirred by the cries of a man shouting for help ; it was the servant of one of Bougainville's officers. Some young Tahitians had thrown themselves on him, laid him on the ground, undressed him and were preparing to do him the civility of Tahitian custom.

A. : What ! these simple souls, these primitive people, so good, so honest. . . ?

B. : You misunderstand. This servant was a woman disguised as a man. Undiscovered by any of the crew, during the whole of a long voyage, the Tahitians had divined her sex at the first glance. Her name was Barré. She was born in Burgundy, was neither ugly nor pretty and was twenty-six years old. She had never before left her village, and her first idea for travelling was to make a journey round the world. She showed wisdom and courage at all times.

A. : These frail creatures often contain heroic spirits.

III. *Discussion between the Almoner and Orou.*

B. : In the sharing of Bougainville's crew among the Tahitians, the almoner was allotted to Orou ; they were about the same age, thirty-five to thirty-six. Orou had then only his wife and three daughters, called Asto, Palli and Thia. They undressed the almoner, bathed his face, hands and feet, and served him a wholesome and frugal meal. When he was about to go to bed, Orou, who had been absent with his family, reappeared, and presenting to him his wife and three daughters, all naked, said : " You have eaten, you are young and in good health ; if you sleep alone you will sleep badly, for man needs a companion beside him at night. There is my wife, there are my daughters ; choose the one who pleases you best. But if you wish to oblige me you will give preference to the youngest of my daughters, who has not yet had any children." The mother added : " Alas ! But it's no good complaining about it ; poor Thia ! it is not her fault."

The almoner answered that his religion, his office, good morals and decency would not allow him to accept these offers.

Orou replied : " I do not know what this thing is that you call ' religion ' ; but I can only think ill of it, since it prevents you from tasting an innocent pleasure to which nature, the sovereign mistress, invites us all ; prevents you from giving existence to one of your own kind, from doing a service which a father, mother and children all ask of you, from doing something for a host who has received you well, and from enriching a nation, by giving it one more citizen. I do not know what this thing is which you call your ' office' but your first duty is to be a man and to be grateful. I do not suggest that you should introduce into your country the ways of Orou, but Orou, your host and friend, begs you to lend yourself to the ways of Tahiti. Whether the ways of Tahiti are better or worse than yours is an easy question to decide. Has the land of your birth more people than it can feed ? If so your ways are neither worse nor better than ours. But can it feed more than it has ? Our ways are better than yours. As to the sense of decency which you offer as objection, I understand you ; I agree that I was wrong, and I ask your pardon. I do not want you to injure your health ; if you are tired, you must have rest ; but I hope that you will not continue to sadden us. See the care you have made appear on all these faces; they fear lest you should have found blemishes on them which merit your disdain. But when it is only the pleasure of doing honour to one of my daughters, amidst her companions and sisters, and of doing a good action, won't that suffice you? Be generous!"

The Almoner : It's not that : they are all equally beautiful; but my religion! my office!

Orou : They are mine and I offer them to you; they are their own and they give themselves to you. Whatever may be the purity of conscience which the thing 'religion' and the thing 'office' prescribe, you can accept them without scruple. I am not abusing my authority at all; be sure that I know and respect the rights of the individual."

Here the truthful almoner agrees that Providence had never exposed him to such violent temptation. He was young, he became agitated and tormented; he turned his eyes away from the lovely suppliants, and then regarded them again; he raised his hands and eyes to the sky. Thia, the youngest, clasped his knees and said : " Stranger, do not distress my father and mother, do not afflict me. Honour me in the hut, among my own people; raise me to the rank of my sisters, who mock me. Asto, the eldest, already had three children; the second, Palli, has two; but Thia has none at all. Stranger, honest stranger, do not repulse me; make me a mother, make me a child that I can one day lead by the hand, by my side, here in Tahiti; who may be seen held at my breast in nine months' time; one of whom I shall be so proud and who will be part of my dowry when I go from my parents' hut to another's. I shall perhaps be more lucky with you than with our young Tahitians. If you will grant me this favour I shall never forget you; I shall bless you all my life. I shall write your name on my arm and on your son's; we shall pronounce it always with joy. And when you leave these shores, my good wishes will go with you on the seas till you reach your own land."

The candid almoner said that she clasped his knees, and gazed into his eyes so expressively and so touchingly ; that she wept ; that her father, mother and sisters withdrew ; that he remained alone with her, and that, still saying "my religion, my office," he found himself the next morning lying beside the young girl, who overwhelmed him with caresses, and who invited her parents and sisters, when they came to their bed in the morning, to join their gratitude to hers.   Asto and Palli, who had withdrawn, returned bringing food, fruits and drink.   They kissed their sister and made vows over her.   They all ate together.

Then Orou, left alone with the almoner, said to him : " I see that my daughter is well satisfied with you and I thank you.   But would you teach me what is meant by this word ' religion ' which you have repeated so many times and so sorrowfully ? "

The almoner, after having mused a moment answered : " Who made your hut and the things which furnish it ? "

Orou : I did.

The Almoner : Well then, we believe that this world and all that it contains is the work of a maker.

Orou : Has he feet, hands and a head then ?

The Almoner : No.

Orou : Where is his dwelling-place ?

The Almoner : Everywhere.

Orou : Here too ?

The Almoner : Here.

Orou : We have never seen him.

The Almoner : One doesn't see him.

Orou : That's an indifferent father, then !   He must be old, for he will at least be as old as his work.

The Almoner : He does not age.   He spoke to our ancestors, gave them laws, prescribed the manner in which he wished to be honoured ; he ordered a certain behaviour as being good, and he forbade them certain other actions as being wicked.

Orou : I follow you ; and one of the actions he forbade them, as wicked, was to lie with a woman or a girl ? Why, then, did he make two sexes ?

The Almoner : That they might unite ; but with certain requisite conditions, after certain preliminary ceremonies in consequence of which the man belongs to the woman and only to her ; and the woman belongs to the man, and only to him.

Orou : For their whole lives ?

The Almoner : For the whole of their lives.

Orou : So that if it happened that a woman should lie with a man other than her husband, or a husband with another woman . . . but that couldn't happen. Since the maker is there and this displeases him, he will know how to prevent them doing it.

The Almoner : No ; he lets them do it, and they sin against the law of God (for it is thus we call the great maker) against the law of the country ; and they commit a crime.

Orou : I should be sorry to offend you by what I say, but if you would permit me, I would give you my opinion.

The Almoner : Speak.

Orou : I find these singular precepts opposed to nature and contrary to reason, made to multiply crimes and to plague at every moment this old maker, who has made everything, without help of hands, or head, or tools, who is everywhere and is not seen anywhere, who exists to-day and to-morrow and yet is not a day older, who commands and is not obeyed, who can prevent and yet does not do so. Contrary to nature because these precepts suppose that a free, thinking and sentient being can be the property of a being like himself. On what is this law founded ? Don't you see that in your country they have confused the thing which has neither consciousness nor thought, nor desire,

nor will ; which one picks up, puts down, keeps or ex-
changes, without injury to it, or without its complaining,
have confused this with the thing which cannot be exchanged
or acquired, which has liberty, will, desire, which can
give or refuse itself for a moment or for ever, which laments
and suffers, and which cannot become an article of commerce,
without its character being forgotten and violence done to
its nature ;[5] contrary to the general law of existence ? In
fact, nothing could appear to you more senseless than a
precept which refuses to admit that change which is a part
of us, which commands a constancy which cannot be found
there and which violates the liberty of the male and female
by chaining them for ever to each other ; more senseless
than a fidelity which limits the most capricious of enjoyments to one individual ; than an oath of the immutability
of two beings made of flesh ; and all that in the face of a
sky which never for a moment remains the same, in caverns
which threaten destruction, below a rock which falls to
powder, at the foot of a tree which cracks, on a stone which
rocks ?[6] Believe me, you have made the condition of man
worse than that of animals. I do not know what your great
maker may be ; but I rejoice that he has never spoken to
our forefathers, and I wish that he may never speak to our
children ; for he might tell them the same foolishness,
and they commit the folly of believing it. Yesterday, at
supper, you mentioned ' magistrates ' and ' priests,' whose
authority regulates your conduct ; but, tell me, are they
the masters of good and evil ? Can they make what is just
to be unjust, and unjust, just ? Does it rest with them to
attribute good to harmful actions, and evil to innocent or
useful actions ? You could not think it, for, at that rate,
there would be neither true nor false, good nor bad,
beautiful nor ugly ; or at any rate only what pleased your
great maker, your magistrates and your priests to pronounce
so. And from one moment to another you would be
obliged to change your ideas and your conduct. One day

someone would tell you, on behalf of one of your three masters, to kill, and you would be obliged by your conscience to kill ; another day, " steal," and you would have to steal ; or " do not eat this fruit " and you would not dare to eat it ; " I forbid you this vegetable or animal " and you would take care not to touch them. There is no good thing that could not be forbidden you, and no wickedness that you could not be ordered to do. And what would you be reduced to, if your three masters, disagreeing among themselves, should at once permit, enjoin and forbid you the same thing, as I believe must often happen. Then, to please the priest you must become embroiled with the magistrate ; to satisfy the magistrate you must displease the great maker ; and to make yourself agreeable to the great maker you must renounce nature. And do you know what will happen then ? You will neglect all of them, and you will be neither man, nor citizen nor pious ; you will be nothing ; you will be out of favour with all the kinds of authorities, at odds even with yourself, tormented by your heart, persecuted by your enraged masters ; and wretched as I saw you yesterday evening when I offered my wife and daughters to you, and you cried out, " But my religion, my office ! "

Do you want to know what is good and what is bad in all times and in all places ? Hold fast to the nature of things and of actions ; to your relations with your fellows ; to the influence of your conduct on your individual usefulness and the general good. You are mad if you believe that there is anything, high or low in the universe, which can add to or subtract from the laws of nature. Her eternal will is that good should be preferred to evil, and the general good to the individual good. You may ordain the opposite but you will not be obeyed. You will multiply the number of malefactors and the wretched by fear, punishment and remorse. You will deprave consciences ; you will corrupt minds. They will not know what to do or what to avoid.

Disturbed in their state of innocence, at ease with crime, they will have lost their guiding star. Answer me sincerely ; in spite of the express orders of your three lawgivers, does a young man, in your country, never lie with a young girl without their permission ?

The Almoner : I should deceive you if I asserted it.

Orou : Does a woman who has sworn to belong only to her husband never give herself to another man ?

The Almoner : Nothing is more common.

Orou : Your lawgivers either punish or do not punish ; if they punish they are ferocious beasts who fight against nature ; if they do not punish, they are imbeciles who have exposed their authority to contempt by an empty prohibition.

The Almoner : The culprits who escape the severity of the law are punished by popular condemnation.

Orou : That is to say, justice is exercised through the lack of common sense of the whole nation, and the foolishness of opinion does duty for laws.

The Almoner : A girl who has been dishonoured will not find a husband.

Orou : Dishonoured ! Why ?

The Almoner : An unfaithful wife is more or less despised.

Orou : Despised ! But why ?

The Almoner : The young man is called a cowardly seducer.

Orou : A coward, a seducer ! But why ?

The Almoner : The father and mother and child are desolated. The unfaithful husband is a libertine ; the betrayed husband shares his wife's shame.

Orou : What a monstrous tissue of extravagances you've just revealed to me ! And yet you don't say everything ; for as soon as one allows oneself to dispose at pleasure of the ideas of justice and ownership, to take away or to give an arbitrary character to things, to attribute or deny good or evil to certain actions, capriciously, then one can be censorious, vindictive, suspicious, tyrannical, envious, jealous, deceitful. There is spying, quarrelling, cheating and lying; daughters deceive their parents, wives their husbands. Girls, yes, I don't doubt it, will strangle their infants, suspicious fathers will hate and neglect theirs, mothers will leave them and abandon them to their fates. And crime and debauchery will show themselves in all their forms. I know all that as if I had lived among you. It is so, because it must be so; and your society, of which your leader boasts because of its good regulations, will only be a swarm of hypocrites who secretly trample all laws under foot; or of unfortunates who are themselves the instruments of their own suffering in submitting; or of imbeciles in whom prejudices have quite stifled the voice of nature; or of abnormal monsters in whom nature does not protest her rights.

The Almoner : So it would seem. But don't you marry, then ?

Orou : Yes, we marry.

The Almoner : But what does it consist in ?

Orou : A mutual consent to live in the same hut and to lie in the same bed for as long as we find it good to do so.

The Almoner : And when you find it no longer good ?

Orou : We separate.

The Almoner : What becomes of the children ?

Orou : Oh stranger ! Your last question finally reveals to me the profound misery of your country. You must understand, my friend, that here the birth of a child is always a good fortune, and its death a subject for regret and tears. A child is precious because he ought to become a man; therefore we have a care for it, quite other than for our animals and plants. A child born causes both domestic and public joy. It is an increase of fortune for the hut and of strength for the nation. It means more hands and arms in Tahiti. We see in him a farmer, fisher, hunter, soldier, husband and father. When she returns from her husband's cabin to that of her parents, a woman takes with her the children which she had taken as dowry ; those born during their companionship are shared ; and as nearly as can be, males and females are divided, so that each one retains an equal number of boys and girls.

The Almoner : But the children are a charge for a long time before they give any service.

Orou : We allot for their maintenance and for that of old people, one-sixth part of all the produce of the country ; this allowance goes with them. Thus you see that the more numerous a Tahitian family is, the richer it is.

The Almoner : A sixth part !

Orou : Yes ; it is a certain means for increasing the population, for securing respect for the aged and for preserving the children.[7]

The Almoner : Your married couples take each other back again sometimes ?

Orou : Very often ; however, the shortest duration of a marriage is from one moon to another.

The Almoner : Unless the woman is pregnant ; must they then live together for at least nine months ?

Orou : You are mistaken ; the paternity, like the allowance, goes with the child everywhere.

The Almoner : You spoke of the children which a woman brought as dowry to her husband.

Orou : Certainly. There's my eldest daughter who has three children ; they are progressing, they are healthy and beautiful, they promise to be strong. If it takes her fancy to marry, she will take them with her, they are hers. Her husband will receive them joyfully, and his wife would only be dearer to him if she were pregnant with a fourth.

The Almoner : By him ?

Orou : By him, or someone else. The more children our girls have, the more they are sought after ; the stronger and more vigorous our lads are, the richer are they. Also, just as much as we are careful to preserve the ones from the approach of men, and the others from commerce with women, before the age of fecundity, after that age we equally exhort them to reproduce, when they are fit to do so. You could not believe the importance of the service you will have done my daughter Thia, if you have given her a child. Her mother will no longer say to her at each moon, " But, Thia, what are you thinking of ? You never get pregnant ; you are nineteen and ought already to have two children, and yet have none at all. Who will look after you ? If you lose all your youth like this, what will you do in your old age ? Thia, you must have some defect which keeps men away from you. Cure yourself of it, my child ; at your age I had been three times a mother."

The Almoner : What precautions do you take to protect your adolescent boys and girls ?

Orou : That is the principal object of education at home and the most important point of public morality. Our boys, until the age of twenty-two, two or three years after puberty, remain covered with a long tunic, their loins girded with a little chain. Before the age of marriage, our girls would not dare to go out without a white veil. Taking off the chain, or lifting the veil are faults which are seldom committed, because we early teach them the unpleasant consequences. But as soon as the male has reached his full growth, when the symptoms of virility are regularly present, and the frequent effusion of the seminal fluid and its quality confirm it ; when the young girl is languid, bored, and is mature enough to feel desires, to inspire them and to satisfy them usefully, then the father takes off his son's chain, and cuts the nail of the middle finger of his right hand. The mother takes off her daughter's veil. The one can then ask of women, and be asked : the other can walk in public with her face uncovered and her breast bare, and accept or refuse the caresses of a man. One merely indicates in advance to the boy which girls, and to the girl which boys, they should prefer. The day of freedom is a great occasion for the boy or girl.

If it is a girl, in the evening the young boys assemble round the hut and the air resounds the whole night through with their songs and the sounds of instruments. On the day, she is led by her father and mother to an enclosure, where there is dancing and exercises of jumping, running and fighting. The man is displayed naked before her, from all aspects and in all attitudes. If it is a boy, it is the young girls who, in his presence, do the ceremonies and honours of the feast, and show him the woman naked, without reserve and without secrecy. The rest of the ceremony is fulfilled on a bed of leaves, as you saw when you first came among us. At the fall of day, the girl goes back to her parent's hut, or to that of the man she has chosen, and stays there so long as it pleases her.

The Almoner : This feast, then, is not at all a wedding-day ?

Orou : Just so. . . .

*   *   *   *   *

A. : What's that I see in the margin ?

B. : It's a note, where the good almoner says that the teachings of the parents concerning the girls' and boys' choices were full of good sense, and very fine and useful observations. But he has suppressed this catechism, which would have appeared to people as corrupt and superficial as ourselves, as unpardonably licentious ; adding, however, that it was not without regret that he had deleted these details, which would have shown, firstly, how far a nation which occupied itself ceaselessly with an important object could be lead in its researches without the aid of physics and anatomy ; secondly, the difference between the ideas of beauty in a country where the forms are related to a momentary pleasure, and among a people where they are appreciated for a more constant utility. There, to be beautiful, a striking complexion, wide forehead, large eyes, fine

171

and delicate features, a slender waist, a small mouth, small hands and feet are required. . . . Here almost every one of these elements does not enter into the calculation. The woman whom everyone regards and whom desire pursues is she who bears promise of many children (the woman of Cardinal d'Ossat) who will be active, intelligent, courageous, healthy and robust. There is almost nothing in common between the Venus of Athens and the Tahitian one; the former is a wanton Venus, the latter a fertile Venus. A Tahitian woman said scornfully one day to another woman of the country: " You are beautiful, but you make ugly children; I am ugly, but I produce beautiful children, and it is me that men prefer."

After this note by the almoner, Orou continues :

Orou : What a happy moment it is for a young girl and for her parents when it is verified that she is pregnant ! She gets up, runs, throws her arms round the necks of her father and mother. With transports of mutual joyfulness she tells, and they learn, of this event. ' Mother, father, kiss me ; I am pregnant !—Is it really true ?—Absolutely true.—And whose is it ?—It was done with so and so ' . . .

The Almoner : How can she name the father of her child ?

Orou : Why do you want her not to know it ? It is the same with the duration of our loves as with that of our marriages ; it is at least from one moon to the following one.

The Almoner : And this rule is really scrupulously observed ?

Orou : You shall judge. In the first place the interval between two moons is not long ; but where two fathers have a well-founded claim to the formation of a child, it no longer belongs to its mother.

The Almoner : Who does it belong to then ?

Orou : To the one to whom it pleases her to give it ; that's her sole privilege. And a child being for its own sake a source of interest and riches, you can imagine that among us, libertines are rare. And that the youths keep away from them.

The Almoner : You have your libertines then ? I am much comforted.

Orou : We have even more than one sort ; but you make me stray from my subject. When one of our girls is pregnant, if the father of the child is a fine young man well built, brave, intelligent, and hard working, the hope that the child will inherit the qualities of the father intensifies the joy. Our child has only the shame of bad choice. You can imagine what value we attach to health, beauty, strength, industriousness and courage ; you can imagine how, without any interference, the prerogatives of blood are bound to be perpetuated among us. You have been in many countries, now tell me if you have seen in any of them as many fine men and beautiful women as in Tahiti ! Look at me ; what do you think of me ? Well, there are ten thousand men here, who are taller and more robust ; but not one braver than I ; therefore the mothers often nominate me to their daughters.

The Almoner : But of all these children that you can have produced outside your own hut, how many come back to you ?

Orou : One fourth, male or female. There is established among us a circulation of men, women and children or of hands of all ages and functions, which is of quite other importance than the circulation of your commodities, which are only the products of them.[8]

The Almoner : So I conceive. What are these black veils that I've noticed from time to time ?

Orou : The sign of sterility, either a defect of birth or a consequence of advanced age. She who discards the veil and mingles with men, is a libertine ; he who lifts this veil and approaches a sterile woman, is a libertine.

The Almoner : And these grey veils ?

Orou : The sign of the periodic indisposition. She who

discards this veil, and mingles with men, is a libertine ; he who lifts it and approaches the indisposed woman, is a libertine.

The Almoner : Have you punishments for such licentiousness ?

Orou : Nothing except the blame !

The Almoner : Can a father lie with his daughter, a mother with her son, a brother with his sister, a husband with another's wife ?

Orou : Why not ?

The Almoner : We'll let fornication pass ; but adultery, incest ! . . .

Orou : What do you mean by your words : "fornication," " adultery," " incest " ?

The Almoner : Crimes, horrible crimes, for any one of which people are burnt in my country.

Orou : Whether you burn or don't burn in your country doesn't matter to me. But you will not judge the morals of Europe by those of Tahiti, nor, consequently, the morals of Tahiti by those of Europe. We must have a more certain rule than that ; and what shall that be ? Do you know any other than the general good and personal utility ? Now tell me what there is in your crime of " incest " which is contrary to these two objectives of our actions. You are mistaken, my friend, if you believe that once a law is published, a dishonourable word invented, a punishment decreed, all is said. Answer me now, what do you understand by " incest ? "

The Almoner : But an incest . . .

Orou : An " incest ? " Was it long ago that your great maker, without head, hands or tools made the world ?

The Almoner : No.

Orou : Did he make the whole human race at once ?

The Almoner : No. He created only one man and one woman.

Orou : Had they any children ?

The Almoner : Assuredly.

Orou : Suppose that the first two parents had had only girls, and that their mother dies first, or that they had had only boys and that the wife had lost her husband.

The Almoner : You embarrass me ; but whatever you say, incest is a horrible crime ; let us speak of something else.

Orou : It pleases you to say so. I am not going to speak as long as you will not tell me what this abominable crime of " incest " is.

The Almoner : Well, I grant you that perhaps incest injures nothing in nature ; but doesn't it suffice that it menaces the political constitution ? What would become of the security of a leader and the tranquillity of a state, if the whole of a nation composed of several million people, should find itself centred about fifty fathers of families ?

Orou : At the worst it would be that where there is only one great society, there would be fifty smaller ones, more happiness and one crime the less.

The Almoner : But I fancy, however, that even here, a son rarely lies with his mother.

Orou : Unless he has much respect for her, and a tenderness which makes him forget the disparity in age and prefer a woman of forty to a girl of nineteen.

The Almoner : And the commerce of fathers with their daughters ?

Orou : Hardly more frequent, unless the girl is ugly and little sought after. If her father loves her, he helps her to prepare her dowry of children.

The Almoner : I imagine from this that the lot of women whom nature has not endowed cannot be a happy one in Tahiti.

Orou : That proves to me that you haven't a high opinion of the generosity of our young people.

The Almoner : As for the union of brother and sister, I do not doubt but that is very common.

Orou : And greatly approved.

The Almoner : To hear you, this passion, which produces so many crimes and evils in our country, must be quite innocent here.

Orou : Stranger ! You are lacking in both judgment and memory ; in judgment, because whenever anything is forbidden one is tempted to do the forbidden thing and one does it ; in memory, because you don't remember what I've told you. We have dissolute old women who go out at night without their black veils, and receive men, when nothing can result from their connection ; if they are recognized or surprised, exile to the north of the island or slavery is their punishment. We have precocious girls who lift their veils in spite of their parents (and we have a closed place for them in the hut) ; youths who remove their chain before the time prescribed by nature and by the law (and we reprove their parents for it) ; women for whom the period of pregnancy seems too long ; women and girls who are not too careful about wearing their grey veils. But, in fact, we do not attach great importance to any of these faults, and you would hardly believe how the idea of personal and public wealth, joined in our minds with the idea of population, purifies our manners in this respect.

The Almoner : The passion of two men for the same woman, or the desire of two women or two girls for the same man, doesn't that ever cause trouble ?

Orou : I have yet seen only four cases of that ; the choice of the man or of the woman settles everything. Violence by a man would be a grave fault ; but a public complaint is necessary and it is almost unheard of that a girl or woman complains. The only thing that I have noticed, is that our women have less compassion for ugly men than our youths have for the women poorly endowed by nature ; and that doesn't worry us.

The Almoner : You hardly know jealousy, from what I can see ; but marital tenderness and maternal love, those powerful and sweet feelings, if they are not strangers here, must be very feeble.

Orou : We have replaced them by another, which in another fashion is quite general, powerful and lasting, namely interest. Now be sincere, leave all that prating about virtues, which is incessantly on your comrades' lips but which is not at all in the depths of their hearts. Tell me, if in any country whatever there is a father who, without shame which checks him, would not rather lose his child, a husband who would not rather lose his wife, than his fortune and ease for the rest of his life. Be sure that wherever a man shall be as attached to the preservation of his fellow man as to his bed, his health, his repose, his hut, his produce, and his fields, he will do for him all that it is possible for him to do. It is here that tears moisten the pillow of a sick child ; it is here that we prize a fertile woman, a daughter ripe for marriage, an adolescent boy. Here it is that we are occupied with their establishment, because their preservation is always a gain, and their loss always a diminution of fortune.

The Almoner : I fear too well that this savage is right. The miserable peasant in our country who wears out his wife to spare his horse, lets his child perish without succour and calls in a doctor for his cattle.

Orou : I don't quite understand what you've just said ; but when you return to your very civilized country try to introduce this motive there ; and it is then that the worth of every child that's born, and the importance of population will be felt. Shall I tell you a secret ? But take care that you do not give it away. You arrive here ; we give our women and girls to you ; you are astonished ; you show a gratitude which makes us laugh ; you thank us when we lay on you and on your companions the heaviest of all impositions. We have not asked for money, we have not thrown ourselves on your merchandise, we have scorned the goods : but our women and our girls have just drawn the very blood from your veins. When you shall be gone, you will have left us children ; do you not think this tribute levied on your person, on your own flesh, is well worth any other ? And if you want to appreciate the value of it, imagine that you had two hundred leagues of coast to sail by, and that at every twenty miles a similar tribute was exacted. We have immense areas of fallow land ; we lack hands to cultivate it ; and we have asked them of you. We have to make up for calamitous epidemics ; and we have used you to fill the void which they have made. We have to fight neighbouring enemies and need soldiers ; and we have begged you to make them for us. Our women and girls outnumber the men, and we have associated you in our task. Amongst these women and girls are some from whom we have not been able to get children, and it is these we have exposed to your first embraces. We have to pay dues in men to a neighbouring oppressor ; it is you and your comrades who will defray this for us ; and in five or six years we shall send him your sons, if they are worth less than the others. Healthier and more robust than you are, we saw at once that you surpassed us in intelligence ; and at once we destined some of our most beautiful women and girls to collect the seed of a race better than our own. It's an experiment that we have made, and one which may prove successful. We have drawn from you and yours the only part of you that we could ; and know that, savages as we are, we know how to scheme. Go where you will ; and you will always find a man as subtle as yourself. He will always give you only what is no good to himself, and will always ask of you something that is useful to him. If he gives you a piece of gold for a piece of iron, it is because the gold is of no value to him and he prizes the iron. But tell me though, why you are not dressed like the others ? What does this long robe that covers you from head to feet signify, and this pointed sack which falls over your shoulders, or which you pull over your ears ?

The Almoner : It is because, as you see me, I belong to a society of men, called monks in my country. The most sacred of their vows is to approach no woman and to beget no children.

Orou : What do you do then ?

The Almoner : Nothing.

Orou : And your magistrate allows that kind of laziness, the worst of all ?

The Almoner : He does more ; he respects it and sees that it is respected.

Orou : My first idea was that nature, some accident, or a cruel art had deprived you of the power of reproducing your like ; and that out of pity they would rather let you live than kill you. But, monk, my daughter tells me that you are a man, and one as robust as any Tahitian, and that she has hopes that your repeated embraces will not be unfruitful. Now that I understand why you cried out yesterday evening " But my religion ! my office ! ", could you tell me the motive of the favour and respect which the magistrates accord to you ?

The Almoner : I do not know.

Orou : You at least know for what reason, being a man, you have freely condemned yourself not to be one ?

The Almoner : That would be too long and too difficult to explain to you.

Orou : And this vow of sterility, is the monk very faithful to it ?

The Almoner : No.

Orou : I was sure of it. Do you also have female monks ?

The Almoner : Yes.

Orou : As wise as the male monks ?

The Almoner : More closely confined, they wither from sadness and perish from boredom.

Orou : And the injury done to nature is revenged. Oh ! What a villanous country ! If everything is arranged there as you tell me, you are more barbarous than we are.

* * * * *

The good almoner then recounts that he passed the rest of the day going about the island, visiting the huts, and that in the evening, after supper, the father and mother having begged him to sleep with the second of their daughters, Palli was presented to him in the same undress as Thia, and that he cried out several times during the night : " My religion ! my office ! " ; that the third night he had been moved by the same remorse with Asto, the eldest ; and that he granted the fourth night, out of politeness, to the wife of his host.

IV. Continuation of the Dialogue.

A. : I like that polite almoner.

B. : I like much more the manners of Tahiti and Orou's discourse.

A. : Although a little on the European model.

B. : I don't doubt it. You see, here the good almoner complains of the briefness of his stay in Tahiti, and of the difficulty of knowing better the customs of a people wise enough to have stopped themselves of their own accord at a median level of development, or happy enough to live in a climate where the fertility assures them a long torpid existence, active enough to provide the necessities of life, and sufficiently indolent for their innocence, repose and happiness to have nothing to fear from a too-rapid progress of enlightenment. Nothing was evil there by law or opinion, there was only what was evil in itself. Labour and the harvests were done collectively. The accepted meaning of the word property was very narrow. The passion of love, reduced there to a simple physical appetite, produced none of our disturbances. The whole island seemed like one large family, where each hut represented the different apartments of one large mansion. He ends by declaring that these Tahitians will always be in his thoughts, that he was tempted to fling his vestments into the ship and pass the rest of his days among them, and that he feared very much that he would rue more than once not having done so.

A. : But in spite of all this praise, what useful conclusions are to be drawn from the strange manners and customs of an uncivilized people ?

B. : I see that as soon as some physical causes, for example, the necessity for conquering the barrenness of the soil, have stimulated man's sagacity, this impetus carries him much beyond his immediate objective, and that when the period of need has passed, he is carried off into the limitless realm of fantasy, from which there is no coming back. May the happy people of Tahiti stay where they are ! I see that except in this remote corner of our globe, there has never been morality and perhaps never will be anywhere.

A. : Then what do you understand by morality ?

B. : I understand a general submission, and a conduct consequent on good or bad laws. If the laws are good, morals are good ; if the laws are bad, morals are bad ; if laws, good or bad, are not observed at all, that worst condition of a society, then there is no morality at all. Now, how can laws be observed if they contradict one another ? Examine the history of various epochs and nations, both ancient and modern, and you will find men subjected to three codes of law, the laws of nature, civil law and the law of religion, and constrained to infringe alternately all these codes, which have never been in agreement. From this it follows that there has never been in any country, as Orou guessed of ours, either man, or citizen or truly pious person.

A. : From which you conclude, no doubt, that in basing morality on the eternal relations which exist between men, the law of religion may become superfluous, and that civil law ought only to be the enunciation of the laws of nature.

B. : And that, under pain of multiplying the wicked instead of making the good.

A. : Or that, if it be judged necessary to keep all three codes, the last two should only be exact copies of the first, which we carry always graven in our hearts and which will always be the most powerful.

B. : That's not very exact. We have at birth only a similarity of organization with other beings, the same needs, an attraction towards the same pleasures, a common aversion for the same pains ; that is what makes man as he is, and which ought to be the basis of the morality suitable for him.

A. : That's not easy.

B. : It is so difficult that I would willingly believe the most primitive people on earth, a Tahitian, who has held scrupulously to the laws of nature, nearer to a good code of laws than any civilized people.

A. : Because it is easier for him to get rid of his too-great primitiveness, than it is for us to retrace our steps and remedy our abuses.

B. : Above all, those which have to do with the relations between men and women.

A. : That may be. But let's begin at the beginning. Let us sincerely question nature and see what answer she gives us about this.

B. : I agree.

A. : Does marriage exist in nature ?

B. : If by marriage you understand the preference which one female gives to one male above all other males, or which a male gives to one female above all other females, a mutual preference, in consequence of which they form a more or less lasting association which perpetuates the species by the reproduction of individuals, then marriage does exist in nature.

A. : I think as you do ; for this preference is observed not only in the human species, but also in other species of animals, as witness the host of males who pursue one female in our countryside in spring, of whom only one obtains the title of husband. What about love-making ?

B. : If by this you understand those means, forcible or

delicate, which passion inspires, both in the male and in the female, in order to obtain that preference which leads to the sweetest, most important and most general of pleasures, then love-making does exist in nature.

A. : I think so too. Witness the variety of pretty tricks done by the male to please the female ; and by the female to excite and secure the desire of the male. And coquetry ? . . .

B. : . . . Is a lie, which consists in feigning a passion that is not felt and in promising a preference that will not be granted. The male flirt plays with the female ; the female flirt plays with the male ; a contemptible game which sometimes leads to terrible catastrophes ; a ridiculous performance for which the deceiver and deceived are equally punished by the loss of some of the most precious moments of their lives.

A. : According to you, then, coquetry is unnatural.

B. : I don't say that.

A. : And constancy ?

B. : I can tell you nothing better about it than what Orou said to the almoner : the poor vanity of two children who don't understand themselves, whose momentary intoxication blinds them to the mutability of everything which surrounds them !

A. : And faithfulness, that rare phenomenon ?

B. : In our country, almost always the infatuation and torture of the honest man or honest woman ; a chimera in Tahiti.

A. : Jealousy?

B. : The passion of a destitute and avaricious animal which fears a lack ; in man an unjust feeling, a consequence of our false morals and of a property-right extended to a feeling, thinking, desiring and free object.

A. : Jealousy, then, you think, does not exist in nature ?

B. : I don't say that. Vices and virtues equally exist in nature.

A. : The jealous man is melancholy.

B. : Like a tyrant, because he is conscious of it.

A. : What about modesty ?

B. : Ah ! Now you involve me in a course on the morality of love-making. A man wants to be neither disturbed nor distracted in his pleasures ; those of love are followed by a weakness which would leave him at the mercy of his enemy. That is all there can be natural in modesty ; all the rest is custom.—The almoner remarks in a third piece which I have not read to you, that the Tahitian does not blush for the involuntary movements which are excited in him when near his wife, surrounded by his daughters ; that the latter see this, are moved, but never embarrassed. As soon as women became the property of men and the furtive enjoyment of a girl was regarded as a theft, then the words " modesty," " reserve," " propriety " were born, and imaginary virtues and vices. In a word, it was wished to raise between the two sexes barriers which should prevent them from a mutual invitation to violate these laws which had been imposed on them, and which often produced the opposite effect, by heating the imagination and exciting desires. When I see trees planted round our palaces, and clothes arranged so as both to show and to hide part of a woman's breast, I seem to recognize a secret return to the forest and an appeal for the liberty of our primeval dwelling. The Tahitian would say to us : " Why do you hide yourself ? What are you ashamed of ? Are you doing evil when you bow to the most powerful impulse in nature ? Man, offer yourself frankly if it pleases you. Woman, if this man is agreeable to you, receive him with the same freedom."

A. : Don't worry yourself. Even if we begin like civilized men, it is rare if we don't finish like the Tahitian.

B. : Yes. These conventional preliminaries consume half the life of a man of character.

A. : Yes, I agree ; but what does it matter, if this pernicious urge of the human mind against which you were inveighing just now, is the more moderated because of it ? A philosopher, in our days, when asked why men courted women, and not women, men, answered that it was natural to ask from the one who could always give.

B. : That reason has always appeared to me more ingenious than sound. Nature, indecently if you like, drives one sex indiscriminately towards the other ; and in some conceivable condition of animal and primitive mankind, perhaps not existing anywhere. . . .

A. : Not even in Tahiti ?

B. : No . . . the gap which should separate man from woman would be crossed by the most amorous. If they wait and flee, pursue and escape, attack and defend, it is because the passion, unequal in its progress, does not operate in them with equal force. From which it follows that sensual pleasure develops, is consummated and is extinguished on the one side, while it has hardly begun to arise on the other, and both remain miserable because of this. That is a faithful picture of what would happen with two free and perfectly innocent young people. But when the woman has learnt, either by experience or education, the more or less cruel consequences of a delicious moment, her heart chills at the approach of the man. The man's heart does not shiver ; his senses command him and he obeys. The woman's senses make themselves understood, but she fears to heed them. It is the man's role to make her forget her fears, to intoxicate her and to seduce her. The man keeps whole his natural urge towards the woman ; the natural urge of the woman towards the man, a geometrician would say, was directly proportional to the intensity of her passion and inversely proportional to the magnitude of her fears ; a ratio which is complicated by a myriad different elements in our society, which practically all conspire to increase the faint-heartedness of the one sex and the duration of the pursuit by the other. It is a kind of tactics in which the resources of the defence and the means of attack are about on a level. The resistance of the woman has been consecrated ; the violence of the man is considered contemptible. Violence which would be only a trifling injury in Tahiti, becomes a crime in our cities.

A. : But how has it happened that an act whose end is so solemn, and to which nature invites us by the most powerful attraction, that the noblest, most delicious and most innocent of pleasures should have become the most fruitful source of our depravities and our evils ?

B. : Orou explained it at least ten times to the almoner ; now listen again and try to remember it. It is by the tyranny of man, who has converted the possession of a woman into the possession of a chattel ;[9] by the manners and customs which have overloaded with stipulations the union of marriage ; by civil laws which have subjected marriage to an infinity of formalities ; by the very nature of our society, where the diversity of fortune and rank has instituted privileges and rules of what is and is not done ; by a peculiar contradiction common to all existing societies, whereby the birth of a child, always regarded as an increase of wealth for the nation, more often and more certainly means an increase of poverty to the family ;[10] by the political opinions of sovereigns who relate everything to their own interest and security ; by religious institutions which have applied the names vices and virtues to actions which were not susceptible to any morality.

How far we are from naturalness and happiness ! The empire of nature cannot be destroyed ; you may try to thwart it with obstacles, but it will prevail. Write as much as you please on the tablets of bronze—to use an expression of wise Marcus Aurelius—that the voluptuous movement of two bellies together is a crime, but the heart of man will only be torn between the menace of your proscription and the violence of his feelings. But the unruly heart will not cease to demand ; and your terrifying inscription will disappear from our eyes a hundred times during the course of a lifetime. Chisel it in marble : Thou shalt not eat of ixion or of griffon ; thou shalt know only thy wife ; thou shalt not be a husband to thy sister. But you will not fail to increase the punishment in proportion to the oddity of your prohibitions ; you will become ferocious, but you will never succeed in making me contrary to nature.

A. : How short the law of nations would be, if it conformed exactly to the law of nature ! How many errors and vices would man be spared !

B. : Would you like to know the condensed history of almost all our miseries ? Here it is. There existed a natural man ; an artificial man was introduced within this man ; and within this cavern a civil war breaks out, which lasts for life. Sometimes the natural man is stronger ; sometimes he is felled by the artificial, moral man ; and in both cases the miserable monster is plagued, tortured, tormented, stretched on the rack ; ceaselessly lamenting, always wretched, whether a false enthusiasm of glory transports him and intoxicates him, or a false shame bows him and casts him down. Nevertheless there are extreme circumstances which bring man back to his original simplicity.

A. : Want and sickness, two great exorcists.

B. : You have named them. In reality, what becomes of all these conventional virtues then ? In want, a man is remorseless ; and in sickness a woman is without shame.

A. : So I have observed.

B. : But another phenomena which will not have escaped you either, is that the return of the artificial and moral man follows step by step the progress from illness to convalescence, and from convalescence to a state of health. The moment when the bodily infirmity ceases is the one when the internal civil war begins again, and almost always to the disadvantage of the invader.

A. : That's true. I have myself experienced in convalescence, that the natural man had deadly strength against the artificial and moral man. But now tell me, must we civilize man or abandon him to his instincts ?

B. : Must you have a precise answer ?

A. : Undoubtedly.

B. : If you propose to be his tyrant, then civilize him, persecute him all you are able with a morality contrary to nature ; fetter him in all ways ; impede his actions with a thousand obstacles ; frighten him with phantoms, make eternal the war in the cavern, and let the natural man be always shackled at the feet of the moral man. But do you want him to be happy and free ? Then don't meddle with his affairs ; plenty of unforeseen events will lead him towards understanding and to corruptness. And always remain convinced, that it is not for your sake but for theirs that these cunning law-givers have moulded you and made you unnatural like you are. I appeal to all political, civil, and religious institutions ; examine them deeply ; and I shall be greatly deceived, if you don't find the human race bowed century after century under the yoke which a handful of scoundrels resolved to put upon it. Beware of anyone who wants to order things. To regulate, is always to make oneself master of the others by hampering them ; and the Calabrians are almost the only ones on whom the flattery of legislators has not yet imposed.

A. : Does this anarchy of the Calabrians please you ?

B. : I appeal to experience ; and I wager that their barbarism is less vicious than our courtesy. How many trifling rascalities here counterbalance the atrociousness of a few great crimes about which so much is made. I look upon uncivilized men as a multitude of scattered and isolated springs. Doubtless if it happened that some of these springs collided, one or other of them would break. To obviate this difficulty, an individual of profound wisdom and sublime genius assembled these springs and made a mechanism of them. And in this mechanism called society, all the springs were set acting and reacting against one another, endlessly fatigued ; and he broke more of them in a day under this state of control, than he would have broken in a year under the anarchy of nature. But what a smash ! What devastation ! What enormous destruction of the little springs when two, three, or four of these enormous machines clashed violently !

A. : So you prefer the condition of brute and primitive nature ?

B. : I should not dare pronounce on it ; but I know that many times the townsman has been known to leave all and go back to the forest ; and that one has never seen the man of the forest clothe himself and establish himself in the town.

A. : I have often thought that the sum of good and evil varied for each individual ; but that the joy and pain of any species of animal had its limit which it could not exceed, and that perhaps our efforts gave us, in the last analysis, as many inconveniences as advantages ; so that we have only tormented ourselves in increasing the two sides of an equation between which there existed an eternal and necessary equality. Nevertheless I do not doubt that the average life of the civilized man is not longer than the average life of a savage.

B. : And if the time a machine lasts is not a true measure of its degree of wear, what would you conclude ?

A. : I see that on the whole, you would incline to believe men the more wicked and unhappy the more they are civilized.

B. : I shall not review all the countries of the earth ; but I will warn you that you will only find the condition of man a happy one in Tahiti, and supportable in one corner of Europe. There suspicious masters, jealous of their security, are occupied in keeping him in what you call brutishness.

A. : In Venice, perhaps ?

B. : Why not ? You will not deny, at least, that nowhere is there less acquired understanding, less artificial morality, and fewer chimerical vices and virtues.

A. : I wasn't expecting such praise of that government.

B. : And I'm not giving it. I am showing you a kind of compensation for slavery, that every traveller has felt and commended.

A. : A poor compensation !

B. : Perhaps. The Greeks proscribed the man who added a string to the lyre of Mercury.

A. : And that prohibition is a bloody satire on their first law-givers. It is the first string that must be cut.

B. : You understand me. Wherever there is a lyre there are strings. So long as the natural appetites are adulterated, count on evil women.

A. : Like La Reymer.

B. : Or horrible men.

A. : Like Gardeil.

B. : And on people ill-fated for no reason at all.

A. : Like Tanié, Mademoiselle de la Chaux, the Chevalier Desroches and Madame de la Carlière.[11] It's certain one would seek in vain in Tahiti for examples of depravity like the first two, and of misery like the last three. What shall we do then ? Shall we return to nature, or submit to the laws ?

B. : We must speak against insane laws until they are reformed ; while waiting, we must submit to them. Anyone who infringes a bad law by his own private authority authorizes all others to infringe the good ones. There is less inconvenience in being mad among madmen, than in being wise alone. Let us tell ourselves, let us cry out unceasingly, that shame, punishment and dishonour have been attached to actions innocent in themselves ; but let us not commit these actions, because shame, punishment and dishonour are the greatest of all evils. Let us copy the good almoner, a monk in France, a primitive man in Tahiti.

A. : Take the dress of the country one's going to, and keep that of the country where one is.

B. : And above all be scrupulously honest and sincere with those fragile beings who cannot delight us without renouncing the most precious advantages of our society. . . . And now, what's become of that thick fog ?

A. : It has disappeared.

B. : And shall we be free again, after dinner, to go out or remain here ?

A. : That will depend, I think, rather more on the ladies than on us.

B. : Always these women ! One can't take a step without meeting them somewhere.

A. : What if we should read the discussion between the almoner and Orou to them ?

B. : What do you think they would say about it ?

A. : I know nothing about that.

B. : And what would they think about it ?

A. : Perhaps the opposite of what they would say.

(1772)

VII

CONVERSATION

ABBÉ BARTHÉLEMY AND DIDEROT

Diderot : However, Abbé, you would not like to converse with someone who never answered ?

Barthélemy : Certainly not.

Diderot : Well then, when you pray, that is to say, when you address words to God or to the Virgin Mary, what answer do you get ?

Barthélemy : But I don't expect an answer.

Diderot : What's the good of conversing, then ?

Barthélemy : You are confused, my dear philosopher, you misapprehend. Prayer is not a conversation.

Diderot : It is a monologue ?

Barthélemy : If you like. It is an elevation of our soul to God, it is an effusion, it is the evidence and the tribute of our adoration and our gratitude ; very often also it is an entreaty, a supplication.

Diderot : But what is the object of this petition, what is its guarantee and its sanction, since it always remains obstinately and invariably without an answer ? Your God, in fact, my dear Abbé, is ETERNAL SILENCE. The phrase is Flechier's, I believe. You never hear his voice. You may well cry to him : " My Father, my Father ! Have pity ! . . . Mercy ! I beseech you ! . . ." Never, however ardent and vehement, however tearful, moving and irresistible your prayers may be, you will never draw from him even a single acknowledgment, you will never hear this Father, so much besought and so merciful, answer you :

" My child ! " Do you recall that woman we saw one
afternoon, at Saint Roch, prostrate before a statue of the
Virgin, praying, weeping, sobbing ? . . . It was enough
to break one's heart. It moved you so much that you
approached her, and questioned her.

Barthélemy : I remember. She was praying for her
daughter, a child of fifteen, who was dying.

Diderot : How she prayed and sobbed, the poor thing !
She would have softened a heart of stone. But the stone
Virgin did not wince, did not flinch . . . or at least we
did not notice anything like that, I think. And was the
child saved ?

Barthélemy : No, she died ; died precisely while the
mother was kneeling there.

Diderot : No doubt God had hastened to call this young
soul to him. He lacked angels.

Barthélemy : Perhaps. To a certainty, she went to
heaven. That is a favour which the Lord did to her.

Diderot : To the mother ?

Barthélemy : To the mother and to the daughter, both of
them. Do we know our needs ? Does not the All-
Powerful, in his infinite wisdom, know better than we what
is good for us ?

Diderot : Why doesn't he tell us then ? Why leave this
poor woman to lament and sigh and to be wrung with
anguish ? You remember ? It was heart-rending, frightful. And one word would have been enough : " I take
back to me those I value. Rejoice therefore, woman,
instead of grieving."

Barthélemy : Yes, that is the truth. It is indeed.

Diderot : And that is what this mother did not admit,
what she could not understand. And how many others
share her blindness, and like to keep their children near
them in this vale of tears, rather than see them carried off
to the heavenly dwelling-place ! Moreover, when I say
see, " see them carried off," that's just a way of speaking,

for we see nothing at all. . . . The eyelids fall, the voice becomes weak and stilled, the mind darkens and becomes nothing, there is no movement, nothing. . . .

Barthélemy : In fact, for you, Diderot, death is the end of everything.

Diderot : Don't make me say that, Abbé. Don't let us go so far. Although I might very well quote against you a certain legend, a corollary of the resurrection of Lazarus by the Christ : " What did you see down there, when you were dead ? "—" Nothing, Master ; there is nothing," answered Lazarus. And Jesus whispered in his ear : " No, there is nothing ; but do not tell."

Barthélemy : Legend, assuredly ! Pure legend !

Diderot : Agreed ! But for myself, I hold to what we have before our eyes. Our soul, its essence, its origin, its destiny, what it will become after us, and in the very first place, if we really have one . . . for, indeed, I don't know. I can affirm nothing about it, and I've an idea that those who speak so freely and so willingly about it *ex cathedra* do not know any more about it than I do.

Barthélemy : However, if you abolish the soul . . .

Diderot : I abolish nothing at all : I do not know.

Barthélemy : . . . it will be necessary for you to abolish God.

Diderot : That would not be a reason. But, once again, I want to abolish nothing, Abbé, I am only an ignorant person who has the frankness and courage of this ignorance ; I dare to say : " I do not know."

And I remark we are discussing endlessly a number of things which we not only do not know, but cannot know, which are beyond our understanding—which ought, it may be said in parenthesis, to convince us that they are hardly necessary to us, for everything which is an everlasting subject of dispute, is necessarily of everlasting uselessness for us, as Voltaire wrote recently. And, by a sort of calamity, it is precisely those things which are most spoken about that are least understood. How many of our most common phrases mean absolutely nothing ! " God has recalled her to Him." How do you know ? Has God taken you into His confidence ? " God has hastened to have him near Him." Not so much haste, since this dead man had seen ninety-one spring-times. " She has ascended to heaven " you just said to me, about the little girl torn from her pious mother. But what is heaven ? Where is it situated ? Does one go up at first ? You say " above." But " above " now will be " below " this evening, since the earth revolves. At least, you don't deny the movement of the earth, with Pope Urban and the Holy Inquisition ?

Barthélemy : I have not come to that, dear friend.

Diderot : The ancients knew at least where to put their paradise, or at least they tried. . . . For some, it was in the Canary Islands, which they called the Fortunate Isles, *Arva beata ;* for others, higher up, in Ireland ; for others. . . .

Barthélemy : In fact, there was hardly any agreement among them, on this point as on so many others.

Diderot : Just like us, Abbé. I was reading this morning in a history of Sweden, that the king, the king of that country, had triumphed over his enemies by *Providential* good fortune ; while, for the same victory, contested and denied by the Turks, the latter declared that Providence had not allowed . . . and that the Spaniards claimed in the same way that the aforesaid Providence had remained dumb. . . . See how each one judges Providence after his own fashion, gauges it by his own standards, makes it act and express itself after his own fancy ! There should be a Lutheran Providence, a Spanish Providence, without counting all the others, Russian Providence, Polish Providence, English Providence, French Providence. Just think a little of the embarrassment of Providence, if there were only one, when each nation invoked it for the same purpose, with opposed interests and contrary intentions ! And would it not first be necessary to be certain that this sovereign with so many and diverse faces, this Divine Providence, consents to be troubled with our little affairs, which appears to me to be excessively problematical ; for how many crimes, shames and abominations we should then have to place on the shoulders of this sacrosanct princess— Providence ! The easiest thing, in my opinion, would be to concern ourselves with her no more than she concerns herself with us. Yes, Abbé, that's the great thing wrong with us, and it will be so for a long time I fear ; we discuss ceaselessly numerous subjects beyond our understanding, beyond our faculties, consequently without being able to attain the least certain and practical conclusion, and getting no other result but discord and hatred— horrible hatreds accompanied by the cruellest persecutions. Aren't these hatreds between nations most often engendered by religious differences, and in direct proportion to the zeal for the cause of God which animates these people ? If only we had the good wit and the good sense to stop ourselves in time on this odious slope, and not to tear each other, cut throats or burn each other alive because we do not envisage the Absolute from the same point of view, or do not think the same about the mystery of the incarnation or the sacrament of the eucharist ! Why lose ourselves in the clouds and not keep ourselves quite frankly to questions of current life, to what we can see, observe and control. It is the pursuit and passion for the supernatural which causes misery to so many people.

Barthélemy : And their consolation also, and their joy.

Diderot : There are consoling errors, I don't deny. A doctor tells a sick man that he is better, a dying man that he will get back his health and that he will be on his feet within a week, and he dies the same evening ; but during that day a ray of hope has warmed his heart and comforted him. The doctor's lie has sweetened the last moments of the patient. That is something. But don't let the good prevent us from recognizing that it comes from something wrong, a lie.

Barthélemy : Wait a moment ! The consolations of religion and the promises which accompany them are not in the least lies.

Diderot : Evidently, Abbé, and I shall be far from contesting it. . . . But, these promises are without guarantee and without proof ; without evident and tangible proofs, I mean. You assure this mother we were talking of just now, that her daughter has gone straight to heaven, and rests in the bosom of the Eternal. These are simply words, this : *hæc sunt verba,* nothing more. In reality, the poor child has been nailed up in a pine or oaken box, then buried in the earth. That is all that it is permissible to say. All the rest beyond that is an affair of the imagination, of supposition, of hope. . . . It is dreaming ! That you have consoled the mother by guaranteeing resurrection and the salvation of her daughter "whom she will one day find again above, in the home of the blessed," is very fine, it is perfect ; but, once more, you have asked to be believed on your word. Now, the wise man is not content with a simple assertion : *Sapiens nihil affirmat quod non probet.* . . . *Quod gratis asseritur gratis negatur.** We may permit a little latin between ourselves, may we not, Monsignore ?

Barthélemy : You will never prevent the crowd from seeking these superior consolations, from having a liking for the supernatural and delighting therein.

Diderot : It's possible ! But are these always consolations which you offer to your flock ? Oh, no, not always ! See our poor friend Dumahis : he, with so cheerful, gracious and charming a character, so naturally happy, there now, if he isn't in a blue funk at going to grill in hell, imagining even that he's grilling and roasting already, plunged in eternal flames for the expiation of his sins ? Isn't it horrible ?

---

* The wise man affirms nothing which he does not prove. . . . What costs nothing to affirm, costs nothing to deny.

Barthélemy : It is madness.

Diderot : Madness or not, do you believe that he will be
consoled, he ? And how many, how many others like him,
experience this very explicable but abominable terror of
the aforesaid eternal flames? Think of Massillon preaching
at St-Eustache his sermon " On the small number of
the elect." Many are called but few are chosen, Abbé.
Then it is always, in spite of all the merits of our Redeemer,
always Master Satan who carries him off? . . . Yes, the
general fear, the terrible panic which seized the congrega-
tion at this sermon of Massillon! They did not think
themselves consoled, those people. You offer to your
clients two perspectives, two solutions, paradise and hell.
It is hell which imposes itself and triumphs ; you do not
console, you terrify, you appal. Now, in order to abolish
radically these very legitimate fears and to play a trick on
Satan, as soon as a newborn has received this sacrament of
baptism which makes a Christian of him and opens wide
the gates of heaven to him, wouldn't it be more prudent,
wiser, to send him speedily above or below. . . ?

Barthélemy : Send him ? How's that ? Kill him ?

Diderot : Quite simply. The English writer Jonathan Swift
demanded, not long ago, in his *Modest Proposal* relative
to the poor children of Ireland, that the little children
of indigent Irish families, destined to die of hunger, should
be carefully fattened, then they should be bled like calves
or sheep, and butcheries for infants'-flesh should be
established for the use of gentlemen whose taste is particularly delicate. I am not so exacting, and I spare you
the fattening. I only ask you to dispatch all these little
angels to the good God as promptly as possible, in order to
spare them the half-certainty which they have, by living
on earth, of going after their death to boil and roast for all
eternity. The thing is worth the trouble, Abbé. Eternal
flames ! Where there shall be wailing and gnashing of
teeth ! And for ever ! for ever ! Now see, would it not

be a thousand times better to dispatch them to the good God at once? . . . I go even further. Could we not act in the same way towards adults, charge a confessor to put them in a state of grace, and as soon as the absolution is received, hasten them off. . . . Ah! There must be no dallying, there!

Barthélemy: But this is madness!

Diderot: An error! On the contrary, it would be very wise. Torture for all eternity, think of it! And would it not be the best method—a supremely radical method I agree, but, once more, to flame for all eternity!—whereby to cheat, to get the better of and beat the angel of darkness, Satan, always on the watch for souls which he can clutch and impale on his prongs? You have not forgotten the criminal at the theatre in Rouen who stabbed his neighbour, a young girl he did not know and had never seen before, who killed her without any motive, except so as to be condemned to death and to be able, before being broken on the wheel or hanged, to receive absolution, while if he had committed suicide, he would have departed this life in a state of mortal sin?

Barthélemy: Let us talk seriously, Diderot.

Diderot: But that is what we are doing.

Barthélemy: You wriggle and chop logic in vain. I tell you again you will never take from the crowd its taste for the supernatural. The human mind is made that way; it is carried of itself towards what is beyond it, beyond its understanding. . . .

Diderot: Yes, everything that dazzles and enchants it. The crowd loves the marvellous, and the more strange, inconceivable and fabulous the miracle is, the better it is pleased and is delighted. But we philosophers, whose role it is to see clearly in our business—which is devilish difficult, I agree—we try to reduce the number of these dupes as much as possible. We think that the greatest service to be done to men is to teach them to use their reason, only to hold for truth what they have verified and proved. You are compelled to agree, aren't you, that the more a nation educates itself and improves itself, the more the belief in the supernatural is moderated and grows less ? Greater or lesser belief in the supernatural is always the index of lesser or greater civilization. Consider the savages encountered by Bougainville : everything was witchcraft, magic, sorcery and miracle with them. Miracles, a rare commodity with us, eh, Abbé ? in spite of this craze for the marvellous, the incomprehensible ? But there are miracles wherever they are believed in, and the more they are believed in, the more there are of them. Is that true ? You see, Abbé, once one sets foot in this realm of the supernatural, there are no bounds, one doesn't know where one is going nor what one may meet. Someone affirms that five thousand persons have been fed with five small loaves ; this is fine ! But to-morrow another will assure you to have fed five thousand people with one small loaf, and the following day a third will have fed five thousand with the wind. Medallions hung from the neck and other amulets guard you from all accidents or cure you from all ills. If one wants to calm the attack of madness of one of those lunatics called " possessed," a clyster of holy water is administered ; infallible remedy. In the countryside, in many places, it is sufficient to carry round the relics of a saint—in Burgundy, those of St. Potentien, for example—to obtain sun or rain, warmth or moisture, at will. And good St. Denis walks, carrying his cut-off head in his hands, a phenomenon which St. Savinien hastened to reproduce after his decapitation by the Emperor Aurelius. And St. Nicolas who began to fast from the day of his birth : Wednesdays and Fridays he only took the breast of his nurse once a day. And that pious noblewoman who, finding herself pregnant during the absence of her husband, obtained from her celestial patroness, with the aid of God, that her pregnancy not only disappeared, but passed into the body of the said patroness, St. Pelagia or someone, who would thus take the sin upon herself, or at least the consequences of sin. And what do you think about the two skulls of St. Pancras, which are honoured and feasted in two of our rival parishes, his skull when he was twenty-two and his skull when he was thirty-six ? There is nothing more diverting than the lives of the saints, my dear Abbé, and I've often wished to write all that. . . . But it's already done : we have the *Golden Legend*.

Barthélemy : Which nothing obliges you to believe.

Diderot : I beg your pardon ! It is your most eminent hagiographers who utter this nonsense to us.

Barthélemy : These are not articles of faith.

Diderot : There you are, already backing out ; Abbé, you are shirking. If, among all your prodigies and miracles, one can choose . . .

Barthélemy : Certainly, one can choose ; one ought, even.

Diderot : Go and persuade our clergy in the country of that ! They all have their St. Potentiens. And even your dogmas, obligatory to faith, your God in three people, your wicked angels who revolt against their Creator and try to dethrone Him, your Eve drawn out of Adam's side, your Virgin who receives the visit of a young man and a bird and who becomes pregnant, not by the young man, but by the bird ; this virgin who bears a child and remains a virgin ; this God who dies on the cross to appease God, then comes to life again and ascends into heaven (where, to heaven ?), all that is mythology, my dear Abbé, it is paganism, it is worthy of Uranus, Saturn and the Titans, Minerva springing fully armed from the head of Jupiter, Juno pregnant with Mars from having breathed the perfume of a flower, Phœbus-Apollo driving the chariot of the sun. . . . These are the same delirious adventures. Our friend d'Holbach[1] freely declares that the supernatural does not interest him. No, it tells him nothing ; it is aberration, unreason. Isn't it really folly, now, to go imagining that with simple words, that is to say, moving the air with the tip of the tongue, one is going to change the laws of the universe and what one calls the decrees of Providence?

Barthélemy : No, philosopher, indeed no, for these words are addressed to a supreme Being, all-powerful, infinitely perfect, a Father infinitely good, who listens to them, notes them . . .

Diderot : And grants them; so be it! Example: the unfortunate woman we noticed at St-Roch. But where is the proof that he hears you, this Father, so good and so merciful, to whom you have recourse? No one has this proof, which, for my part, I should be truly delighted to possess. But nothing, always nothing, always the unfathomable and inviolable silence. I do not recall what governor of a province it was or even some bishop or cardinal perhaps, who reproached another bishop for having exceeded his instructions. "Monseigneur, I have prayed, I have asked God's advice," the accused replied with noble assurance, "I have consulted my crucifix. . . ." "Well then, imbecile, you must do what God and your crucifix answered to you," interrupted the other. That is to say, keep silent and do nothing at all. What is God but a word, a simple vocable to explain the existence of the world? And note well that after all, this word explains nothing; for if you object that no clock has ever been made without a clock-maker, I shall ask you who made the clock-maker, so that we are back at the same mark—at the same mark of interrogation.

Barthélemy : However, haven't you yourself, Diderot, sometimes proclaimed the existence of this clock-maker?

Diderot : Proclaimed! That is saying a great deal.

Barthélemy : A certain letter of yours has been circulated in which you clearly say: "I believe in God, although I get along very well with the atheists."

Diderot : A letter to Voltaire. . . . That was to please him. . . . Ah! so you saw that scribble. This is what happens Abbé: when I am with atheists, since there are atheists, all the arguments in favour of the existence of God spring up in my mind ; when I happen to be with believers, it's the opposite : I see rise up before me, and in spite of me, everything that combats, saps and demolishes the Divinity.

Barthélemy : After this avowal, you will no longer say, my dear Diderot, that you are not endowed with the spirit of contradiction ?

Diderot : It is certain that contradiction, or at least opposition, is the stimulant, also the embellishment and spice of conversation. If we were always of the same opinion, what monotony, what feebleness, what platitude ! The world would not be habitable. Diversity of opinion is as necessary, as inevitable, as diversity of features and characters. It is necessary to recognize and to admit that what pleases some cannot please all the others. But no, my dear friend, no ; it is not only for the vain pleasure of contradicting that I thus see rise up in my mind all the arguments contrary to the thesis of my opponent ; it is because of a peculiarity of my nature, a queerness which I record, which I suffer, without being able to explain it at all. That's how it is !

Barthélemy : See all the advantages of faith ! If you possessed it. . . .

Diderot : All difficulties would disappear, evidently. That is the way Pascal reasoned : whether it is true or false, you never risk anything in believing our holy religion to be true, and you risk everything in believing it false. But a Jew can say as much, a Moslem even, and similarly a Huguenot. It's a saddle that fits all horses, a barber's chair that suits all behinds. Unfortunately, dear Abbé, I do not possess this sovereign remedy, this panacea which you call faith, that is to say, the ability to believe things which we know are manifestly false, inadmissible, unbelievable. A table for me is only a table, a chair only a chair, bread is only bread, and wine, equally, is only wine.

I cannot tell you that this lack of faith bothers me **very**
much, that it obsesses, distracts, poisons and torments my
days and nights, and that I lose the desire to eat and drink
because of it! No, alas! I cannot tell you that, for, on the
contrary, this incredulity or ignorance leaves me absolutely
calm and indifferent. But to affirm and maintain certain
facts which are beyond our reason, which escape us entirely ;
to certify and to proclaim them stubbornly, that is what
seems as arrogant as it is ridiculous. And if one furiously
sets about imposing these supernatural things on people,
as always happens with those who are convinced that they
alone hold the innate science, the absolute truth, the truth
on which depends our eternal happiness then . . . " Think
as I do, or the good God will damn you. . . . Think as I
do or I kill you ! " That is the necessary conclusion and
final point. Does not the Bible, in Deuteronomy,* command the massacre of those of our fellow-citizens who do
not share our religious beliefs ? " Brother, son, daughter,
mother, wife ; do not discuss with them : kill them at
once ! " It is clear and plain. A charming plan, and drawn
up in the name of the Lord ! And note well, Abbé, that
in thus demanding that someone should change his religious
beliefs, you ask him, in brief, to do something which you
yourself refuse to do. What logic, eh ?

Barthélemy : But . . .

Diderot : Yes, I know, I guess what you are going to say.
It's that your own cult is the good one, the true one, the
only true and the only good one, while mine is not worth
a fig. Do you recall the letters once exchanged between the
Pope and the Duke of Sully ? The Holy Father compli-
mented the Huguenot minister on his politics and his
excellent government, and he finished, like a good shepherd
who wants to bring back a strayed ewe into the fold, by
beseeching him to open his eyes to the divine light, to see
the truth where it is, and to re-enter the bosom of the

* Deuteronomy xiii, 6.

Church. "Exactly, this is also what I pray to Heaven for, about you," Sully replied to him. "I never cease to pray for the conversion of Your Holiness."

Barthélemy : What cynicism !

Diderot : It is the answer of the shepherdess to the shepherd. But let's return . . . return to our other sheep. Now, every consideration and reflection being taken into account, does God manifest himself to us otherwise than through the worship we offer Him ? Do you see Him manifest Himself otherwise, Abbé ?

Barthélemy : But, my dear philosopher, one needs only open one's eyes and look around. The whole of nature . . .

Diderot : Then the blind who, never having seen anything, cannot render an account to themselves. . . .[2]

Barthélemy : Let's leave the blind out of it.

Diderot : Very well then, for us, for all who can see, isn't it our prayers, our offerings, our religious practices solely, you understand, Abbé, *solely*, which attest to us the existence of God ? Now, I will not hide from you that for myself and from some others, this is not enough. We wish that these evidences should not always come from ourselves, but sometimes a little from this Divinity, so much celebrated and glorified, hymned and entreated.

Barthélemy : These evidences have already been collected. They exist in the holy books.

Diderot : Yes, but your holy books are not those of other nations, and they differ even among themselves. And then, I should very much like to have been there, to verify for myself. . . . For, after all, it is always men who speak in the name of God, who claim to be the representatives here on earth of the Most High ; but these representatives never show us their credentials, never !

Barthélemy : Indeed they do ! Only you obstinately refuse to see them.

Diderot : I would only ask this, however, that they should be only the least bit clear, precise and convincing—which they never are, alas! And again, note this, which is hardly to the credit of the Divinity, at least as it shows itself to us : that wherever there is a God, there is a religious cult, and wherever there is a cult, the natural order of moral duties is overturned.

Barthélemy : Overturned? But how is that?

Diderot : Without any doubt. To go without Mass on Sunday or to eat a slice of veal on Friday becomes a more horrible crime than to steal a neighbour's purse or to debauch his daughter. And that is to be understood! In the first case it is God personally whom you offend ; in the second case it is only your neighbour. You have read the story of that herdsman on the outskirts of Naples who carried on brigandage on every possible occasion, and at confession only accused himself of having broken a fast by inadvertently drinking a little soup. At the tribunal of penitence it was never a question of his ravages, shootings and killings. That didn't count. And that other man, all stained with blood his dagger had just shed, scrupling on a Friday to put any bacon on his bread. With us it is sufficient to receive absolution before dying in order to go straight to heaven, whatever life one may have led, whatever scandals and horrors one may have perpetrated. With the Indians, provided that one dies on the banks of the Ganges so that one's ashes are thrown into that river, then you are saved, admitted straight away into paradise. See just a little, my dear Abbé, how much this idea of God and of religion falsifies and vitiates all our reasoning. Isn't it precisely this, according to the *Spirit of Laws*[3], which by making us regard as necessary what is or ought to be indifferent, makes us consider as indifferent what is absolutely necessary? Again, isn't it this which drives us to massacre thousands of men because they haven't the same beliefs as ourselves? The Vaudois, the Albigenses, St. Bartholomew's Night, the Inquisition, the Dragonades, how many others, are the proof of it. And what about human sacrifices designed to appease the Supreme Being, the God of clemency and mercy ? I remember in one of your memoirs that you yourself, Abbé, said : " For long no better way for averting celestial anger was known than shedding on the altars the blood of men. . . ."

Barthélemy : Those were pagans.

Diderot : We have not changed, and we have burnt enough Jews, tortured enough infidels. . . . Even one of your colleagues and rivals, the Abbé of Longuerue, who is concerned with Chaldeans and ancient France, as you are with the Greeks, estimates that religions, by all the blood which they have caused to be shed, have caused more evil than good in the world.

Barthélemy : Longuerue, a learned man, yes, but a hot-head. In any case, my dear philosopher, you cannot do without these religions, whatever they are.

Diderot : We cannot ?

Barthélemy : No, and you never will be able to. People will always want some ceremonial for their marriages and their births, funeral hymns and the trappings of mourning at the burial of their dead, and holy water on their tombs. Otherwise they would fear to resemble too closely the animals who couple and who die without any ceremony and are flung on the dung-heap.

Diderot : Now let us see, Abbé, don't we procreate exactly like animals ? Don't we breathe, don't we eat and function in everything, exactly as they do ? Did not Solomon teach us that the condition of man in no way differs from that of animals, and that what remains of the one is no more than remains of the other ? Then why this demarcation and this contempt ? Animals are, and ought to be, only younger brothers for us, having a little less reason, but the same needs, the same appetites and the same passions. . . . According to you, then, in order not to resemble animals, we ought not to eat ?

Barthélemy : We ought to make ourselves not resemble

their bad sides, but to uplift our intellect as high as possible towards heaven.

Diderot : And our looks also : *Os sublime dedit.*

Barthélemy : Yes, certainly.

Diderot : There is yet another point which troubles me : among all these millions and billions of stars which race through space, and which, like our little terrestrial globe, are inhabited worlds—one supposes so at least—have their inhabitants also committed the original or queer—yes queer!—sin? do they also need a Messiah, a virgin birth? . . .

Barthélemy : You ask too much of me, my dear philosopher, and it is for inquisitive people of your kind that hell was created.

Diderot : Ass ! You're confusing me with Desmahis.

Barthélemy : Not at all. But I ask you, since you yourself recognize that these questions have been discussed without any result as long as the universe has existed, what is the good of discussing them again ?

Diderot : Ah ! now you are speaking wisely, Abbé. We are wasting our time. Pascal has clearly forewarned us of it : all philosophical discussion, the whole of philosophy even, is not worth an hour's trouble.

Barthélemy : Our human and earthly philosophy ; but . . .

Diderot : Oh ! theology ; that's a thousand times worse !

Barthélemy : But instinctively, inevitably, once again, man looks, and will ever look, higher than himself ; his hope for the Beyond will never leave him, and will never be quenched. And note, moreover, that we Christians have a base of operations, we have a body of doctrines, a code, a catechism to give it its proper name ; while you do not and cannot have one.

Diderot : Hey ! Hey !

Barthélemy : No, impossible ; for one does not make laws and one converts nobody with negation and doubt. In order to teach and to make laws there must be a collection of incontestable facts, above all concerning those things which affect us most closely, our most constant and essential preoccupations, our origin, our creation, the creation of the universe. . . .

Diderot : In six days, and rest the seventh day.

Barthélemy : We possess a catechism, and it is this which gives us our strength.

Diderot : And you also have those ceremonies of which you were speaking just now, your processions, your feasts, your hymns, your organs, all your music, all these shows, so well contrived to attract the crowd, to ensnare and to keep it. That is another of the elements of your success, of your power. I am not hiding from myself, my dear Abbé, any of your advantages. But neither let us deny our own, those of the philosophers, and let us testify that we are making progress, the greatest and most incontestable progress. Recently at Grandval, Father Hoop told me that he had seen in a Swiss village when the curé was away or ill, a Protestant pastor replace the curé in his offices, teaching the catechism to the Catholic children in the evening, after having given his lesson of religious instruction to the little Protestants in the morning ; and thus in the same locality serving at the same time, or rather, successively, the church and the temple.

Barthélemy : This pastor did not go so far as to celebrate Mass, I imagine ?

Diderot : Not yet, but we are coming to it. Tolerance is permeating and penetrating little by little everywhere. Catholics and Huguenots are beginning not to burn one another ; that's something. And since tolerance necessarily leads to indifference, I calculate that Christianity has still two or three centuries. . . .

Barthélemy : For a little longer, if you please. *Tu es Petrus et super hanc petram.**

Diderot : Alas ! there is nothing everlasting here below,

* " You are Peter (rock) and on this rock I build." A pun on word *Petrus* meaning Peter or rock.

Abbe. Montesquieu gives you still five hundred years existence as a maximum ; the Scotsman, John Craig, dead, it is true over a century and a half ago, allowed you three hundred and fifty years ; for myself, I am less generous, I grant you two or three hundred. Perhaps I am wrong, and you deserve more. What is certain is that everything changes, everything varies on our globe, everything fades, weakens, is extinguished, falls and disappears. That is the general law, and you will not escape it, in spite of your predictions, your *Tu es Petrus*. What a fall you had there ! Where are the days when through your popes and their influence and preponderance, you were as masters of the earth ! And before you, wasn't Jupiter also enthroned in his Olympus with all his fellow-gods ? He reigned so well and was so powerful that during the Council of Trent, that is to say barely two centuries ago, two learned men testified to it and besought him, and actually at Trent : " They may well perorate and do all that in there. We shall be obliged to return to thy worship sooner or later. Yea, Jupiter, we have faith in thee. When thou shalt have regained thy rank and grasped thy sovereignty again, in thy turn forget us not ! Deign, oh Jupiter ! deign to remember that we have remained faithful unto thee ! "

Barthélemy : Dreamers ! Visionaries !

Diderot : Yes, certainly ! But so far as dreamers and visionaries go, to you the palm, to you and yours, monsieur l'Abbé ! And is it necessary to recall to you all the metamorphoses which your Church has undergone since St. Peter, how much it differs to-day from what it was at its beginning ? . . . St. Peter himself would not recognize it ; you know it just as well as I do. And you who know very well that this code or catechism which makes your strength is a tissue of impossibilities, of humbug, of . . .

Barthélemy : Of whatever you please, my dear philosopher. But this tissue holds together from one end to the other. It forms a solid whole. . . .

Diderot : Solid !

Barthélemy : For the masses it answers and suffices for everything ; while as for you others, you gentlemen of the *Encyclopedia,* you answer and can answer none of the great questions which haunt the human mind : " How was the world created ? By whom ? What is God ? How did man appear on earth ? " And so on. You philosophers, or at least part of you . . . oh ! I don't accuse you of being swollen with pride and boasting ! No, on the contrary ! You have for ever on your lips your, " I do not know . . . I am ignorant ! "

Diderot : That is true, and I am the most often like that, among them. But with you, Abbé, it's just the opposite ; you always know everything, you others, and you never question anything.

Barthélemy : Precisely !

Diderot : You continually affirm things which are contradicted more and more by science. . . .

Barthélemy : Human science !

Diderot : Don't speak ill of it. . . . You have recourse to it when you discourse and debate. And you, least of all, Abbé, should disparage science, you who pass your life surrounded with your books and manuscripts, your medallions and all the remains of Roman and Greek antiquity. You know in what high esteem you are held by those whom you call the Encyclopedists ?

Barthélemy : I know how forbearing you are, Diderot, how sensitive and tender your soul is.

Diderot : Well, would you believe, my dear friend, sometimes I suspect you of having, besides your profound learning, too much good sense not to be enlightened about the value of these Catholic dogmas, and to be decided, in this respect, just as I am ? Naturally you will not agree to this, and in your conscience you think me terribly indiscreet. . . . But finally, yes—why are you a Catholic ?

Barthélemy : What ! Why ?

Diderot : Yes !

Barthélemy : But . . .

Diderot : Well then, I'll tell it you. It is solely—*solely* —because you were born in France and were brought up, " nourished," by Catholics. Exactly ! Suppose yourself for a moment a native of the Antipodes, of Zanzibar, of Cathay, of Patagonia, and see what would have become of you. You would be perhaps not even an Israelite, Lutheran, Calvinist or Moslem, but very likely a Buddhist, Brahmin, idolator, or animal-worshipper for all I know ! We have the choice. You see, my dear Abbé, all that is an affair of latitude, a pure hazard, luck.

Barthélemy : You said the word, Diderot : luck ! So be it. And I profit by this luck.

Diderot : Much good may it do you ! But state with me that the most important thing for man, his eternal salvation, his religion in other words, depends solely on chance, on a caprice of fate. What fine deserts, eh ?

Barthélemy : So I bless Providence. . . .

Diderot : And you are right Abbé. I don't profit from this windfall, an infidel like me. . . . But, pardon me, forgive my questions. . . . I hardly ever restrain myself, and speak freely what is in my mind.

Barthélemy : I live apart from all discussions. I work and associate more with the sages of Athens and of Rome and indeed with those of Palestine, than with my contemporaries.

Diderot : Work, eh ? yes, that's our lot and our role here below. To try to leave after us a little more light and comfort than there was before, to improve and increase the heritage we have received ; it is to that we should apply ourselves. I add : to do as much good as possible, and to spare as much suffering as possible around us, to all our companions on the way. Benevolence is better than any-thing. Work and benevolence, there are my sole two articles of faith, Abbé. For the rest. . . . For myself, no more than for d'Holbach, the infinite does not preoccupy me, not in the least. When and by whom was the world created? Where shall we go after our death? What shall we become? All these problems which you think of such capital importance, don't in the least disturb my sleep. For hundreds and thousands of centuries, nobody has been able to solve them, but only to clarify them. So I . . . God, the soul, the future life. I neither believe nor disbelieve them; I eliminate these questions, I stick to life in the present, and I consider, with Spinoza, that all meditation about the Beyond and about death is useless, vain and depressing.

Barthélemy: Ah, my poor Diderot! how far we are out in our reckoning! Is not true wisdom, on the contrary, continual meditation on death, as our Bourdaloue has demonstrated in such masterly fashion?

Diderot: The Lord bless him! As for myself, I haven't got such penetrating and far-seeing vision, and limit myself to the present, to what I am and what I see, and I do not feel any more in despair at not knowing what to think about the existence of the Supreme Being and of the immortality of the soul, than at not having two heads, three arms or four legs. I take existence as it is, trying to pass through it as honestly and as comfortably and agreeably as I can, and if later on I encounter what I hardly expect, I confess it, namely a judge beyond the Styx, I have confidence in his wisdom and mercy; he will not punish me for my ignorance and my humility, any more than for my frankness. Otherwise I should have the right to answer him: " You had only to speak more clearly, Lord. Is it my fault that I know not how to unravel these enigmas? How could I suspect that in order to guide myself through the darkness into which you plunged me, I ought to have begun by blowing out my lantern, my sole torch, this feeble candle-end, this poor little reason with which you have favoured me? "

(1772–1773?)

213

VIII

DISCOURSE OF
A PHILOSOPHER TO A KING

SIRE, if you want priests you do not need philosophers,
and if you want philosophers you do not need priests ; for
the ones being by their calling the friends of reason and the
promoters of science, the others the enemies of reason and
the favourers of ignorance, if the first do good, the others do
evil.

You have both philosophers and priests ; philosophers
who are poor and not very formidable, priests who are very
rich and very dangerous. You should not much concern
yourself with enriching your philosophers, because riches
are harmful to philosophy, but your design should be to
keep them ; and you should strongly desire to impoverish
your priests and to rid yourself of them.

You will most surely rid yourself of them, and with them
of all the lies which they inflict on your nation, by im-
poverishing them ; because, impoverished, they will soon
be degraded, and who would want to enter a calling, where
there will be neither honour to be acquired, nor fortune
to be made ? But how shall you impoverish them ? I am
going to tell you. You will be very careful not to attack
their privileges, nor to seek at first to reduce them to the
general level of your citizens. That would be unjust and
clumsy—unjust, because their privileges belong to them as
your crown belongs to you ; because they possess them and
if you touch their deeds of possession, your deeds of
possession will be touched ; because there is nothing that
you can better do than respect the law of prescription which

is at least as favourable to you as to them ; because these are the gifts of your ancestors and of the ancestors of your subjects, and nothing is more holy than a gift ; because you have been raised to the throne only on condition of leaving each calling its prerogatives ; because if you fail in your oath to one of the estates of your kingdom, why should you not forswear yourself to the others ? because you would then alarm all ; there would no longer be anything stable around you, you would shake the foundations of property, without which there is no longer king nor subjects, there is only a tyrant and slaves ; and it is in that, moreover, that you would be clumsy. What shall you do then ? You will leave things in the state as they are. Your arrogant clergy prefer to accord you " freewill offerings " rather than pay you taxes : ask " freewill offerings " then.

Your celibate clergy, who care very little for their successors, will not want to pay out of their purses, but they will borrow from your subjects. So much the better ; let them borrow. Help them to contract an enormous debt with the rest of the nation. Then do one just thing : force them to pay. They will be able to pay only by using a portion of their treasure. This treasure may well be sacred, but be sure that your subjects will have no scruple in taking it, when they find themselves in the necessity either of accepting it in payment or of ruining themselves by losing what they advanced.

Thus, by freewill offering after freewill offering, you will make them contract a second debt, a third, a fourth, which you will force them to discharge until they are reduced to mediocrity or poverty, which will make them as vile as they are useless. It will rest only with you and your successors whether one day they are seen in rags under the porticos of their sumptuous buildings, offering their prayers and their sacrifices to the people at reduced prices.

But, you will say to me, I shall no longer have any religion. You are deceived, Sire, you will always have one ; for

215

religion is a climbing and lively plant which never perishes ; it only changes form. That religion which will result from the poverty and degradation of its members will be the least troublesome, the least sad, the most tranquil and the most innocent. Do against the reigning superstition what Constantine did against paganism : he ruined the pagan priests, and soon only an old woman with a prophetic goose telling fortunes to the lowest of the populace was seen within their magnificent temples ; at the doorway, only wretches lending themselves to vice and amorous intrigues. A father would have died with shame to have let his child become a priest.

And if you deign to listen to me, I shall be the most dangerous of all philosophers for the priests. For the most dangerous is he who brings to the monarch's attention the immense sums which these arrogant and useless loafers cost his state ; he who tells him, as I tell you, that you have a hundred and fifty thousand men to whom you and your subjects pay about a hundred and fifty thousand crowns a day to bawl in a building and deafen us with their bells ; who tells him that a hundred times a year, at a fixed hour, these men speak to eighteen millions of your assembled subjects, disposed to believe and to do all that they enjoin them to do in God's name ; who tells him that a king is nothing, nothing at all, when someone can command within his realm, in the name of a Being recognized as the master of the king ; who tells him that these makers of feast-days shut the shops of the nation every day when they open theirs, that is to say, a third of the year ; who tells him that, if he knew how to act, it would be easier to discredit the whole of his clergy than one maker of good cloth, because cloth is useful and Masses and sermons are more easily done without than shoes ; who strips from these holy personages their pretended sacred character, as I am doing now, and who teaches you to devour them without scruple when you are driven by hunger ; who counsels you, while waiting for the main bulk, to seize the multitude of their rich benefices as they become vacant, and to nominate to them only those who will take them at a third of their revenue, reserving for yourself and the urgent needs of your state the other two-thirds, for five years, ten years, for ever, as you please; who demonstrates to you that if you have been able without unpleasant consequences, to make your magistrates liable to dismissal, there is very much less inconvenience in making your priests liable to dismissal; that as long as you think you have need of them, you must pay them stipends because a stipendary priest is only a craven who fears to be kicked out and ruined; who shows you that the man who gets his subsistence from your bene-factions no longer has any courage and dares do nothing great and bold, as witness those who fill your academies, and in whom the fear of losing their post and their pension awes them to the extent that they would be unknown, if it were not for the works which had previously made them famous.

Since you have the secret of making a philosopher hold his tongue, why not employ it to silence the priest? The one is of quite different importance from the other.

(1775–1776 ?)

IX

CONVERSATION OF A PHILOSOPHER WITH THE MARÉCHALE DE X[1]

I HAD some business or other with the Maréchal de X. I went to his mansion one morning ; he was absent ; I had myself announced to Madame la Maréchale. She is a charming woman ; she is as beautiful and as devout as an angel ; sweetness is clearly expressed on her countenance ; and she has, moreover, a tone of voice and a candour in discussion quite in keeping with her expression. She was at her toilette. A chair is drawn up for me ; I seat myself and we chat. Following some remarks, which enlightened and surprised her (for she was of the opinion that whoever denies the very Holy Trinity is a complete scoundrel who will end by hanging) she said :

" Aren't you Monsieur Crudeli ? "

Crudeli : Yes, Madame.

The Maréchale : Then it's you who believes in nothing ?

Crudeli : The same.

The Maréchale : Your morals, though, are those of a believer.

Crudeli : Why not, when he is an honest man ?

The Maréchale : And do you practise this morality ?

Crudeli : As best I can.

The Maréchale : What ! You don't steal, you don't kill, you don't plunder ?

Crudeli : Very rarely.

The Maréchale : What do you gain, then, by not believing ?

Crudeli : Nothing at all, Madame la Maréchale. Does one believe because there is something to be gained ?

The Maréchale : I don't know ; but the motive of personal interest harms nothing in the affairs of this world or of the next.

Crudeli : I am a little sorry, then, for the credit of our poor human species. It doesn't say much for us.

The Maréchale : What ! you don't steal at all ?

Crudeli : No, on my honour.

The Maréchale : If you are neither thief nor assassin, at least agree that you are not consistent.

Crudeli : But why not ?

The Maréchale : Because it seems to me that if I had nothing to hope or to fear when I shall no longer exist in this world, then there are many little pleasures which I should not forego, as I do now that I am in it. I admit that I lend to God at a high rate.

Crudeli : You imagine you do !

The Maréchale : It is not imagination at all. It is a fact.

Crudeli : And might one ask what are those things you would permit yourself if you were an unbeliever ?

The Maréchale : Please don't ; that is one article I keep for my confession.

Crudeli : For myself, I never expect to see my capital again. I never invest.

The Maréchale : That's the resource of beggars.

Crudeli : Would you rather I were a usurer ?

The Maréchale : Certainly ; one can charge God with interest to any extent ; one cannot ruin him. I well know that is not very delicate, but what does it matter ? Since the point is to get to heaven, either by skill or force, it's necessary to take everything into account, to neglect no profit. Alas ! Whatever we do, we shall try in vain, our stake will always be very paltry in comparison with the return we expect. And you expect nothing ?

Crudeli : Nothing.

The Maréchale : That is sad. You must agree then, that you are very wicked or quite mad!

Crudeli : Truly, I could not, Madame la Maréchale.

The Maréchale : What motive can an unbeliever have for being good, if he is not mad ? I should very much like to know.

Crudeli : And I am going to tell it you.

The Maréchale : I am much obliged.

Crudeli : Don't you think that one might be so fortunately born that one finds a great pleasure in doing good ?

The Maréchale : I think so.

Crudeli : That one can have received an excellent education which strengthens the natural inclination for doing good ?

The Maréchale : Assuredly.

Crudeli : And that, in after-life, experience may have convinced us that taking everything into consideration, it were better, for one's happiness in this world, to be an honest man rather than a rogue ?

The Maréchale : Yes, to be sure ; but how to be an honest man when bad principles combine with the passions to lead into evil ?

Crudeli : One is inconsistent : and is there anything more common than being inconsistent ?

The Maréchale : Alas ! Unfortunately no. One believes, and every day one behaves as if one did not.

Crudeli : And without believing, one behaves almost as if one did.

The Maréchale : So be it ; but what inconvenience would there be in having one reason more, religion, for doing good, and one reason less, unbelief, for doing evil ?

Crudeli : None at all, if religion were a motive for doing good, and unbelief a motive for doing evil.

The Maréchale : But is there any doubt about that ? Isn't the spirit of religion to oppose this villainous corrupted nature, and the spirit of unbelief to abandon it to its malice, by freeing it from fear ?

Crudeli : This, Madame la Maréchale, is going to lead us into a big discussion.

The Maréchale : What does that matter? The Maréchal won't be returning just yet ; and it's better that one should get clear than speak ill of one's neighbours.

Crudeli : It will be necessary for me to take things up somewhat further back.

The Maréchale : As far as you like, provided I can understand you.

Crudeli : If you don't understand me, it will be entirely my fault.

The Maréchale : That is very polite ; but you should know that I've never read anything except my Book of Hours and that I've hardly had time to do anything except practise the teaching of the Gospel and bear children.

Crudeli : Those are two duties at which you have well acquitted yourself.

The Maréchale : Yes, as concerns the children ; you have seen six about me, and in a few days will be able to see another on my lap. But begin.

Crudeli : Madame la Maréchale, is there any good thing in this world which is without some disadvantage ?

The Maréchale : None at all.

Crudeli : And any evil thing which may not have some advantage ?

The Maréchale : None.

Crudeli : Then what do you call good or evil ?

The Maréchale : An evil thing will be that which has more disadvantages than advantages ; a good thing, on the contrary, will have more advantages than disadvantages.

Crudeli : Will Madame la Maréchale have the goodness to remember her definition of good and evil ?

The Maréchale : I will remember it. You call that a definition ?

Crudeli : Yes.

The Maréchale : That's philosophy, then ?

Crudeli : Excellent philosophy.

The Maréchale : Then I've done some philosophizing!

Crudeli : Thus, you are persuaded that religion has more advantages than disadvantages ; and it's because of that that you call it good?

The Maréchale : Yes.

Crudeli : For myself, I don't doubt at all that your steward steals from you a little less on the eve of Easter than the day after the feast ; and that from time to time religion prevents a number of small evils and produces a number of small beneficial effects.

The Maréchale : Little by little, all adds up.

Crudeli : But do you believe that the terrible ravages which it has caused in the past, and which it will cause in the future are sufficiently compensated by these paltry advantages? Think of the most bitter antipathy between nations which it has created and perpetuated. There is not a Moslem who doesn't imagine doing an action agreeable to God and the Holy Prophet, by exterminating all Christians, who, on their side, are hardly more tolerant. Think of the divisions within a nation which it has created and perpetuated, which are rarely extinguished without bloodshed. Our history offers us examples only too recent and too terrible. Think of the most bitter and most constant hatreds which it has created and perpetuated in society among the citizens, and among near relations in the family. Christ has said that he came to divide husband from wife, mother from children, brother from sister, and friend from friend ; and his prediction has only too faithfully come to pass.

The Maréchale : Those are indeed abuses ; but that is not the thing itself.

Crudeli : It is the thing itself, if the abuses are inseparable from it.

The Maréchale : And how will you show me that the abuses of religion are inseparable from religion.

Crudeli : Very easily. Tell me, if a misanthrope had proposed to do evil to the human race, what could he have invented better than the belief in an incomprehensible being about whom men would never have been able to agree and to whom they would have attached more importance than to their own lives ? Now, is it possible to separate from the conception of divinity, the most profound incomprehensibility and the most profound importance ?

The Maréchale : No.

Crudeli : Draw the conclusion then.

The Maréchale : I conclude that it is an idea which is not without importance in the heads of fools.

Crudeli : And add that the fools have always been and will always be the most numerous ; and that the most dangerous fools are those made so by religion, and of whom the disturbers of society know how to make use on occasion.

The Maréchale : But there must be something which terrifies men for evil actions which escape the severity of the law ; and if you destroy religion what will you put in its place ?

Crudeli : If I should have nothing to put in its place, that would of course be one terrible prejudice the less : without counting the fact that in no century and in no nation have religious opinions served as basis for the national morality. The gods whom those old Greeks and Romans, the most honest people on earth, adored, were the most dissolute rabble ; a Jupiter who ought to have been burnt alive ; a Venus to be shut up at the *Hôpital* ; a Mercury to be put in the Bicêtre. [2]

The Maréchale : And you think it is quite immaterial whether we are Christians or pagans ; that as pagans we should be equally good and as Christians we are no better ?

Crudeli : My oath, I'm sure of it, except that as pagans we should be a little more lively.

The Maréchale : That can't be.

Crudeli : But, Madame la Maréchale, are there any Christians ? I've never seen any.

The Maréchale : You ask *me* that, me ?

Crudeli : No, Madame, I don't ask you ; I asked a neighbour of mine, who is as honest and pious as you are, and who believes herself a Christian of the most sublime faith in the world, just as you do.

The Maréchale : And you made her see that she was wrong.

Crudeli : In an instant.

The Maréchale : How did you do it ?

Crudeli : I opened a New Testament, which she had used a great deal, for it was very worn. I read her the Sermon on the Mount, and at each article, I asked her, " Do you do that, and this, and again this ? " I went further. She is beautiful, and although she may be very modest and very devout, she is not ignorant of the fact. She has a very white skin, and although she does not attach great value to this frail advantage, she is not displeased if it is praised. She has as fine a bosom as it is possible to have, and, although she is very modest, she is not averse to its beauty being observed.

The Maréchale : So long as only she and her husband know it.

Crudeli : I believe that her husband knows it better than anyone else, but for a woman who prides herself on her strict Christianity, that is not enough. I said to her : " Isn't it written in the Gospel that he who has coveted his neighbour's wife has committed adultery in his heart " ?

The Maréchale : She answered, yes ?

Crudeli : I said to her, " And does not adultery committed in the heart damn as surely as adultery actually committed ?

The Maréchale : She answered, yes ?

Crudeli : I said to her : " And if the man is damned for the adultery he has committed in his heart, what will be the fate of the woman who invites all who come near her to commit this crime ? " This last question embarrassed her.

The Maréchale : I understand ; it was because she did not veil very carefully that bosom of hers, which was as fine as it is possible to have.

Crudeli : That is true. She answered me that it was a customary thing, as if nothing were more customary than to call oneself a Christian and not to be one ; that " it was not necessary to dress ridiculously," as if there were any comparison to be made between a little bit of ridicule and her eternal damnation and that of her neighbour ; that " she let her dress-maker dress her," as if it were not better to change her dress-maker than to renounce her religion ; that it was " her husband's fancy," as if a husband was so absurd as to exact from his wife forgetfulness of decency and her duties, and as if a true Christian ought to carry obedience to an extravagant husband to the length of sacrificing the will of her God and of disregarding the threats of her Redeemer.

The Maréchale : I guessed all those puerilities in advance ; I should perhaps have said them, just as your neighbour did. But both she and I would have been insincere. But what decision did she take after your remonstrance ?

Crudeli : The day after this conversation—it was a feast day—I was just going into my house, and my devout and beautiful neighbour was coming out of hers to go to Mass.

The Maréchale : Dressed as usual ?

Crudeli : Dressed as usual. I smiled, she smiled, and we passed each other without speaking. Madame la Maréchale, an honest woman ! a Christian ! a devout woman ! After this example, and a hundred thousand others of the same kind, what real influence on conduct can I give to religion? Almost none, and so much the better.

The Maréchale : What, so much the better ?

Crudeli : Yes, Madame : if it suddenly took the fancy of twenty thousand inhabitants of Paris to conform strictly to the Sermon on the Mount. . . .

The Maréchale : Well ! there would be several other beautiful bosoms more covered.

Crudeli : And so many lunatics, that the police wouldn't know what to do with them ; for our asylums wouldn't be large enough. In the inspired books there are two moralities : one is general and common to all nations and all religious cults, and which is followed, more or less ; the other is peculiar to each nation and each religious cult, which is believed, preached in the churches, and extolled in the home, and which is not followed at all.

The Maréchale : And how does this queer situation arise ?

Crudeli : Because it is impossible to subject a whole people to a rule which only suits a few melancholic men, who have stamped their own characters on it. It is with religious as with monastical institutions, that with time, everything becomes slackened. These are follies which cannot stand against the constant impulses of nature, which brings us all back under its law. Make it so that the good of individuals is so closely tied to the general good that a citizen can hardly harm society without harming himself. Assure virtue its recompense as you have assured wickedness its punishment ; and assure that, with no discrimination of religious belief, merit in whatever condition of man it is found may lead to the highest positions in the state. Then no longer expect any wicked people, except a few men whose perverse nature, which nothing can correct, leads into crime. Madame la Maréchale, temptation is too close and hell is too far away ; don't expect anything which is worth the trouble of a wise law-maker, from a system of bizarre opinions which wouldn't deceive children ; which encourages crime by the facility of expiation ; which sends the culprit to ask God to pardon an injury done to man, and which degrades the behests of natural duties and morals by subordinating them to the command of chimerical duties.

The Maréchale : I don't understand you.

Crudeli : I'll explain ; but I think that's the coach of Monsieur le Maréchal, who's returned just in time to stop me saying something foolish.

The Maréchale : Say it, say your foolishness, I shan't hear it ; I am accustomed to hearing only what pleases me.

Crudeli : I leaned towards her ear and whispered : Madame la Maréchale, ask the vicar of your parish, of these two crimes, which is the most atrocious : to piss in a sacred vessel or to blacken the reputation of an honest woman. He will shudder with horror at the first, will cry sacrilege ; and civil law, which hardly takes notice of the calumny, while it punishes sacrilege by burning, will finish by confusing ideas and corrupting minds.

The Maréchale : I know more than one woman who would scruple to eat luxuriously on a Friday, and who would. . . . But I was going to say something foolish also. Continue.

Crudeli : But Madame, I absolutely must speak to M. le Maréchal.

The Maréchale : Just one moment more, and then we will go to see him together. I hardly know what to answer you ; but you haven't persuaded me, however.

Crudeli : I have not proposed to persuade you. It is the same with religion as with marriage. Marriage, which has been the misfortune of so many others, has made your happiness and that of M. le Maréchal ; you did well to marry each other. Religion, which has made, which is making and will make so many evil-doers, has rendered you even better ; you do well to keep it. It is pleasant for you to imagine beside you, above your head, a great and powerful Being who sees you walking on earth, and this idea strengthens your steps. Madame, continue to enjoy this august surety for your thoughts, this spectator, this sublime model for your actions.

The Maréchale : From what I see, you haven't the mania for making converts.

Crudeli : Not in the least.

The Maréchale : I esteem you the better for that.

Crudeli : I let everyone think as they like, provided they let me think my way ; and besides, those who are destined to be delivered of these prejudices, hardly need to be catechized.

The Maréchale : Do you believe that man can do without superstition ?

Crudeli : Not so long as he remains ignorant and full of fears.

The Maréchale : Well then ! one superstition is as good as another, as well ours as another one.

Crudeli : I don't think so.

The Maréchale : Tell me frankly, isn't it repugnant to you to be nothing, after your death ?

Crudeli : I would rather prefer to exist, although I don't know why a Being, who has been able to make me miserable without reason, should not thus amuse himself twice over.

The Maréchale : If, in spite of this inconvenience, the hope of a life to come seems sweet and consoling even to you, why deprive us of it ?

Crudeli : I haven't got this hope because the desire hasn't in the least concealed from me the emptiness of it ; but I deprive no one of it. If one can believe that one will see, when one shall no longer have eyes, will hear with no ears, will think without a head ; that one will love when one no longer has a heart, will feel when one no longer has senses ; that one will exist when one will be nowhere ; that one will be something, without occupying extent or position in space, then I'll grant it you.

The Maréchale : But this world of ours, who made it ?

Crudeli : I ask you that.

The Maréchale : God made it.

Crudeli : And what is God ?

The Maréchale : A spirit.

Crudeli : If a spirit can make matter, why could not matter make a spirit ?

The Maréchale : But why should it make it ?

Crudeli : I see it do it every day. Do you believe that animals have. souls ?

The Maréchale : Certainly I believe it.

Crudeli : And would you tell me what becomes of the

soul of a Peruvian serpent, for example, while it becomes dried, hung in a chimney, exposed to the smoke for a year or two continuously?

The Maréchale : I don't care what happens to it ; what has it to do with me?

Crudeli : Madame la Maréchale doesn't know that this dried and smoked serpent, revives and is alive again.

The Maréchale : I believe none of that.

Crudeli : It is a clever man, however, Bouguer, who asserts it.

The Maréchale : Your clever man has lied about it.

Crudeli : And if he had spoken truly?

The Maréchale : I should have to believe that animals are machines.

Crudeli : And man, who is only an animal a little more perfect than others. . . . But M. le Maréchal. . . .

The Maréchale : Just one more question, and it's the last. Are you really quite at peace in your unbelief?

Crudeli : One could not be more so.

The Maréchale : But what if you've deceived yourself?

Crudeli : If I should have deceived myself?

The Maréchale : All that you believed false would be true, and you would be damned. Monsieur Crudeli, it is a dreadful thing to be damned ; to burn for all eternity, that's terribly long.

Crudeli : La Fontaine believed that we should be like fish in water there.

The Maréchale : Oh yes, yes ; but your La Fontaine became very serious in his last moments ; it's then I wait for you.

Crudeli : I shall answer for nothing when my brain is no longer clear, but if I finish by one of those illnesses which leave the man at point of death with all his reason, I shall not be any more troubled at the moment you wait for than you see me now.

The Maréchale : This fearlessness abashes me.

Crudeli : I find much more in a person who believes in a

229

stern judge who weighs even our most secret thoughts and in whose balance the most just man would lose himself by his vanity if he did not tremble to find himself found wanting. If this dying man then had the choice, either to be annihilated or to present himself at this judgment-seat, his fearlessness would impress me much more if he hesitated to take the first choice ; at least if he were not madder than the companion of St. Bruno, ᵔr more intoxicated with his own merits than Bohola.

The Maréchale : I have read the story of St. Bruno's companion ; but I've never heard of your Bohola.

Crudeli : He was a jesuit of the college of Pinsk in Lithuania, who left a coffer full of money and a memorandum, written and signed with his own hand, when he died.

The Maréchale : And this memorandum ?

Crudeli : Was drawn up in these terms : " I beg my dear colleague with whom I have deposited this coffer, to open it after I shall have performed miracles. The money it contains will serve to defray the costs of my beatification. I have also added some authentic memoirs for the confirmation of my virtues, which will be useful to those who shall undertake to write my life."

The Maréchale : How killingly funny.

Crudeli : For me, Madame la Maréchale ; but not for you, your God doesn't know how to take a joke.

The Maréchale : You are right.

Crudeli : Madame la Maréchale, it is very easy to sin grievously against your law.

The Maréchale : I agree.

Crudeli : The justice which will decide your fate is very stern.

The Maréchale : That is true.

Crudeli : And if you believe the oracles of your religion about the number of the elect, it will be very small.

The Maréchale : Oh ! I'm not a Jansenist ;[3] I only see the medal on its consoling side ; the blood of Jesus Christ covers a multitude of sins; and it would seem very peculiar to me that the devil, who has not delivered his son to death, should, however, have the larger share of mankind.

Crudeli : Do you damn Socrates, Phocion, Aristides, Cato, Trajan, Marcus Aurelius ?

The Maréchale : Fie, fie ! Only ferocious beasts could think such a thing. St. Paul said that every man shall be judged according to the law he has known ; and St. Paul is right.

Crudeli : And by what law will the unbeliever be judged ?

The Maréchale : Your case is a little different. You are one of those cursed inhabitants of Chorazin and of Bethsaida who shut their eyes to the light which shone upon them, and stopped their ears that they should not hear the voice of Truth speaking to them.

Crudeli : Madame la Maréchale, these folk of Chorazin and Bethsaida were men who never existed anywhere except there, if they were the masters of believing or not believing.

The Maréchale : They saw marvels which would have sent up the price of sack-cloth and ashes, if they had been done in Tyre and Sidon.

Crudeli : The inhabitants of Tyre and Sidon were clever people, while those of Chorazin and Bethsaida were only fools. But will he who made the fools punish them for being fools ? I have just made a difficulty for you, and I should like to tell you a story. A young Mexican. . . . But M. le Maréchal. . . .

The Maréchale : I'm just going to send to discover if we can see him. Well now, your young Mexican ?

Crudeli : Wearied by his work, was walking one day beside the sea. He saw a plank which had one end dipping in the water and the other resting on the beach. He sat himself on this plank, and then, casting his eyes over the vast expanse that stretched before him, said to himself : " There's nothing more certain than that my grandmother was raving with her story about some people or other who landed somewhere here, I don't know when, from some country beyond our seas. There's no common sense in it ; and don't I see the sea bordered by the sky ? And can I believe, against the evidence of my senses, an old fable of which the date is unknown and which everyone alters to taste, and which is only a tissue of absurd circumstances about which they eat out their hearts and tear out one another's eyes?" While he was reasoning like this, the movement of the waters rocked him on his plank and he fell asleep. While he slept the wind sprang up, the tide lifted the plank on which he was stretched, and behold, our young reasoner was afloat.

The Maréchale : Alas ! this is indeed our own image ; we are each one on our plank ; the wind blows and the tide carries us away.

Crudeli : He was already far from the land when he awoke. Who was surprised to find himself at sea ? Our Mexican. Who was then still more surprised ? He again when, having lost sight of the shore on which he had been walking a short while ago, the sea appeared to him bounded by the sky on all sides. He suspected then that he might well have deceived himself ; and that, if the wind remained in the same quarter, he would perhaps be carried to that shore and among those inhabitants about whom his grandmother had so often conversed.

The Maréchale : You don't say a word about his anxiety.

Crudeli : He had none. He said to himself : " What does it matter, so long as I land ? I reasoned like a fool ; so be it. But I have been sincere with myself, and that's all that can be expected of me. If it is not a virtue to be clever, it is no crime not to be." However, the wind held, the man and the plank voyaged on and the unknown shore began to appear ; he touched land, and there he was.

The Maréchale : We shall meet there again one day, Monsieur Crudeli.

Crudeli : I hope so, Madame la Maréchale ; wherever it is, I shall always be delighted to pay my respects to you. He had hardly stepped off his plank on to the sand, when he noticed a venerable old man standing beside him. He asked of him where he was and to whom he had the honour of speaking. " I am the sovereign of this country," the old man answered him. (Instantly the young man prostrated himself.) " Get up," said the old man. " You have denied my existence ?—That is true—And that of my empire ?— That is true—I pardon you because I am he who sees to the bottom of hearts, and I have read in the depths of yours that you are one of good faith ; but the rest of your actions and thoughts are not equally innocent." Then the old man, who was holding him by the ear, recalled to him all the errors of his life ; and at each article the young Mexican bowed, struck his breast and asked pardon. . . . Now, Madame la Maréchale, put yourself for a moment in the old man's place and tell me what you would have done ? Would you have taken this absurd young man by the hair ; and would you have taken pleasure in dragging him up and down on the shore for all eternity ?

The Maréchale : In truth, no.

Crudeli : If one of these six children of yours, after having escaped from the house of their father and having done very foolish things, came back very repentant ?

The Maréchale : I, I should run to meet him ; I should fold him in my arms and wet him with my tears ; but M. le Maréchal, his father, would not take things so easily.

Crudeli : M. le Maréchal is not a tiger.

The Maréchale : He is far from it.

Crudeli : He would perhaps scold a little ; but he would pardon.

The Maréchale : Certainly.

Crudeli : Especially if he considered that before causing this child to be born, he knew the whole of its life, and that punishment of its faults would be without any use, either for himself, or for his brothers.

The Maréchale : The old man and M. le Maréchal are two different people.

Crudeli : You wish to say that M. le Maréchal is better than the old man. Ah ! Madame ! You don't see the consequence of this answer. Either the general definition holds equally for you, for M. le Maréchal, for myself, for the young Mexican, for the old man ; or else, I no longer know what it is, and I am ignorant of how one pleases or displeases the latter.

(We were just there, when we were informed that M. le Maréchal was awaiting us. I gave my hand to Madame la Maréchale who said to me) : " That's enough to make one's head swim, isn't it ? "

Crudeli : Why so, when one has a good one ?

The Maréchale : After all, it's simplest to behave as if the old man existed.

Crudeli : Even when one doesn't believe it ?

The Maréchale : And when one does believe it, not to count on his goodness.

Crudeli : If this is not the most candid, it is at least the most sure.

The Maréchale : If you had to render an account of your principles to our magistrates, would you confess them ?

Crudeli : I should do my best to spare them from committing an atrocious deed.

The Maréchale : Ah ! you coward ! And if you were at the point of death, would you submit to the ceremonies of the Church ?

Crudeli : I should not fail to.

The Maréchale : Oh ! You villainous hypocrite !

(1776)

X

RAMEAU'S NEPHEW [1]

*" Vertumnis, quotquot sunt, natus iniquis."**
(Horat. Lib. II. Sat. VII.)

BE the day fair or foul, it is my custom, towards five in the evening, to walk in the Palais-Royal gardens. I am that man who may be seen, always alone, day-dreaming on d'Argenson's bench. I converse with myself on politics, love, taste, and philosophy. I give my mind full licence; I leave it free to follow the first notion, wise or foolish, that occurs to it, as one may see in the Allée de Foy our dissolute young gallants walk close on the heels of some courtesan with giddy air, laughing face, bright eye and pert nose, then leave her for some other, tackling them all and adhering to none. My thoughts are my wantons.

If the weather is too cold or too wet, I take refuge in the Café de la Régence ; there I find entertainment in watching the chess-players. Paris is the place in all the world, and the Café de la Régence the place in all Paris, where this game is played best. It is at Rey's that Légal, the profound player, the subtle Philidor, and the sound Mayot are pitted against one another ; that you will see the most astonishing play and hear the worst conversation ; for, if one may be a man of sense and a great chess-player, like Légal, it is also possible to be a great chess-player and a fool, like Foubert and Mayot.

One afternoon I was there, watching a great deal, speaking little, listening as little as possible, when I was accosted by one of the queerest figures ever seen in this country where

* Born with the enmity of all the gods.

235

God has made no lack of them. He is a mixture of fineness and baseness, of good sense and folly. Ideas of right and wrong must be very strangely confused in his head ; for he displays his natural good qualities without ostentation and his bad ones without shame. He is endowed, moreover, with a vigorous constitution, a rare imaginative fervour and an uncommonly powerful pair of lungs. If ever you meet him, and you are not stopped by his eccentricity, either you will put your fingers in your ears or you will run away. Heavens, what terrible lungs ! Nothing can be more unlike him than he is himself at times. Sometimes he is thin and haggard, like a sick man in the last stages of consumption ; you might count his teeth through his cheeks. You would say he had gone without food for several days, or had just come from a Trappist monastery. The month after, he is plump and stout, as if he had been a constant guest at a financier's dinner-table, or had been shut up in a Cistercian monastery. One day, with his linen soiled, his breeches torn, his clothes in rags and his shoes in pieces, he will go about hanging his head, avoiding people, and you feel inclined to call him and offer him alms. Next day, powdered and curled, well clad and shod, he holds his head high, shows himself off, and you would almost take him for a gentleman. He lives from day to day : sad or merry according to circumstances. His first care in the morning, as soon as he is up, is to find out where he is to dine ; after dinner, he thinks where he will get supper. Night, too, brings its problem. Either he goes back on foot to the little attic where he lives, unless the landlady, tired of waiting for her rent, has asked to have the key back ; or else he subsides in a tavern in the suburbs to wait for daylight with a hunk of bread and a pot of beer. When he has not six sous in his pocket, which sometimes happens, he has recourse either to a cabman of his acquaintance or to the coachman of some great noble who lets him sleep on the straw, beside the horses. In the morning he still has part of his mattress in his hair. If the weather is mild, he walks all night along the Cours or the Champs-Elysées. With daylight he reappears in town, still wearing the clothes he had on the night before, and wearing them sometimes for the rest of the week. I have no high opinion of such eccentrics. Some people accept them as familiar acquaintances, even as friends. Once a year they engage my interest when I meet them, because their character is in violent contrast with that of other people, and they break the tedious uniformity introduced by our education, our social conventions, our customary notions of propriety. If one such person appears in a gathering, he acts like a grain of yeast that starts a fermentation, and restores to everyone part of his natural individuality. He shakes and stirs up people ; he calls forth approval or blame ; he brings out the truth ; he shows one which are honest folk, and unmasks rogues. It's then that a man of sense listens and learns to distinguish between people.

I had known this particular eccentric for a long time. He used to visit a household to which his gifts had won him an entry. There was an only daughter ; he used to swear to the father and mother that he would marry their child. They would shrug their shoulders, laugh in his face, tell him he was mad ; and I could foresee the thing being accomplished. He would borrow from me a few crowns which I would let him have. He had found his way, I don't know how, into certain respectable households, where his place was laid at table on condition that he did not speak unless he was given permission. He would keep silence, and eat in a fury. If, seized with a desire to break the contract, he opened his mouth, at the first word everyone at table cried out : " Oh, Rameau ! " Then, his eyes glittering with wrath, he would fall to eating again even more furiously. You were curious to know the man's name, and now you know it. He is the nephew of that celebrated musician, who has delivered us from the plainsong

of Lulli which we had been droning out for over a hundred
years ; who has written so many unintelligible imaginings
and apocalyptic truths on the theory of music, which neither
he nor anyone else has ever understood, and who has given
us a certain number of operas which contain harmony,
fragments of song, disconnected ideas, clamour, flights,
triumphs, spears, glories, murmurs, victories, in breath-
less succession ; dance tunes that will last for ever ; and
who, having buried the Florentine, will himself be buried
by the virtuosi of Italy, which he foresaw and which made
him gloomy, sad and surly ; for there is no one as peevish,
not even a pretty woman who finds a pimple on her nose
when she gets up, as an author in danger of outliving his
reputation : witness Marivaux and the younger Crébillon.

He accosts me . . . " Aha ! so here you are, master
philosopher ; and what are you doing among this gang of
idlers ? Do you, too, waste your time shoving the wood ? "
Thus the games of chess and draughts are contemptuously
referred to.

I : No ; but when I've nothing better to do, it amuses
me to spend a moment watching those who do it well.

He : In that case, you're seldom amused ; except Légal
and Philidor, the rest don't know a thing about it.

I : What about M. de Bissy ?

He : He stands, as a chess-player, where Mlle. Clairon
stands as an actress. Both know all that can be learnt about
these games.

I : You are hard to please : and I see that you only spare
those who are really great.

He : Yes, in such trivialities as chess, draughts, poetry,
eloquence, music ; of what use is the second-rate in such
matters ?

I : Very little, I admit. But there must be a great
number of men practising them in order that the man of
genius may emerge. He is one out of a multitude. But

let us leave that. I haven't seen you for an age; I never think of you when I don't see you, but I am always pleased to see you again. What have you been doing?

He: What you and I and all other men do: some good, some harm, sometimes nothing at all. And then I've been hungry, and eaten when I got the chance; and after eating I've been thirsty, and sometimes I've had a drink. Meanwhile my beard grew; and when it was grown I shaved it off.

I: That was a mistake; it's all you lacked to be a sage.

He: Yes, indeed. I've a high, wrinkled brow; a fiery eye; a prominent nose; broad cheeks; black bushy eyebrows; a big mouth, a curled lip and a square face. If this great chin were covered with a long beard, do you know, I should look very well in bronze or marble?

I: By the side of Caesar, Marcus Aurelius and Socrates?

He: No, I'd be better between Diogenes and Phryne. I have the effrontery of the one, and I'm a frequent visitor of the other.

I: Have you kept well?

He: Yes, usually; but not wonderfully well to-day.

I: What! here you are with the belly of a Silenus and a face. . . .

He: A face that might belong to his antagonist. Well, it seems that the ill-humour that dries up my dear uncle makes his dear nephew grow fat.

I: Speaking of that uncle, do you sometimes see him?

He: Yes, passing in the street.

I: Does he never do you a kindness?

He: If he ever does to anyone, it's by mistake. He is a philosopher after his kind. He thinks only of himself; the rest of the universe doesn't exist for him. His wife and daughter can die whenever they choose; so long as the church bells that toll for them always sound a twelfth and a seventeenth, all will be well. He's lucky in that respect. And that is what I value particularly in people of genius.

They are good at one thing only. Beyond that, nothing.
They don't know what it means to be citizens, fathers,
mothers, relatives, friends. Between you and me, one
ought to resemble them in every respect; but one must
not wish their seed to be common. Men are necessary,
but not men of genius. No, on my word, they are not
wanted at all! It is they who change the face of the globe;
and stupidity about the smallest things is so common and
so powerful that it cannot be reformed without an uproar.
Part of what they plan gets established; part remains as it
was; hence two gospels, a harlequin's coat. The wisdom
of Rabelais' monk is the true wisdom, for his own peace of
mind and that of others: to do one's duty more or less,
always speak well of the reverend prior, and let the world
go as it will. It goes all right, since the majority is satisfied
with it. If I knew any history, I would demonstrate to
you that harm has always come, here below, through some
man of genius. But I know no history, because I know
nothing at all. Devil take me if ever I learnt anything;
and if I am any the worse for having learnt nothing. One
day I was having dinner with a minister of the King of
France, as clever as they're made; well, he proved to us,
as clear as one and one make two, that nothing was more
useful to nations than falsehood; nothing more harmful
than the truth. I don't remember his proofs very well, but
the evident conclusion was that men of genius are detestable,
and that if a child, at birth, bore on its brow the mark of
this dangerous gift of nature, it should either be smothered
or thrown in the river.[2]

I : And yet these people who are so hostile to genius all
claim to possess it.

He : I really think they do in their hearts; but I don't
think they would dare to confess as much.

I : That is through modesty. So you conceived a fearful
hatred for genius there?

He : One which I shall never get over.

I : But I have seen the times when you were in despair at being only a common man. You will never be happy, if the two sides of an argument distress you equally. You must make your decision and keep to it. While agreeing with you that men of genius are usually peculiar, or that, as the proverb says, there is no great wit without a grain of madness, we can't help admiring them, and we shall always despise the centuries that have produced none. They will still be the glory of the nations among whom they have lived ; sooner or later, statues are erected to them, and they are regarded as benefactors of the human race. With all due respect to that wonderful minister whom you quoted to me, I believe that, if falsehood may be useful for a moment, it is inevitably harmful in the long run ; and that, on the contrary, truth is inevitably useful in the long run, though it may do harm for the moment. From which I am inclined to conclude that the man of genius who condemns some general error, or who wins credit for some great truth, is always a being worthy of our reverence. It may so happen that this being falls a victim to prejudice and to law ; but laws are of two kinds ; some are of absolute justice and universality, others are peculiar, and only owe their sanction to human blindness or to the necessity of circumstances. These cast only a passing shame on the man who is guilty of infringing them ; a shame which in course of time is reversed and falls irrevocably on the judges and nations. Who is the dishonoured man to-day, Socrates or the judge who made him drink hemlock ?

He : And is Socrates any the better off for that ? Does it alter the fact that he was condemned, that he was put to death, that he was an unruly citizen ? By despising a bad law, did he any the less encourage the foolish to despise good laws ? Was he any the less a bold, eccentric individual ? You just now came near admitting something not very favourable to men of genius.

I : Listen to me, my dear fellow. A society should have

no bad laws ; and if it had only good ones, it would never have occasion to persecute a genius. I did not say that genius was inseparably attached to perverseness, nor perverseness to genius. A fool is more likely to be bad than a man of intelligence. If a genius should usually be an ill-mannered fellow, difficult to deal with, cantankerous, unbearable, if he should even be evil-natured, what would you conclude therefrom ?

He : That he ought to be drowned.

I : Gently, my dear fellow. Here now, tell me ; I won't take your uncle for an example ; he is a hard man, brutal and inhuman, miserly, a bad father, a bad husband, a bad uncle ; but it is not really certain whether he is a genius, whether he has greatly furthered the progress of his art and whether his works will be talked of in ten years' time. But take Racine ; there's an unquestioned genius for you, and one who was not considered exactly a good man. Take Voltaire. . . .

He : Don't press me too closely ; I am logical.

I : Which would you rather, that he should have been a good man, sticking to his counter like Briasson, or to his yard-measure like Barbier ; a good husband, getting a legitimate child regularly every year from his wife ; a good father, a good uncle, a good neighbour, an honest tradesman, but nothing more ; or that he should have been a knave, treacherous, ambitious, envious, evil-natured ; and yet the author of *Andromaque, Britannicus, Iphigénie, Phèdre, Athalie* ?

He : Why, for his own sake, perhaps, it would have been better if he had been the first of these two men.

I : Indeed, that's infinitely truer than you think.

He : Oh, that's just like you people ! If we say anything sensible, it's bound to be by chance, like madmen or men inspired ; you are the only people who know what you are saying. Yes, master philosopher, I know what I'm saying, just as much as you know what you're saying.

I : Well, then, why—" for his own sake " ?

He : Because all those fine works of his didn't bring him in twenty thousand francs ; whereas if he had been some worthy silk merchant of the rue St.-Denis or St.-Honoré, some worthy wholesale grocer, some apothecary doing good business, he would have collected a huge fortune, and, by collecting it, there's no sort of pleasure he could not have enjoyed ; he would have given a guinea from time to time to some poor devil of a buffoon, like myself, who would have made him laugh, and who would have procured him on occasions a young girl to relieve him from the tedium of eternal cohabitation with his wife ; we should have had excellent meals at his house and played for high stakes, drunk excellent wines, excellent liqueurs, excellent coffee, gone on pleasure-parties ; and so you see I knew what I was saying. You laugh. But let me have my say. He would have been better towards those around him.

I : Undoubtedly ; provided that he did not use in some dishonourable fashion the wealth he gained through legitimate trade ; that he turned out of his house all those gamblers, parasites, insipid flatterers, idlers, perverse hangers-on ; and that he set his shop-assistants to flog soundly the meddler who offers to relieve husbands, by variety, from the boredom of habitual cohabitation with their wives.

He : Flog him, monsieur ! flog him ? In a well-regulated town nobody gets flogged. And it's an honest profession ; many people, even titled people, practise it. And what the devil do you want a man to spend his money on, if not on enjoying good food, good company, good wine, fine women, pleasures of every description, amusements of all sorts ? I'd as soon be a beggar as possess a great fortune and enjoy none of these things. But let us get back to Racine. There's a man who was good only for those who never knew him, when he was no longer alive.

I : Granted. But weigh up the good and the bad. A

thousand years hence, he will still cause tears to flow ; he will awaken men's admiration in all the countries of the earth ; he will inspire compassion, pity, tenderness. Men will ask who he was, of what country, and they will envy France for him. He caused pain to a few beings who are no more, who scarcely interest us to-day ; we have nothing to fear from his vices or his faults. No doubt it would have been better if he had received from nature a good man's virtue, together with a great man's talents. He was like a tree that withers up a few trees planted in its neighbourhood, that chokes the plants growing at its feet, but that lifts its crest into the clouds, and widely spreads its branches ; that grants shade to those who have come, who come still, and who will yet come to rest around its majestic trunk ; that yields fruits of an exquisite savour, which continually renew themselves. One might wish that de Voltaire were also as gentle as Duclos, as ingenuous as the abbé Trublet, as upright as the abbé d'Olivet ; but since that is impossible, let us look at the question from its really significant side ; let us forget for a moment the position we occupy in space and time ; and take a long view over the centuries to come, the remotest regions and peoples yet unborn. Let us consider the good of our species. If we are not generous enough, let us at least forgive nature for having been wiser than ourselves. If you throw cold water over the head of Greuze, you may extinguish his talent at the same time as his vanity. If you render de Voltaire less sensitive to criticism, he will no longer be able to penetrate the soul of Mérope. He will cease to move you.

He : But if nature were as powerful as she is wise, why did she not make them as good as she made them great ?

I : But don't you see that with that line of reasoning you upset the general order of things, and that if all were excellent here on earth nothing would be excellent ?

He : You are right. The important point is that you and I should exist and that we should be you and I. Apart from that, let all go as best it can. The best possible order of things, to my mind, is that which requires that I should exist ; and a fig for the most perfect of worlds, if it doesn't include me. I'd rather exist, and even be an extravagant reasoner, than not exist at all.

I : There is no one who doesn't think as you do, and who nevertheless doesn't condemn the existing order of things, without seeing that he repudiates his own existence.

He : True.

I : Then let us accept things as they are. Let us see what they cost us and what they bring us in ; and let us leave out of account all that we don't understand well enough to praise or blame, and which is perhaps neither good nor evil, so long as it be necessary, as many honest folk imagine it to be.

He : I don't understand much of this harangue of yours. It appears to be philosophy ; and I warn you that I'll have nothing to do with that. All I know is, that I'd like to be someone different, on the chance of being a man of genius, a great man. Yes, I must admit it, there is something within me that tells me so. I've never heard anyone praised without being secretly infuriated at their praise. I am envious. When I'm told something discreditable about their private life, I listen to it with pleasure ; it puts us more on a level. It makes my mediocrity easier to bear. I say to myself : " Assuredly you could never have written *Mahomet* ; but neither could you have praised Maupeou." So then, I have been, I still am, resentful of my mediocrity. Yes, yes, I am mediocre and I resent it. I have never heard the overture to *Indes galantes* played, never heard anyone sing the *Profondes abîmes du Ténare,* or *Nuit, eternelle nuit,* without saying to myself with sorrow, there's something you'll never do. So then, I am jealous of my uncle ; and if there were at his death a few fine pieces for the harpsichord in his portfolio, I shouldn't hesitate between remaining myself and being him.

I : If that's all that distresses you, it's hardly worth it.

He : It's nothing. These moments are soon over.

Then he began to sing once more the overture of *Indes galantes* and the air *Profondes abîmes,* and added :

" The something within that speaks to me says : ' Rameau, you'd be very glad to have written those two pieces ; if you had written those two, you could certainly have written two others ; and when you had written a certain number, you'd be played and sung everywhere ; when you walked, you'd hold your head high ; your conscience would bear witness to you of your own merit ; others would point you out. They would say : ' that's the man who wrote those pretty gavottes.' " And he sang the gavottes. Then, with the air of a man who is moved, who is overjoyed, who has tears of joy in his eyes, he added, rubbing his hands together : " You'd have a good house (he seemed to be measuring its span with his arms), a good bed (he was stretching himself out in it nonchalantly), good wines (and he smacked his tongue as he tasted them), a fine carriage (he lifted his foot to climb into it), pretty women (already he seemed to stroke their bosoms and gaze at them voluptuously), a hundred little snobs would come to flatter me every day " and he imagined them around him ; he saw Palissot,[3] Poinsinet, the Frérons, father and son, La Porte ; he listened to them, swelled with pride, approved them, smiled at them, disdained them, scorned them, dismissed them, recalled them ; then he went on :

" And so you'd be told in the morning that you were a great man ; you'd read in the *History of Three Centuries* that you were a great man ; you'd be convinced, by evening, that you were a great man ; and that great man, Rameau the nephew, would fall asleep to the sweet murmur of the praises echoing in his ear ; even as he slept he would have a satisfied air; his chest would expand, would rise and fall easily; he would snore like a great man."

And, as he spoke, he let himself sink lazily onto a bench; he closed his eyes and mimed the happy sleep he was imagining. Having enjoyed for some minutes the sweetness of this rest, he woke up, stretched his arms and yawned, rubbed his eyes and seemed to be still looking around him for his insipid flatterers.

I: Do you believe then that a happy man sleeps in a special way?

He: Do I not believe it! I, poor wretch, when at night I have gone back to my attic and crawled on to my pallet, I crouch under my blanket; my chest is constricted, I breathe with difficulty—just a sort of feeble murmur that can scarcely be heard; whereas a financier makes his whole lodging resound and astounds the whole street. But what distresses me to-day is not that I snore and sleep so meanly, like a pauper.

I: It's sad, all the same.

He: What has happened to me is far sadder.

I: What's that?

He: You've always taken some interest in me because I'm a good fellow whom you despise at heart, but who amuses you.

I: That is the truth.

He: And so I'll tell you.

Before beginning, he heaved a deep sigh and clasped his head in his hands. Then, resuming an air of calm, he said:

" You know that I'm ignorant, foolish, mad, impertinent, idle, an arrant rogue, as they say in Burgundy, a thief, a glutton. . . ."

I: What a panegyric!

He: It's true in every respect. Not a word to be left out. No discussion on that point, if you please; no one knows

me better than I know myself ; and I'm not saying all
there is to say.

I : I don't want to vex you ; and I'll accept everything.

He : Well ! I was living with some people who'd taken
a fancy to me just because I was endowed to an uncommon
degree with all these qualities.

I : That is odd. Up till now I had believed that one
either concealed them from oneself, or that one excused
them in oneself and despised them in others.

He : How can one conceal them from oneself ? You
may be sure that when Palissot is alone and examines himself, he has plenty to say then. You may be sure that
when he's alone with his colleague, they frankly confess
they're a pair of notorious rascals. As for despising them
in others, my folk were too fair for that, their own character
made me a wonderful success with them. I was in clover.
They made a fuss of me ; they couldn't lose sight of me
for a moment without missing me. I was their little
Rameau, their pretty Rameau, their crazy, impertinent,
ignorant, lazy, greedy Rameau, their buffoon, their great
big fool of a Rameau. And every one of these familiar
epithets brought with it a smile or a caress for me, a little tap
on the shoulder, a box on the ear, a kick, at table a dainty
morsel flung on my plate, away from table some liberty
at which I took no offence. For I never take offence.
People can do what they like to me, with me and in front
of me, and I'll not take exception. And how little presents
rained on me ! Great ass that I am, I've lost everything !
I've lost everything, through having had some common
sense, for the first, the only time, in my life. Ah ! if
ever that happens again !

I : What was it all about ?

He : An incomparable, incomprehensible, unpardonable
piece of stupidity.

I : But what was the stupidity ?

He : Rameau, Rameau, had you been taken on for that ?

The stupidity of having had a little taste, a little wit, a little sense. Rameau, my friend, that will teach you to stay as God made you and as your patrons desired you. And so they took you by the shoulders ; they led you to the door ; they said to you : " Knave, be off with you ; never show yourself again. The creature wants to show sense and reason, it seems ! Be off ! We've enough and to spare of these qualities." You went away biting your fingers ; it's your cursed tongue you should have bitten before. Just for lack of forethought, here you are on the pavement, penniless, not knowing where to bestow yourself. You were fed like a king and you're going back to the garbage-pail ; you had a good home, and now you'll be only too glad if you can have your attic again ; you had a good bed, and now the straw awaits you, between M. de Soubise's coachman and friend Robbé.⁴ Instead of that sweet peaceful sleep you've been enjoying, you will hear with one ear the neighing and trampling of horses, with the other the far more intolerable sound of dry, hard, barbarous verses. Oh thoughtless wretch, possessed of a million devils !

I : But mightn't there be some way of getting back ? Is the fault you have committed so unpardonable ? In your place I would go and see these people again ; they need you more than you think.

He : Oh, I am sure that now they haven't got me to make them laugh they are as dull as ditchwater.

I : I should go and seek them out, then. I should not leave them time to get on without me, to turn to some respectable amusement ; for who knows what may happen ?

He : That is not what I'm afraid of. That won't happen.

I : Sublime though you may be, another can take your place.

He : Hardly.

I : Granted. Nevertheless I should go, with that distracted countenance, those wild eyes, your shirt all gaping at the neck, your hair dishevelled, in that truly tragic state you are in now. I should throw myself at the feet of the goddess ; I should press my face to the ground, and without getting up I should say in a low, sobbing voice : " Forgive me, madame ! I am unworthy and infamous ; it was just an unfortunate moment ; for you know that I am not subject to having common sense, and I promise never to have any again in my life."

To my amusement, as I was holding forth to him, he mimed my words. He fell prostrate ; he pressed his face against the earth ; he seemed to be holding between his hands the tip of a slipper ; he wept, he sobbed, and said : " Yes, my little queen ; yes, I promise, I'll never have any again in all my life." Then getting up suddenly, he added in a grave, reflective tone :

He : Yes, you are right. I think that is the best thing. She is good. M. Vieillard says she is so good. And I know a bit about that too. But still, to go and humiliate oneself before a she-ape ! To beg for mercy at the feet of a little second-rate actress who's followed everywhere by the hisses of the pit ! I, Rameau ! son of M. Rameau, apothecary, of Dijon, a worthy man who has never bent the knee before anyone ! I, Rameau, nephew of him whom they call the great Rameau, who may be seen walking about the Palais-Royal, upright, his arms in the air ever since M. Carmontelle sketched him stooping with his hands under his coat-tails ! I who have composed pieces for the harpsichord that no one plays, but which will perhaps be the only ones to go down to posterity, which will play them ; that I, I should go. . . . I tell you, monsieur, it is impossible. (And, clapping his right hand to his breast, he added :) I feel here something rising up and saying : Rameau, you shall do no such thing. There must be a certain dignity inherent in man's nature, that nothing can suppress. It is aroused for no apparent reason ; yes, for no reason, for on certain other days it would cost me nothing to be as base as you like ; on such days, for a farthing, I'd kiss the arse of little Mlle. Hus.

I : Well, but, my friend, she's white and pretty, young, soft and plump ; and that's an act of humility to which one more fastidious than yourself might sometimes be willing to abase himself.

He : Let us be clear ; there's a literal arse-kissing and a figurative arse-kissing. Ask fat Bergier,[5] who kisses Mme. de la Marque's arse both literally and figuratively ; and I declare, in that particular case, the literal and the figurative would displease me equally.

I : If the expedient I have suggested does not suit you, then have courage enough to be a penniless beggar.

He : It's hard to be penniless while there are so many wealthy fools at whose expense one might live. And then, self-contempt is so unbearable.

I : Is that a feeling you've experienced ?

He : Have I experienced it ! How many times have I said to myself : What, Rameau, there are ten thousand good tables in Paris, each laid for fifteen or twenty, and of all those places not one is for you ! There are purses full of gold being shed right and left, and not one coin falls to you ! A thousand petty wits, without talent or merit ; a thousand little wenches, without any charms ; a thousand dull intriguers go well-clad, and shall you go naked ? Must you be foolish to that extent ? Couldn't you flatter as well as anyone ? Couldn't you lie, swear, perjure yourself, make promises, keep or break them as well as anyone ? Couldn't you crawl on all fours as well as anyone ? Couldn't you assist Madame's intrigue and carry Monsieur's *billet-doux*, as well as anyone ? Couldn't you encourage this young man to speak to Mademoiselle, and persuade Mademoiselle to listen to him, as well as anyone ? Couldn't you indicate to the daughter of some bourgeois that she is ill-dressed, that fine earrings, a little rouge, some lace and a gown *à la polonaise* would suit her to perfection ? That those little feet were not made for walking in the streets ? That a fine gentleman, young and rich, who has a gold-laced coat, a superb carriage and six great footmen, has seen her as he passed by, and been charmed by her, and in consequence from that day on has ceased to touch food and drink, can't sleep, and may die ?—" But my papa ? "—Well, well, your papa may be just a bit angry at first.—" And mamma, who's always exhorting me to be a good girl ? who tells me that honour is all that matters in this world ? "—Old-fashioned talk that means nothing.—" And my confessor ? "—You need not see him any more ; or if you persist in the whim of going to relate all your pastimes to him, it may cost you a few pounds of sugar and coffee.—" He's a strict man, and has already refused me absolution on account of that song, ' *Come into my cell.* ' "—That's because you had nothing to give him. . . . But when you appear before him with all your lace. . . . " Shall I have lace then ? "—Of course, and of every sort. With your fine diamond earrings. . . . " Shall I have fine diamond earrings ? "—Yes.—" Like those of the marquise who sometimes comes to buy gloves in our shop ? "—Exactly. In a fine carriage, with dapple-grey horses, two great footmen, a little negro, and the groom going in front ; with rouge and patches, and your train carried.—" Going to the ball ? "—Yes, to the ball, to the opera, to the play. . . . Already her heart leaps for joy. You play with a scrap of paper you hold between your fingers.—" What's that ? "—Oh, nothing.—" I think it is something."—It's a note.—" And for whom ? "—For you, if you had a little curiosity.—" Curiosity, I've plenty of that. Let me see."—She reads. " An interview ? that is impossible."—On your way to Mass.—" Mamma is always with me ; but if he were to come here, rather early in the morning ; I get up first, and I am at the counter before they're up. . . . "—He comes ; he pleases ; and one fine day, at dusk, the pretty one disappears, and my two

thousand crowns are handed over. . . . What! possessing
that talent, you lack bread? Aren't you ashamed, you
wretch? I remembered a crowd of rascals, who didn't come
up to my ankle, and who were overflowing with riches. I
wore a coat of coarse cloth, and they were clad in velvet ;
they leaned on sticks with golden knobs and curved handles ;
and they had Aristotle and Plato engraved on the signet-
rings they had on their fingers. And yet what used they to
be? Wretched tenth-rate musicians for the most part ;
now they're as good as lords. Then I felt brave, high-
hearted, keen-minded, capable of anything. But it seems
that this happy condition did not endure ; for up till now,
I've not succeeded in making any real progress. However that
may be, that is the text of my frequent soliloquies, which
you may paraphrase as you please ; provided that you conclude therefrom that I do know self-contempt, that torment
of the conscience which springs from the uselessness of the
gifts that Heaven has allotted to us ; it is the most cruel of all
torments. A man might almost as well not have been born.

I listened to him, and while he was acting the scene
between the procurer and the young girl whom he seduces,
my soul was disturbed by two contrary impulses ; I did
not know whether to give way to a longing to laugh or to a
fit of indignation. I was in distress. A score of times a
burst of laughter would prevent my anger from breaking
out ; a score of times the anger rising within my heart
ended in a burst of laughter. I was astounded at such
shrewdness allied with such baseness ; such sound ideas
alternating with such falseness ; such a general perversity
of feeling, such utter corruption, together with such uncommon frankness. He noticed the struggle that was going
on within me and said : "What is the matter?"

I : Nothing.
He : You seem distressed.

I : So I am.

He : But tell me, what do you advise me to do ?

I : To change the subject. Unfortunate creature, to what an abject state you have fallen !

He : I admit it. Nevertheless don't be too much upset about my state. I did not intend, when I confided in you, to distress you. I saved some money at these people's ; remember that I needed nothing, absolutely nothing, and that I was allowed so much for pocket money.

(Then he began once more to beat his brow with his fist, to bite his lip, and to roll his eyes wildly to the ceiling, adding :)

But it's all over and done with. I have set something aside. Time has passed ; and that's always something saved.

I : You mean something lost.

He : No, no, saved. Every instant one grows rich. One day less to live, or one crown to the good, it comes to the same thing. The important point is to go easily, freely, pleasantly, copiously, to the closet every evening : *O stercum pretiosum !** That is the great end of life, for all conditions of men. At the last moment, we are all equally rich ; Samuel Bernard who by dint of thefts, plunder, and bankruptcies leaves twenty-seven million in gold, and Rameau who leaves nothing at all, Rameau for whom charity will provide a bit of packing cloth for a shroud. The dead man hears no bells tolling. In vain do a hundred priests sing themselves hoarse for him ; in vain does a long procession of burning torches go before and behind him ; his soul is not walking beside the master of ceremonies. Whether you rot under marble or under the earth, you still rot. Whether you have round your coffin children in red and children in blue,[6] or no one at all, it makes no difference. And then, just look at this wrist of mine ; it used to be

* O precious excrement.

stiff as the devil. These ten fingers were so many sticks fixed in a wooden metacarpal ; and these tendons were like old strings of cat-gut, drier, stiffer and less flexible than those that have been used on a turner's wheel. But I worried them, broke them, shattered them so ; you won't give way, and I, damn it, I say you shall ; and it's going to be so.

And as he said this, with his right hand he seized the fingers and wrist of his left hand ; and he twisted them over and under till the tips of his fingers touched his arm ; his joints were cracking ; I was afraid the bones would be dislocated.

I : Take care (I told him) you'll injure yourself.

He : Don't be afraid. They are used to it ; for ten years I've been treating them worse than this. And against their will, the b—s had to get accustomed to it, and learn to place themselves on the keys and fly over the strings. And so, now, it's all right ; yes, it's all right.

At the same time he assumed the pose of a fiddler ; he hummed an allegro by Locatelli ; his right arm imitated the movement of the bow ; his left hand and fingers seemed to move up and down the neck ; if he played a note out of tune, he would stop, tune the string up or down, pluck it with his nail to make sure it was in tune, take up the music again where he had left off ; beat time with his feet, throwing about his head, his feet, hands, arms, and whole body. Just as you have sometimes seen, at the Sacred Concert, Ferrari or Chiabran, or some other virtuoso, undergoing the same convulsions, appearing to suffer the same torments, and causing one about the same distress, for is it not a painful thing to behold a man in agony when he is engaged in representing pleasure ? Draw a curtain to hide that man from me, if he must show me a victim on the rack. In the midst of his convulsions and his cries, there would occur

255

a holding-note, one of those passages of harmony in which the bow moves slowly over several strings at once ; then his face would take on an ecstatic look, his voice softened, he listened to himself with delight. There is no question but the chords were sounding in his ears and in mine. Then, putting his instrument back under his left arm, with the same hand with which he was holding it, and letting drop his right hand with the bow : " Well," he said, " what do you think of that " ?

I : Wonderful.

He : It seems to me to be all right ; it sounds about as good as other people. . . .

(And immediately he crouches down like a musician sitting at the harpsichord.)

I : I ask mercy, for your sake and my own !

He : No, no, since I've got you, you shall listen to me. I don't want anyone's approval given in ignorance. You will praise me in a more confident tone, and that may get me a pupil.

I : I mix with so few people ; and you'll tire yourself in vain.

He : I never get tired.

As I saw that it was useless for me to try and take pity on the fellow, the violin sonata having put him all in a lather, I decided to let him have his own way. Behold him then sitting at the harpsichord ; his legs bent, his head lifted towards the ceiling where you would think he saw a musical score set down ; singing, trying out his fingers, performing a piece by Alberti or Galuppi, I don't know which. His voice went like the wind, and his fingers flew over the notes ; now leaving the treble to take up the bass, now dropping the accompaniment to return to the treble. His face expressed various emotions in turn ; you could distinguish tenderness, anger, delight and pain ;

you could feel the soft and the loud passages. And I am sure one more skilled than I could have recognized the piece through its movement and character, through his varied expressions and through some fragments of song which he uttered at intervals. But the oddest thing was, that he fumbled from time to time ; he corrected himself as though he had made some mistake, and grew vexed at no longer having the piece at his fingers' ends.

" So now you see," he said, standing up again and wiping the drops of sweat that ran down his cheeks, " that we too know how to place an augmented fourth or a superfluous fifth, and are familiar with the sequence of dominants. Those chromatic passages about which dear uncle makes so much ado, they're nothing so tremendous, we can deal with them."

I : You've given yourself a great deal of trouble to show me how very clever you are ; I was willing to take your word for it.

He : Very clever ? oh, no ; I know my job more or less, and that's more than enough. For in this country is one obliged to know what one teaches ?

I : Not more than to know what one learns.

He : That is true, damn it, very true. Come, now, master philosopher, speak honestly, with your hand on your heart. Wasn't there a time when you weren't as well-off as you are to-day ?

I : I'm none too well off even yet.

He : But now you wouldn't go to the Luxembourg in summer, don't you remember. . . .

I : Don't talk of that ; yes, I remember.

He : Dressed in a grey plush coat. . . .

I : Yes, yes.

He : All worn out on one side ; with torn cuffs, and black woollen stockings sewn up behind with white thread.

I : Oh, yes, all right, just as you please.

He : What did you do then in the Allée des Soupirs ?

I : I cut a sorry figure.

He : When you left there you'd pace the pavement.

I : That's so.

He : You taught mathematics.

I : Without knowing the first thing about it ; isn't that what you were coming to ?

He : Exactly.

I : I learnt while teaching others, and I made a few good students.

He : That may be, but music isn't the same as algebra or geometry. Now that you've become a fine gentleman. . . .

I : Not so fine !

He : That your pockets are well-lined. . . .

I : Not so well !

He : You have masters for your daughter.

I : Not yet. Her mother sees to her education, since one needs peace in the home.

He : Peace in the home ? Good Lord, one only has that when one is the servant or the master ; and master is what one should be. I've had a wife, God rest her soul ; but when at times she happened to answer back, I'd get on my high horse ; I'd wield my thunder ; I'd say, like God, " Let there be light," and there was light. And so, in four years, we never once had to raise our voices against each other ! How old is your child ?

I : That has nothing to do with it.

He : How old is your child ?

I : What the devil, let's leave my child and her age out of it, and get back to the teachers she will have.

He : On my oath, I know nothing so obstinate as a philosopher. If one were to beg very humbly, could one find out from my lord philosopher, about what age is mademoiselle his daughter ?

I : You may assume she is eight.

He : Eight ! She should have had her fingers on the keyboard four years ago.

I : But perhaps I was none too anxious to include in the plans for her education a study that takes up so much time and serves so little purpose.

He : And what will you teach her then, if you please ?

I : To reason correctly, if I can ; a very uncommon thing among men and rarer still among women.

He : Oh ! let her talk nonsense as much as she likes, provided she be pretty, amusing and a flirt.

I : Since nature has been so unkind to her as to give her a delicate constitution together with a sensitive spirit, and to expose her to the same troubles in life as if she had a strong constitution and a heart of bronze, I will teach her, if I can, to bear them with courage.

He : Eh ! Let her weep and suffer, make a fuss and have her nerves on edge like all of them, provided she be pretty and amusing and a flirt. What, no dancing ?

I : No more than is necessary to make a curtsey, to have a decent carriage and presence, and to know how to walk gracefully.

He : No singing ?

I : No more than is necessary to pronounce correctly.

He : No music ?

I : If there were a good teacher of harmony, I'd willingly put her in his charge, for two hours a day during a year or two ; no more.

He : And in the place of the essential things you are suppressing ?

I : I put some grammar, fables, history, geography, a little drawing and a good deal of moral instruction.

He : How easy it would be for me to prove to you the uselessness of all such learning in a world such as ours ; uselessness, nay, perhaps even danger. But for the moment I'll restrict myself to one question ; won't she need one or two teachers ?

I : No doubt.

He : Ah, now we're back again. And these teachers, do you expect they will know the grammar, the fables, the history, the geography, the morality about which they will give her lessons ? Nonsense, my dear sir, nonsense. If they knew these things well enough to teach them, they would not be teaching them.

I : And why so ?

He : Because they would have spent their whole lives studying them. One needs a profound knowledge of art or science in order to have a good grasp of their elements. Works of classic rank can only be produced by those who have grown grey in harness. The middle and the end illuminate the obscurity of the beginnings. Ask your friend M. d'Alembert, who leads the chorus in mathematical science, if he is too good to deal with its elements. It was only after thirty or forty years of practice that my uncle perceived the first glimmerings of musical theory.

I : O madman ! archmadman ! (I cried), how comes it that in your wild head there should be so many sound ideas mingled with so many extravagant ones ?

He : Who the devil can tell ? Chance flings them to you, and they stick. The fact remains, that as long as one doesn't know everything, one knows nothing well. One cannot tell whither one thing goes, whence another comes, where each of them should be put, which should go first, which would be better second. Can one teach well without method ? And how does method come ? I tell you, my dear philosopher, I have a conviction that physics will always be a wretched science ; a drop of water taken up on a needle's point out of the vast ocean, a grain of sand detached from the chain of the Alps. And what about the causes of phenomena ? Truly it would be better to know nothing than to know so little, and that so ill ; and that is precisely where I'd got to, when I became a teacher of accompaniment and composition. What are you thinking about ?

I : I am thinking that all you have just said to me is specious rather than sound. But let us leave that. You say you have taught accompaniment and composition ?

He : Yes.

I : And you knew nothing at all about them ?

He : No, on my word ; and that is why there were others who were worse than I—those who thought they knew something. At least I spoilt neither the taste nor the hands of the children. When they passed from me to a good teacher, as they had learnt nothing, at any rate they had nothing to unlearn ; and that was always so much money and time saved.

I : How did you set about it ?

He : Like everyone else. I would arrive, throw myself into a chair : " What dreadful weather ! How tiring the pavements are ! " I would chatter and gossip a little : " Mlle. Lemierre was to have played the part of a vestal in the new opera, but she's pregnant for the second time. It's not known who is to understudy her. Mlle. Arnould has just left her little count. They say she's begun to negotiate with Bertin. Still, the little count found M. de Montamy's porcelain. At the last amateur concert there was an Italian woman who sang like an angel. That Préville is a remarkable creature. You should see him in the *Mercure galant* ; the riddle scene is priceless. Poor Dumesnil, she's no longer responsible for her words and actions. Come, Mademoiselle, take your book." While Mademoiselle, without hurrying, looks for her book which she has mislaid, while a maid is sent for and scolded, I I go on : " Really there's no understanding la Clairon. I've heard talk of a most absurd marriage, that of Mademoiselle what d'you call her, a little creature that he kept, by whom he'd had two or three children, and who had been kept by so many others." "Come, Rameau, that's impossible, you're talking nonsense." "I'm not talking nonsense. They even say that the thing is done. There's a rumour that Voltaire is dead; all the better. . . ." "Why all the better?" "Because it means he's going to produce some good joke. He usually dies a fortnight before." What else shall I tell you? I would repeat a few low stories, that I'd picked up in the houses I had been in; for we are all great tale-bearers. I would play the fool. They would listen, they would laugh, they'd exclaim: "He is always delightful." Meanwhile Mademoiselle's book would at last be found under an arm-chair where it had been dragged about, chewed and torn by a young puppy or kitten. She would sit down to her harpsichord. At first she'd make a noise on it by herself. Then I would draw near, after making some sign of approval to the mother. The mother: "It's not going too badly: if we'd only try, but we won't try. We prefer to waste our time chattering, prinking, running around and Heaven knows what. No sooner are you gone than the book is shut, not to be opened till you return. But then you never scold her. . . ." Meanwhile as something had to be done, I would take her hands and place them differently. I would lose my temper, I'd cry "G, G, Mademoiselle, it's a G." The mother: "Mademoiselle, have you no ear? Without being at the harpsichord, or seeing your book, I can tell that it should be a G. You give Monsieur an infinite amount of trouble. I cannot think why he is so patient. You don't remember anything he tells you. You make no progress. . . ."

Then I would abate the violence of my attack somewhat, and shaking my head, say: "Forgive me, Madame; it would go better if Mademoiselle would try, if she would study a little; but it's not going badly." The mother: "In your place, I'd keep her a year at the same piece." "Oh, for that matter, she's not going to leave it until she

has mastered all the difficulties ; and that won't be as
long as Madame thinks." The mother : " Monsieur
Rameau, you flatter her ; you are too good. That's the
only thing she'll remember from her lesson, and she'll
certainly be able to repeat it to me when the opportunity
arises." The hour would pass, my pupil would offer me
the fee for the lesson with the graceful gesture of the arm
and the curtsy that she had learnt from the dancing-
master. I'd put it in my pocket, while the mother said :
" Very nice, Mademoiselle. If Javillier were there he'd
applaud you." I would gossip for a moment longer, out of
politeness ; then I'd disappear, and that's what used to be
called a lesson in accompaniment.

I : And are things different to-day ?

He : Good heavens, I should think so. I arrive. I look
grave. I hastily remove my muff. I open the harpsichord.
I try the keys. I am always in a hurry ; if I'm kept waiting
one minute, I yell as though I'd had five shillings stolen.
In an hour's time I have to be at such and such a place ;
in two hours, at the house of the Duchess of so and so. A
beautiful marquise expects me to dinner ; and after that
there's a concert at the Baron de Bagge's in the rue Neuve-
des-Petits-Champs.

I : And yet you're not expected anywhere ?

He : True.

I : And why use all these base little tricks ?

He : Base ! Why base, if you please ? They are customary among people in my condition. I don't abase myself
by doing as everyone else does. I didn't invent them ;
and it would be queer and clumsy of me not to conform
with them. Of course, I know that if you are going to
apply in this case certain general principles of Lord knows
what morality, which everyone talks about and no one
practises, what's white will appear black and what's black
will appear white. But, master philosopher, there is a
general conscience just as there is a general grammar ; and

then in every language there are exceptions, which you scholars, I believe, call . . . help me out. . . .

I : Idioms.

He : Exactly. Well, then, each condition has its exceptions to the general conscience ; I'd like to describe them as professional idioms.

I : I understand. Fontenelle speaks well, writes well, although his style abounds in French idioms.

He : And the sovereign, the minister, the financier, the magistrate, the soldier, the writer, the lawyer, the attorney, the merchant, the banker, the artisan, the singing-master and the dancing-master are all highly respectable people, although their conduct deviates on several points from the general conscience, and is full of moral idioms. The older established things are, the more idioms there are ; the worse times are, the more the idioms multiply. The trade is as good as the man ; and contrariwise, in the long run, a man is as good as his trade. So a man must make the most of his trade.

I : All that I can understand clearly from this tangled argument is that few trades are practised honestly, or else few men are honest in their trade.

He : Well, none of them are ; but, on the other hand, few men are rogues outside their shop ; and all would go fairly well, but for a certain number of people who are said to be assiduous, precise, exact in the fulfilment of their duties, strict, that is to say, always inside their shops, following their trade from morning till night and doing nothing else. And so they are the only people who get rich and who are respected.

I : Thanks to idioms.

He : Just so ; I see you have understood me. Now then, one idiom that belongs to all conditions, since certain idioms are common to all countries and all times just as certain follies are, one common idiom is to procure for oneself the widest possible custom, and one common folly is to believe

264

that the man with the widest custom is the cleverest. There are two exceptions to the general conscience to which one is obliged to conform. It is a kind of credit; a thing worth nothing in itself, but which takes its value from public opinion. They say that " Good fame is better than a belt of gold "; and yet he who has good fame hasn't got a golden belt, and from what I can see these days, he who has a golden belt is never without fame. As far as possible one should have both fame and the belt. And that is my object when I make the most of myself by what you describe as base tricks and mean little ruses. I give my lesson and I give it well; there's the general rule. I create the impression that I have more lessons to give than the day has hours, there's the idiom.

I : And do you give the lessons well?

He : Yes, not badly, tolerably well. Dear uncle's fundamental bass has made all that much simpler. Formerly I used to steal my pupil's money; yes, I stole it, that's certain. To-day I earn it, at least as much as anyone else.

I : And used you to steal it without remorse?

He : Oh, without any remorse. They say that " when one thief robs another, the devil laughs." The parents were bursting with wealth, acquired God knows how; they were courtiers, financiers, big merchants, bankers, business-men. I helped them to make restitution, I and a crowd of others whom they employed like myself. In nature, all species devour one another, in society all conditions of men devour one another. We mete out justice to one another, without interference from the law. Formerly through la Deschamps, to-day through la Guimard, the prince gets his revenge on the financier; and through the dressmaker, the jeweller, the upholsterer, the sempstress, the swindler, the ladies'-maid, the cook, and the harness-maker, the financier has his revenge on la Deschamps. In the midst of all this, only the imbecile or the idler is in-

jured, without having offended anyone ; and serve him right.
Whence you see that these exceptions to the common
conscience, these moral idioms about which so much fuss
is made, and which are described as " jugglers' tricks,"
are nothing at all, and that, on the whole, all that is needed
is to have good sight.

I : I admire yours.

He : And then, there's poverty. The voice of conscience
and honour is very weak when the bowels are crying out.
It's enough that if I ever grow rich I shall certainly have
to make restitution, and that I'm firmly resolved to do so
in every possible way, through good fare, gaming, wine and
women.

I : But I fear you'll never grow rich.

He : I suspect as much.

I : However, if things should turn out otherwise, what
would you do ?

He : I should believe as all re-clad beggars do ; I should
be the most insolent rascal ever seen. It's then that I
should remember all they made me suffer ; and I should
pay them back for all the outrages they inflicted on me. I
love to give orders, and I shall give them. I love to be
praised, and people shall praise me. I shall have the whole
of Vilmorien's gang in my service, and I shall say to them,
as they said to me, " Now then, rogues, amuse me," and
they will amuse me. " Get your claws into honest folks,"
and the honest folks, if there are any left, will be torn to
shreds. And then we shall have women ; we'll call each
other " thou " when we are drunk ; we shall get drunk ;
we'll tell tall stories ; we'll have all sorts of perversions
and vices. It will be delicious. We shall prove that
Voltaire has no genius ; that Buffon, always mounted on
stilts, is just an inflated ranter ; that Montesquieu is
nothing but a society wit ; we shall pack d'Alembert back
to his mathematics ; we shall rain blows on all you little
Catos who despise us out of envy, in whom modesty is

the cloak of pride, and who are sober from sheer necessity. And as for music, then's the time we shall make music !

I : From the noble use you'd make of your riches, I can see what a pity it is that you should be a beggar. Such a way of living would contribute greatly to the honour of the human race, to the benefit of your fellow-citizens, and to your own glory !

He : I believe you are laughing at me, master philosopher. You don't know with whom you are dealing ; you don't suspect that I represent the most important section of society, in town and at court. All our rich folks, in every profession, may or may not have said to themselves just what I've been telling you in confidence ; but the fact is that the life which I should lead, were I in their shoes, is exactly the life they do lead. I'll tell you what you're like, you fellows, you think that the same happiness suits everyone. What a strange fantasy ! Your sort of happiness presupposes a certain romantic turn of mind which we haven't got, an unusual temperament, peculiar tastes. You decorate this eccentricity with the name of virtue ; you call it philosophy. But do virtue and philosophy suit everyone ? He has them who can, and maintains them if he can. Imagine the universe grown wise and philosophical ; admit that it would be devilish dull ! Look here, long live philosophy, long live the wisdom of Solomon : to drink good wine, to guzzle delicate food, tumble pretty women and rest on soft beds ! Except for this, all is vanity.

I : Ah ! but to defend one's country ?

He : Vanity. There's no longer any such thing as one's country. From one pole to the other I can see only tyrants and slaves.[7]

I : To help one's friends ?

He : Vanity. Does one have friends ? And if one had them, ought one to make them guilty of ingratitude ?

For, look at it closely, you'll see that is all one's reward for services rendered. Gratitude is a burden ; and all burdens are meant to be shaken off.

I : To have some position in society and fulfil the duties thereof ?

He : Vanity. What does it matter whether or not one has a position, so long as one is rich ; since one only takes up the position in order to become rich ? And where does fulfilling one's duties lead to ? To jealousy, trouble, persecution. Is that how one gets on in the world ? No, good heavens, but by playing the courtier, frequenting great folks, studying their tastes, humouring their whims, pandering to their vices, subscribing to their unjust actions ; there's the secret.

I : To attend to the education of one's children ?

He : Vanity. That's the business of a tutor.

I : But if that tutor, steeped in your principles, neglects his duties ; who will be the sufferer ?

He : Well, not I, but perhaps some day my daughter's husband or my son's wife.

I : But if both of them rush headlong into debauchery and vice ?

He : That befits their social position.

I : If they forfeit their honour ?

He : Whatever one does, one can't forfeit one's honour when one is rich.

I : If they are ruined ?

He : So much the worse for them.

I : I see that if you dispense with attending to the conduct of your wife, your children and your servants, you are quite liable to neglect your business affairs.

He : Excuse me ; it is sometimes hard to find money ; and it is prudent to set about that well in advance.

I : You won't take much care of your wife ?

He : None at all, please. The best way of dealing with one's beloved mate, to my mind, is to do just what suits

one. Don't you think society would be most amusing if
everyone followed his own bent ?

I : Why not ? The evening is always most beautiful
to me when I am pleased with the way I've spent the
morning.

He : And to me too.

I : It is their utter idleness that makes society people so
fastidious about their pleasures.

He : Don't you believe that ; they are constantly on the
go.

I : As they never weary themselves they never find relief
from weariness.

He : Don't you believe that ; they are always exhausted.

I : Pleasure is always a business for them, never a need.

He : All the better ; a need is always disagreeable.

I : They wear out everything. Their souls grow stupefied, boredom overtakes them. Surrounded as they are by
an abundance that oppresses them, they would be grateful
to anyone who took their life from them. For all they know
of happiness is that part that is soonest dulled. I do not
despise the pleasures of the senses. I have a palate too,
and it can savour a delicate dish, a fragrant wine ; I have a
heart and eyes, and I like to see a pretty woman. I love to
feel beneath my hand her firm round breast, to press my
lips to hers, to drink delight in her glances and to die of it
in her arms. I can enjoy an occasional wild party with my
friends, even if it be somewhat riotous. But I won't
conceal the fact that it is infinitely sweeter to me to have
been of help to someone in distress, to have concluded some
difficult piece of business, or given wholesome advice ;
to have read a pleasant book, walked awhile with a man or
woman who is dear to me ; spent a few hours teaching my
children, written a good page, fulfilled the duties of my
profession ; or said to her whom I love a few tender affec-
tionate words that make her clasp her arms around my neck.
I know of certain deeds to have done which I'd give all I

possess. *Mahomet* is a noble work ; I'd rather have rehabilitated the memory of the Calas family [8] A man I know had taken refuge at Carthagena. He was a younger son of a family, in a land where custom bequeaths the whole of a fortune to the eldest. There he learnt that his elder brother, a spoilt child, after robbing his over-indulgent father and mother of all their goods, had driven them from their country home, and that the poor old folks were pining away in poverty in some small provincial town. What did he do then, this younger son, whom his parents' harsh treatment had driven to seek his fortune in a far country ? He sent them help ; he hastily settled up his business. He came home, a rich man ; he brought back his father and mother to their house. He married his sisters. Ah, my dear Rameau, this man considered this period as the happiest of all his life. Tears stood in eyes as he told me of it ; and I myself, as I tell you the story, feel my heart stirred with joy, and delight interrupts my words.

He : What extraordinary creatures you are !

I : What unfortunate creatures you are, if you cannot conceive that a man may rise superior to his fate, and that it is impossible to be unhappy under the aegis of two such noble deeds.

He : That's a species of happiness with which I shall not easily become familiar, for one meets it very seldom. But according to you, then, people ought to behave decently ?

I : In order to be happy ? Most certainly !

He : Yet I see an infinite number of decent folk who are not happy, and an infinite number who are happy without being decent folk.

I : So it seems to you.

He : And isn't it all through being sensible and sincere for one minute that I've nowhere to go for supper to-night ?

I : Why no, it's through not being so always. It's through not realizing early enough that one should first provide one-self with some means of livelihood independent of servitude.

He : Independent or not, what I've provided for myself is at least the most comfortable.

I : And the least certain, and the least decent.

He : But best suited to my character, which is that of an idler, a fool, and a worthless blackguard.

I : No doubt.

He : And, since I can be happy through vices that are natural to me, acquired without labour and maintained without effort, vices that fit in with the customs of my fellow-countrymen, that please the taste of my patrons and suit their petty personal requirements better than virtues, which would embarrass them by accusing them from morning till night ; it would be most odd for me to go torturing myself like a lost soul, in order to distort myself and make myself other than I am ; to take on a character that's foreign to my own ; worthy qualities, I grant you, we won't quarrel about that ; but qualities which it would cost me much to acquire and to practise, which would lead to nothing or maybe worse than nothing, by exposing me to the continual satire of the rich folk among whom beggars like myself have to make a living. Virtue is highly praised, but she is hated and shunned ; she is cold as ice, and in this world we must keep our feet warm. And then, it would inevitably make me bad-tempered ; for why are pious people so often hard, disagreeable, unsociable ? Because they have imposed on themselves a task that's not natural to them. They suffer, and when one suffers one makes others suffer. That doesn't suit me, nor my patrons either ; I have to be gay, pliable, amusing, comic, absurd. Virtue commands respect ; and respect is uncomfortable. Virtue commands admiration ; and admiration is not amusing. I'm dealing with people who are bored, and I have to make them laugh. Now absurdity and craziness arouse laughter, so I have to be crazy and absurd ; and if nature had not made me so, the quickest way would be to pretend to be so. Luckily I've no need to be a hypocrite ; there are so many

already of every variety, not counting those who are hypo-
critical with themselves. That Chevalier de La Morlière who
cocks his hat over his ear, bears his head so bravely, looks
down over his shoulder at passers-by, wears a long sword
dangling on his thigh, has an insult all ready for anyone
that goes swordless, and seems to challenge all comers,
what's he doing? Trying his utmost to persuade himself
that he's a brave man ; but he is a coward. If you offer
him a fillip on the nose, he'll receive it meekly. If you want
to make him talk less loudly, raise your own voice. Show
him your stick, or kick his behind ; astonished to discover
himself a coward, he will ask you who told you he was?
how you found it out? He didn't know it himself, a
minute ago ; a long habit of aping bravery had taken him
in. He had assumed the airs of it so much that he believed
in its reality. And that woman who mortifies her flesh
and visits prisons, who is present at all meetings in aid of
charity, who goes about with downcast eyes and would not
dare look a man in the face, always on her guard against the
seductions of the senses ; in spite of all this, her heart
throbs, she heaves sighs, her passions are awakened, desires
obsess her, and her imagination calls up, night and day,
scenes from the *Portier des Chartreux*, postures from Aretino.
What happens to her then? What does her chambermaid
think when she gets up in her nightgown and flies to the
help of her dying mistress? Go back to bed, Justine ; it's
not you that your mistress was calling in her delirium. And
as for friend Rameau, if one day he began to show contempt
for wealth, women, good fare and idleness, to be censorious,
what would he be? A hypocrite. Rameau must stay what
he is ; a happy robber among rich robbers ; and not a
braggart of virtue or even a virtuous man, gnawing his crust
of bread alone or among beggars. And, to speak plainly,
I've no use for your sort of felicity, for the happiness that
suits a few visionaries like yourself.

   I : I see, my dear fellow, that you don't know what

that happiness is, and that you're not even capable of learning.

He : All the better, good God, all the better. It would make me die of hunger, boredom, and maybe remorse.

I : Accordingly the only advice I have to give you is to get back quickly into the house from which you rashly let yourself be turned out.

He : And to do what you don't disapprove of in the literal sense, and what rather repels me in the figurative sense ?

I : That's what I think.

He : Apart from this metaphor, what I dislike at the present moment, and what I shan't mind the next.

I : How very peculiar !

He : There's nothing peculiar about that. I'm quite willing to be abject, but it must not be under constraint. I'm willing to lower my dignity—you're laughing ?

I : Yes, " your dignity " makes me laugh.

He : Every man has his own ; I'm willing to forget mine, but at my own discretion, and not at anyone else's orders. Have I got to crawl when they say " crawl " to me ? That's the worm's way of moving, and it's mine ; we both assume it when we're allowed to go as we like ; but we rise up when our tails are trodden on. My tail has been trodden on, and I shall rise up. And then you've no conception of what a bedlam the place is. Imagine a sullen, melancholy person, a prey to nerves, swathed in a dressing-gown that goes two or three times round him ; who's disgusted with himself and everything else ; whom you can hardly get to smile, though you contort yourself, body and mind, in a hundred different ways ; who watches coldly while I twist my face into quaint grimaces, and my wit into even quainter ones ; for, between ourselves, Father Noel, that unpleasant Benedictine whose grimaces are so famous, is, despite his success at Court, a mere wooden puppet compared to me—and I'm not flattering myself nor him either. In vain do I torture myself—striving to reach

the sublime heights of bedlam ; it's no use. Will he
laugh or won't he ? That's what I have to keep saying to
myself, in the midst of my contortions ; and you can see
how much all this uncertainty hinders one's talent. My
hypochondriac, his face buried in a nightcap that comes down
over his eyes, looks like a motionless Chinese puppet that
has a string fastened to its chin, the end of which hangs
down below its chair. You wait for the string to be pulled ;
and it isn't pulled ; or if it happens that the jaw gapes a little,
it is to utter some distressing word, some word that tells
you that you haven't been noticed, that all your monkey-
tricks are wasted. That word is in answer to a question you
put to him four days ago ; once it's said, the mastoid
muscle relaxes, and the jaw closes again.

(Then he began to imitate the man in question ; he sat
in a chair, his head rigid, his hat pulled down to his eyelids, his eyes half closed, his arms dangling, moving his jaw
like an automaton and saying :)
" Yes, you are right, Mademoiselle. Delicacy is needed
there." And that is decisive ; always and irrevocably,
evening and morning, when he's dressing or dining, at the
café or the card-table, at the theatre or at supper, in bed,
and, God forgive me, I believe in his mistress's arms. I'm
never within earshot in the last-named circumstances, to
hear him make his decisions ; but I'm devilish tired of all
the others. Gloomy, obscure and peremptory, like fate :
such is our patron.
    On the other hand, there's a prude who puts on airs of
importance ; one could submit to telling her she's pretty,
because she still is, although she has a few scabs here and
there on her face, and is emulating the bulk of Madame
Bouvillon. I like flesh when it's handsome flesh, but then,
too much is too much, and movement is so essential to
matter ! *Item*, she's prouder, stupider, and more ill-
humoured than a goose. *Item*, she has pretensions to wit.

Item, one has to persuade her that one thinks her wittier than anyone else. *Item*, she knows nothing, and yet her word has to be decisive too. *Item*, one has to applaud her decisions, clap hands and stamp feet, jump for joy, be in ecstasies of admiration : " How fine, how delicate, how well expressed, what subtlety of observation, what originality of feeling ! How do women do it ? Without study, through sheer instinct, by the light of nature ; the thing's miraculous. And then people want you to believe that experience, study, reflection and education have something to do with it ! " And such like nonsense ; and one weeps for joy. Ten times a day one must bow down, one knee bent forward, the other leg drawn back, arms stretched out towards the goddess, one must try to read her wish in her eyes, hang on her lips, await her orders, and then be off like a flash. Who can submit to playing such a part, except the wretch who finds thereby, twice or thrice a week, the wherewithal to quieten the affliction of his intestines ? What is one to think of the others, like Palissot, Fréron, Poinsinet, Baculard and company, who haven't the rumble of a hungry belly to excuse their servility ?

I : I'd never have thought you were so fastidious.

He : I'm not. To begin with I saw what others did, and I did the same, even rather better because I am more frankly impudent, a better play-actor, hungrier and stronger in the lung. I seem to be a direct descendant of the famous Stentor.

And to give me a correct notion of the strength of that organ, he began to cough with enough violence to shake the windows of the café and attract the attention of the chess-players.

I : But what use is that talent ?

He : Can't you guess ?

I : No, I am a bit stupid.

He : Suppose a quarrel has begun and its outcome is

uncertain ; I get up, and loosing my thunder, I say :
" That is so, as Mademoiselle declares. That's what I
call good judgment. I defy all our wits to equal it. It's
expressed with real genius." But one must not always
show approval in the same way. That would be monotonous, and seem insincere. One would become tedious.
It takes tact and resourcefulness to save one from that ;
one must know how to prepare and where to place such
major tones, such peremptory utterances, how to seize the
right occasion and the right moment. When, for example,
feelings are divided ; when the quarrel has reached its
peak of violence ; when no one listens to anyone else, and
everyone is speaking at once ; one should be standing aloof,
in the corner of the room furthest from the battlefield, and
having prepared for one's explosion by a long silence, fall
suddenly like a bomb into the midst of the combatants.
No one has that art to the same degree as I. But where I
really excel is in the opposite direction ; I can produce
gentle noises accompanied by a smile, an infinite variety
of facial expressions marking approval ; nose, mouth,
forehead, eyes come into play ; I have such supple loins,
a way of twisting my spine, of lifting and dropping my
shoulders, of spreading out my fingers, bending my head,
closing my eyes, showing as much bewilderment as though
I had heard the voices of angels and divinities speaking from
heaven. That's real flattering. I don't know if you grasp
the full force of that particular pose. I didn't invent it,
but no one has surpassed me in performance. Just look.

I : It's unique, that is true.

He : Do you think any tolerably vain woman has a head
to withstand that ?

I : No. It must be admitted that you have carried the
art of making fools and behaving basely as far as it can be
carried.

He : Try as they will, the whole lot of them, they'll
never get so far. The best of them, Palissot for instance,

will never be more than a good scholar at it. But, though it's amusing at first to play such a part, and though one gets a certain enjoyment from laughing inwardly at the stupidity of those whom one's making drunk, the pleasure palls in the long run ; and then, after a certain number of discoveries, one is obliged to repeat oneself. Wit and art have their limits ; only God and a few rare geniuses find their road grow wider, the further they go. Bouret[9] may be one of these. Certain inventions of his strike me, even me, as truly sublime. The little dog, the *Book of Happiness*, the torches on the Versailles road, are things that amaze and humiliate me. It's enough to make one throw up one's job in disgust.

I : What do you mean by " the little dog " ?

He : Where do you come from ? What, seriously, don't you know how that remarkable man managed to divert the affection of a small dog from himself to the Lord Chancellor, who had taken a liking to it ?

I : I confess I don't know.

He : All the better. It's one of the most beautiful things ever thought of ; all Europe was astonished at it, and it aroused the envy of every courtier. Let's see how you, who aren't lacking in shrewdness, would have set about it in his place. Remember that the dog loved Bouret. Remember that the minister's strange garments frightened the little creature. Remember that there was only a week in which to overcome all the difficulties. One needs to know all the conditions of the problem in order to appreciate fully the beauty of its solution. Well ?

I : Well, I must confess that I should find the simplest things of that sort perplexing.

He : Listen, (he said to me, with a little tap on the shoulder, for he takes these liberties), listen and admire. He gets a mask made in the likeness of the Lord Chancellor ; he borrows the voluminous robe from a valet. He covers his face with the mask, he puts on the robe. He calls his dog. He gives it biscuits. Then suddenly, changing his attire, he is no longer the Lord Chancellor, he is Bouret, calling his dog and beating it. By repeating this exercise from morning till night, before two or three days were up he's taught the dog to fly from Bouret, the Farmer-General and to run to Bouret the Lord Chancellor. But I'm too kind ; you are an unbeliever and don't deserve to learn of the miracles that are performed around you.

I : In spite of that, I beg of you, what about the book and the torches ?

He : No, no. Ask the pavements, and they'll tell you about those things ; and take advantage of the circumstance that has brought us together to learn things that are known only to me.

I : You're right.

He : To have borrowed the robe and the wig—I'd forgotten about the wig !—of the Lord Chancellor ! To have had a mask made in his likeness ! That mask, particularly, leaves me dizzy. And, in consequence, this man enjoys the highest respect ; he owns millions. There are some who've won the Cross of St. Louis, but who have no bread ; so why run after the Cross, at the risk of getting one's neck broken, instead of turning to an occupation that involves no danger and never fails to bring its reward ? That's what I call doing things on the grand scale. Such models are discouraging ; one pities oneself, and one gets bored. That mask, that mask ! I'd give one of my fingers to have thought of the mask.

I : But with such enthusiasm for fine things, and such a fertile genius as you possess, have you invented nothing ?

He : Oh, excuse me, yes ; for example, that admiring attitude of the back, of which I spoke to you ; I consider that as my own, although the envious might perhaps dispute my claim to it. I believe, indeed, that it has been used before ; but who else has realized how convenient it is for laughing up one's sleeve at the vain fellow one is admiring ?

I've over a hundred ways of embarking on the seduction of a young girl, by her mother's side, without the latter noticing, and even of involving her as an accomplice. While I was still a beginner in this career, I rejected with scorn all the vulgar methods of passing a *billet-doux*. I've ten ways of getting it snatched from me ; and among these ways I dare flatter myself some are original. Above all, I have the gift of encouraging a timid young man ; I've made some succeed, who had neither wit nor presence. If all this were written down, I think I should be granted some measure of genius.

I : Would you be singled out for praise ?

He : I don't doubt it.

I : In your place, I should set down these things on paper. It would be a pity to lose them.

He : True, but you don't guess how low an opinion I have of method and precept. The man who needs a text-book will never go far. Men of genius read little, practise much and are self-made. Look at Caesar, Turenne, Vauban, the Marquise de Tencin, her brother the cardinal and his secretary, the abbé Trublet. And Bouret ? Who gave Bouret lessons ? No one. Such rare men as these are formed by nature. Do you think the story of the dog and the mask is written down anywhere ?

I : But in your idle hours, when the gnawing of your empty stomach or the exhaustion of your overloaded stomach prevents you from sleeping. . . .

He : I'll think it over ; it's better to write great things than to perform trivial ones. Then one's soul is uplifted ; one's imagination is excited, inflamed and expanded ; whereas it merely shrinks when used to convey to the little Hus woman one's astonishment at the applause the foolish public persists in lavishing on that simpering Dangeville, whose acting is so dull, who walks almost bent double on the stage, who's always gazing affectedly into the eyes of the person to whom she's speaking, and acting in a sly manner, and who mistakes her own grimaces for subtlety, her mincing walk for grace ; and on that declamatory Clairon, who is leaner, stiffer, more affected, more artificial than you'd think possible. The idiotic audience claps them with wild enthusiasm, and never notices that we are a little bundle of charms ;—it's true that the bundle is getting a bit plump, but what matter ?—that we have the loveliest skin, the loveliest eyes, the sweetest mouth ; not much passion, it's true, and a walk that's certainly not light, though it isn't so clumsy as they make out. On the other hand, there's no one to come near us on the matter of feeling.

I : What do you mean by all this ? Are you speaking sincerely or ironically ?

He : The trouble is that this confounded feeling is all within, and that not a glimpse of it can be caught from outside. But I who am talking to you, I know she's got it, and I know it well. If it's not feeling exactly, it's something like it. You ought to see, when the temper takes us, how we treat our valets, how we box our chambermaids' ears, what great kicks we deal out to the Treasurer of the *Parties Casuelles** if he fails in the slightest degree to pay us the respect that's due to us. I tell you she's a little imp packed with feeling and dignity. . . . Why, you're bewildered, aren't you ?

I : I admit that I can't make out whether you are speaking sincerely or maliciously. I'm a simple fellow ; be good enough to deal more frankly with me, and leave aside your art.

He : Well, that's how we hold forth to the little Hus, on the subject of la Clairon and la Dangeville, with just a few words interspersed to put you on your guard. I'll allow you take me for a knave, but not for a fool ; and only a fool, or a man crazy with love, would say such ridiculous things seriously.

* Bertin was " *Trésorier des Parties Casuelles.*"

I : But how can one bring oneself to say them at all ?

He : It can't be accomplished suddenly ; but little by little, one reaches the point. *Ingenii largitor venter.**

I : One needs to be driven by a very cruel hunger.

He : Maybe. Yet, exaggerated as they seem to you, believe me, those to whom these phrases are addressed are more accustomed to hear them than we are to venture on saying them.

I : Is there anyone amongst you brave enough to share your opinion ?

He : Anyone, you say ? It's the way the whole group thinks and speaks.

I : Those of you who aren't great knaves must be great fools.

He : Fools, amongst us ? I swear there's only one ; the man who makes much of us, in order that we may deceive him.

I : But how can anyone let himself be so grossly deceived ? For, after all, the superior talent of Dangeville and Clairon is an unquestioned fact.

He : A lie that flatters is swallowed whole ; truth, if it tastes bitter, is only sipped little by little. And then, we wear such an air of conviction and sincerity !

I : Yet you must at some time have infringed the principles of art, and let slip by mistake one of those bitter truths that hurt; for, despite the wretched, abject, base and abominable role you have assumed, I believe you have a sensitive soul at bottom.

He : I ? Not at all. Devil take me if I know what I am at bottom. On the whole, I'm plain-minded and frank-natured ; never dishonest, if there's anything to gain by being honest ; never honest, if there's anything to gain by dishonesty. I say things just as they occur to me ; if they're sensible so much the better ; if they're absurd, no one heeds them. I make full use of my freedom of speech.

* The belly is the dispenser of wit.

I've never in my life taken thought before speaking, while speaking or after speaking. And thus I offend nobody.

I : And yet you did happen to offend those good folks amongst whom you were living and who had been so exceedingly kind to you.

He : Ah, well, it can't be helped ; it's a misfortune, such as one expects in life. There's no such thing as continual happiness ; I was too well off, it could not last. As you know, we are a large and well-chosen band. You can get your training in humanity there ; the antique tradition of hospitality is renewed. We pick up all poets who fall flat ; we got Palissot after his *Zarès*, Bret after the *Faux Généreux* ; all unpopular musicians ; all unread authors ; all actresses that get hissed ; all actors that get hooted at ; a gang of shame-faced wretches, of mean parasites, at whose head I have the honour to be, the gallant leader of a timid band. I'm the person who urges them to eat, the first time they come ; who calls for drinks for them. They take up so little room ! A few ragged youths who don't know which way to turn, but who've got a good appearance ; others, scoundrels who wheedle the patron and send him to sleep, so as to enjoy after him the favours of the patroness. We seem gay, but at bottom we're all bad-tempered and hungry. Wolves are not more ravenous, nor tigers more cruel. We devour like wolves when the ground has long been covered with snow ; like so many tigers, we tear up everyone who is successful. Sometimes Bertin's mob, and Monsauge's and Vilmorien's get together ; and then there's a fine din in the menagerie. Never before were seen in one place so many sullen, peevish, mischievous and angry animals. You hear nothing but the names of Buffon, Duclos, Montesquieu, Rousseau, Voltaire, d'Alembert, Diderot ; and God knows with what epithets they're accompanied. We won't credit anyone with intelligence who's not as stupid as ourselves. The comedy of the *Philosophes*[10] was first planned here ; the scene of the pedlar was supplied by me, from out of the *Théologie en quenouille*. You're not spared in it, any more than the others.

I : All the better. Perhaps that does me more honour than I deserve. I should feel humiliated if those who speak ill of so many clever and decent folk should venture to speak well of me.

He : There are many of us, and every one must contribute his share. After the larger animals have been sacrificed, we slaughter the others.

I : You earn your bread dearly if you insult science and virtue for a living.

He : I've already told you that we don't count. We abuse everyone and we hurt nobody. Sometimes the ponderous abbé d'Olivet is one of us, or the fat abbé LeBlanc, or Batteux the hypocrite. The fat abbé is only spiteful before dinner. When he's had his coffee he flings himself into an arm-chair, propping his feet against the mantelpiece, and goes to sleep like an old parrot on its perch. If the din becomes violent, he yawns, stretches his arms, rubs his eyes and says, " Well, what's the matter ? " " We're arguing as to whether Piron has more wit than Voltaire." " Let's get this clear. Wit, you said ? You're not discussing taste ? for, as regards taste, your Piron has no notion of it." " Has no notion ? " " No." And there we are embarked on a dissertation about taste. Then the patron raises his hand to show that we must listen to him, for taste is what he particularly prides himself upon. " Taste," says he, " taste is a thing. . . ." I declare I don't know what sort of thing he said it was, and neither did he.

Sometimes friend Robbé is with us. He entertains us with his cynical stories, with descriptions of the miracles worked among the convulsionaries of St. Médard, of which he was an eye-witness : and with some cantos of his poem on a subject with which he is saturated. I hate his verse, but I love to hear him recite. He looks like a fanatic. Everyone round him exclaims : " There's a real poet for you." Between you and me, such poetry is a mere medley of noises of all sorts, the barbaric clamour of the Tower of Babel. And sometimes, too, there comes one who looks a dull and stupid fool, but who's as witty as the devil and more cunning than an old monkey. One of those faces that calls for jokes and jeers and that God made to teach a lesson to those who judge by appearances, when their mirror should have taught them that it's as easy for a clever man to look a fool, as for a fool to be concealed behind a clever face. It's a very common weakness to sacrifice a good man for the sake of amusing the others ; and this fellow is always made a victim of it. We lay this trap for all new-comers, and I've hardly ever seen one avoid it.

(I was sometimes surprised by the exactness with which this madman observed men and characters ; and I told him so. He answered me :)

He : One can profit by bad company, you see, just as by licentiousness. The loss of one's prejudices compensates for the loss of one's innocence. In the company of bad men, where vices appear unmasked, one gets to learn all about them. And then I've read a bit.

I : What have you read ?

He : I've read, and I read and re-read constantly, Theophrastus, La Bruyère and Molière.

I : Those are excellent books.

He : They are far better than people think ; but who knows how to read them ?

I : Everyone, according to his degree of intelligence.

He : Scarcely anyone. Can you tell me what people look for in these books ?

I : Amusement and instruction.

He : But what sort of instruction ? That's the important point.

I : To know one's duties, to love virtue and to hate vice.

He : Whereas I learn from them all that one should do and all that one shouldn't. Thus when I read *L'Avare* I say to myself : Be a miser if you like ; but take care not to speak like a miser. When I read *Tartuffe* I say: Be a hypocrite if you like, but don't talk like a hypocrite. Keep vices that are useful to you, but avoid the manner and appearance that express them, for these would make you ridiculous. To preserve oneself from that manner and those appearances one needs to be familiar with them ; now these authors have drawn excellent portraits of them. I am myself and I remain as I am : but I act and speak as it suits me. I'm not one of those people who despise moralists. There's much to be gained from them, especially from those who have put their morality into practice. Vice only hurts men at intervals ; the outward signs of vice hurt them from morning till night. Perhaps it is better to be insolent than to look insolent ; if you've an insolent character, you only insult people from time to time ; if you've an insolent face, you insult them all the time. For that matter, you mustn't suppose that I am the only reader of this kind. My only merit here lies in doing systematically, intelligently, from a reasonable and correct view of things, what most others do from instinct. As a result, their reading does not make them better than me, but they remain ridiculous against their will, whereas I am so only when I please, and then I leave them far behind me ; for that same art that teaches me to avoid being ridiculous on some occasions, also teaches me to be ridiculous in masterly fashion on other occasions. Then I remember all that others have said, all that I've read, and I add all I can of my own invention, which is astonishingly fertile in that kind of style.

I : It's a good thing you have revealed these secrets to me, otherwise I might have thought you inconsistent.

He : I'm not that at all ; for luckily, if there's one occasion on which one must avoid being ridiculous, there are a hundred on which one needs to play the fool. It's the best role to assume in the company of the great. For a long time there was an official king's fool; there has never been an official king's wise man. I'm the fool of Bertin and of many others, perhaps yours at this moment; or perhaps you are mine. A really wise man would have no fool. So then, he who has a fool is not wise; if he is not wise, he is a fool; and perhaps, were he the king himself, his fool's fool. Moreover, you must remember that, where something as variable as morality is concerned, nothing is absolutely, essentially, generally true or false, except that one must be as it is to one's interest to be: good or bad, wise or foolish, respectable or ridiculous, honest or vicious. If by any chance virtue had led to fortune, either I should have been virtuous, or I should have pretended to be, like anyone else. I was asked to be ridiculous, and I made myself so; as for vice, nature had seen to that by herself. I say vice, because I'm speaking your language; for if we were to have it out, we might find that you call vice what I call virtue, and virtue what I call vice.

Then we have the authors of the *Opéra Comique*, their actors and actresses; and often their producers, Corby, Moette —all people of great resourcefulness and merit! And I was forgetting the great literary critics: the *Fore-Runner*, the *Little Notices*, the *Literary Year*, the *Literary Observer*, the *Weekly Censor*, the whole clique of pamphleteers.

I: The *Literary Year*, the *Literary Observer*? That isn't possible. They detest one another.

He: True; but all beggars make friends over the platter. That damned *Literary Observer*! I wish the devil had carried him off with all his leaflets! That dog of a little priest, that miserly stinking usurer was the cause of my disaster. He appeared on our horizon yesterday, for the first time. He arrived at the hour that drives us all from our lairs, the dinner-hour. When the weather's bad, he's a lucky one amongst us who has a florin in his pocket to pay for a

286

cab! The man who has sneered at his colleague for arriving in the morning muddied up to the backbone and wet to the skin, may be in the same plight himself when he gets home at night. One of us, I don't remember who, had a violent quarrel a few months ago with the Savoyard sweeper who had installed himself outside the door. They had a current account; the creditor wanted his debtor to settle up, and the debtor had no money and yet couldn't avoid his creditor if he wanted to go upstairs.

Well, dinner was served; the abbé was in the place of honour, near the head of the table. I came in and noticed him. "How's this, abbé," said I, "you're presiding? That's all very well for to-day, but to-morrow you will please go down one place, the next day one more place, and so on from one place to another, either to the right or to the left, from the seat that I occupied once before you, Fréron once after me, Dorat once after Fréron, Palissot once after Dorat, until you come to a halt beside me, who am a poor wretched b—— like yourself, *qui siedo sempre come un maestoso cazzo fra duoi coglioni.*"* The abbé, who's a good-natured fellow and takes everything in good part, began to laugh. Mademoiselle, impressed with the truth of my remark and the exactness of my comparison, began to laugh; all those who were sitting to the right and left of the abbé, and who'd been sent down one place by him, began to laugh; everyone laughed except Monsieur, who grew angry and spoke to me in terms that would have meant nothing if we had been alone. "Rameau, you are an impertinent fellow." "I know that well; it was on that condition that you took me up." "A scoundrel." "No more than another." "A beggarly wretch." "Should I be here otherwise?" "I'll have you kicked out." "After dinner I'll go of my own accord." "You had better." We had dinner; I didn't miss a single bite. After eating well and drinking freely, since after all that made no difference, and Sir Belly

* An insulting anatomical simile.

is a gentleman to whom I've never borne ill-will, I made up my mind and got ready to go. I had given my word in presence of so many people that I was bound to keep it. I took a considerable time prowling about the room looking for my stick and my hat where they were not, and all the time expecting that the patron would let loose a fresh flood of insults, that someone would step in, and that, after getting really angry, we should end by making it up. I roamed round and round, for I myself wasn't in the least upset ; but as for the patron, he strode up and down, his fist under his chin, his cap pulled down even lower than usual, gloomier and blacker than Homer's Apollo letting fly his arrows over the Grecian army. Mademoiselle came up to me. " But, Mademoiselle, what is it that's so unusual? Have I been unlike myself to-day ? " " I insist on his going." " I'll go . . . I've not been wanting in respect to him." " Excuse me ; Monsieur l'abbé was invited and. . . ." " He has been lacking in respect to himself, by inviting the abbé, and by receiving me and other rascals like me." " Come now, Rameau dear, you must beg Monsieur l'abbé's pardon." " I don't want his pardon." " Come, come, it'll all blow over." I was taken by the hand and led to the abbé's chair ; I stretched out my arms and gazed at the abbé with a sort of admiration, for who has ever begged the abbé's pardon? " Abbé, abbé," I said to him, " all this is very silly, isn't it ? " And then I burst out laughing, and so did the abbé. Thus I was forgiven in this quarter ; but now I must approach the other, and what I had to say to him was quite a different matter. I can't really remember how I worded my apology. . . . " Monsieur here's this madman." " He's been vexing me for too long ; I never want to hear of him again." " He's very sorry he annoyed you." " Yes, he annoyed me very much." " It won't happen to him any more. . . ." " Nor to any other rascal."

I don't know if it was one of his bad-tempered days,

when Mademoiselle is afraid to go near him and daren't touch him except with velvet gloves on, or if he couldn't hear what I said, or if I said the wrong thing ; but it was worse than before. What the devil, doesn't he know me ? Doesn't he know that I'm a child and on some occasions let loose everything under me ? And then I believe, God forgive me, that they wouldn't let me have a moment's respite. It would wear out a steel puppet to have its strings pulled from morning till night and from night till morning. I've got to distract them, that's the condition ; but I've got to amuse myself sometimes. In the middle of this confusion, a fatal thought came into my head, a thought that gave me arrogance, a thought that inspired me with pride and insolence ; namely, that they couldn't get on without me, that I was an essential person.

I : Yes, I believe you are very useful to them, but that they are still more so to you. You won't find such a good house again for the asking ; but they'll find a hundred fools for one that fails them.

He : A hundred fools like me ! Master philosopher, they're not so common. Dull fools, yes. People are harder to please in the matter of folly than in the matter of talent or virtue. I am rare in my kind, yes, very rare. Now that they haven't got me, what's happened to them ? They are as dull as ditchwater. I'm an inexhaustible treasury of impertinence. I had a sally for every moment, which would make them laugh till they cried, I was a complete mad-house for them.

I : And for your part you had board and bed, coat, waistcoat and breeches, shoes and a guinea a month.

He : That was the good side of it. That was the profit ; but you don't mention the costs. To begin with, if there was a rumour of any new play, whatever the weather I had to ferret about all the attics in Paris until I'd found the author of it ; I had to get leave to read the work, and I had to insinuate adroitly that there was one part in it

289

which would be admirably played by someone of my acquaintance. " And by whom, if you please ? " " By whom ? What a question ! By the most gracious, charming, delicate. . . ." " You mean Mademoiselle Dangeville ? Do you know her, by any chance ? " " Yes, a little ; but she's not the person." " Who then ? " I'd murmur the name. " She ! " " Yes, she," I'd repeat it, somewhat embarrassed ; for I have a certain shame, and when this name is repeated, you should see what a long face the poet pulls or how, at other times, he bursts out laughing in my face. Nevertheless, I had to bring my man along to dinner, whether he liked or no ; and he, afraid of committing himself, would make excuses, proffer thanks. You should have seen how I was treated when I didn't succeed in my negotiation ; I was a clumsy brute, a fool, a dolt, I was good for nothing ; I wasn't worth the glass of water I was given to drink. It was far worse when a play was on, and I must go fearlessly, amidst the hoots of an audience which, whatever they say, is a good judge, and clap my solitary pair of hands ; draw all eyes towards me ; sometimes draw on to myself the hisses that were meant for the actress ; and hear whispered beside me : " That's one of her lover's valets in disguise ; won't the rascal be quiet ? " People don't know what drives one to such conduct, they think it's sheer idiocy, whereas there is a motive that excuses everything.

I : Even the violation of civil laws.

He : In the end, however, people got to know me, and they'd say : " Oh, it's Rameau." My expedient was to fling out a few ironical words that saved my solitary applause from appearing ridiculous, by inviting a contrary interpretation. You must admit that it needed a powerful interest to make one brave the assembled audience in this fashion, and that each of these labours was worth more than half-a-crown.

I : Why didn't you get some assistance ?

He : That happened sometimes, and I made a little profit over that. Before going to the scene of my torture, I must load my memory with the purple passages, where I should have to give the lead. If I chanced to forget them and make a mistake, I was all trembling when I went home ; you've no conception what an uproar there'd be. And then, there was a pack of dogs to look after in the house ; it's true that I'd stupidly imposed this task on myself ; cats that I had to superintend ; and it was lucky for me if Micou did me the favour of tearing my cuff or my hand with his claws. Criquette was a victim to colic, and I had to rub her belly. Formerly Mademoiselle used to suffer from the vapours ; to-day she calls it nerves. I won't mention other trifling disorders which she discusses freely in front of me. Let that pass ; I've never attempted to restrain anyone. I've read somewhere or other that a certain monarch, surnamed the Great, would sometimes stand leaning against the back of his mistress's commode. One behaves without restraint with one's intimates, and I was that, more than anyone, in those days. I'm the apostle of familiarity and ease. I preached them there by my example, and nobody took offence ; they had only to leave me alone. I've sketched the patron for you. Mademoiselle is beginning to grow heavy ; you should hear the good stories they tell on that subject.

I : You're not one of those people ?

He : Why not ?

I : Because it is unseemly, to say the least, to laugh at one's benefactors.

He : But is it not worse still to assume that one's benefactions give one the right to debase one's protégé ?

I : But if that protégé were not base in himself, nothing would give the protector such a right.

He : But if the people in question were not ridiculous in themselves, there'd be no good stories told about them. And then, is it my fault if they keep low company ? Is it my fault if, when they keep low company, they are betrayed and made fools of? A man who can bring himself to live with the likes of us, if he has common sense, must be prepared for any amount of wickedness. When they take us up, don't they know us for what we are, for selfseeking, vile, perfidious souls? If they know us it's all right. There's a tacit agreement that they'll do good towards us, and that sooner or later we shall repay that good with evil. Does not such an agreement exist between a man and his monkey or his parrot? Brun cries out in horror because Palissot, his friend and his guest, has written verses against him. Palissot had to write the verses and it's Brun who is wrong. Poinsinet cries out in horror because Palissot has attributed to him the verses he wrote against Brun. Palissot had to attribute the verses to Poinsinet; and Poinsinet is in the wrong. Little abbé Rey cries out in horror because his mistress was stolen by his friend Palissot to whom he'd introduced her. But either he should never have introduced her to a man like Palissot, or else he should have resigned himself to losing her. Palissot did his duty; and the abbé Rey is in the wrong. The bookseller David cries out in horror because his colleague Palissot slept or wanted to sleep with his wife; the wife of the bookseller David cries out in horror because Palissot has let it be understood by anyone who wanted to listen that he'd slept with her; whether or not Palissot did sleep with the bookseller's wife is a difficult question to settle, because the wife was bound to deny what may have happened, and Palissot may have given us to believe something that didn't happen. However that may be, Palissot played his part, and David and his wife are in the wrong. Let Helvétius[11] cry out in horror because Palissot represents him on the stage as a dishonest man, Palissot who still owes him the money he lent him for treatment of his ill-health, for food and clothing; what other conduct could he have expected from a man stained with every kind of infamy, who just

to amuse himself induces his friend to abjure religion,
who embezzles the fortune of his associates, who knows no
loyalty, no law, no feeling ; who seeks after wealth *per
fas et nefas* ;* who measures his days by his misdeeds ; and
who has represented himself on the stage as one of the most
dangerous of rascals, a stroke of impudence unprecedented,
surely, in the past, and unrepeatable in the future. No ;
it's not Palissot but Helvétius who is in the wrong. If a
young provincial is taken to the menagerie at Versailles,
and out of stupidity ventures to thrust his hand through the
bars of the tiger's cage, or the panther's ; if that young
man leaves his arm between the jaws of the savage beast,
which is in the wrong ? All that is written down in the
tacit agreement. So much the worse for whoever doesn't
know it or forgets it. By reference to that universal, sacred
agreement, I could justify any number of people whom we
accuse of wickedness, when we should rather accuse ourselves of stupidity ! Yes, fat Countess, it's you who are
in the wrong when you gather around you what people of
your sort call " creatures," and these creatures act basely
towards you, make you act basely yourselves, and expose
you to the indignation of decent folk. Decent folk do their
duty, and these creatures do theirs ; it's yourselves who are
in the wrong to take them up. If Bertinhus† lived quietly
and calmly with his mistress, if through the honesty of
their characters they had won the acquaintance of honest
folk, if they had drawn around them men of talent, men
known in society for their virtue ; if they had devoted to a
small, well-chosen and enlightened group such leisure hours
as they could spare from the pleasure of each other's company, of mutual love confessed in the silence of seclusion ;
do you think there would be any stories, good or bad, told
about them ? What, then, has happened to them ? Just
what they deserved. Their imprudence has been punished ;

* By fair means or foul.
† Nickname of Bertin, whose mistress was Mlle. Hus.

and we were destined by Providence, from all eternity, to deal justice to the Bertins of our day ; and our fellows among posterity are destined to deal justice to the Bertins and Monsauges to come. But while we carry out her just decrees against these fools, you, who depict us as we are, you carry out her just decrees against ourselves. What would you think of us if, with our immoral ways, we aspired to enjoy the respect of the public?—that we were crazy. And those who expect decent conduct from men born vicious, men of vile degraded character, are they wise? Everything has its right price in this world. There are two public prosecutors ; one, at your door, chastizes crimes against society. Nature is the other. She takes cognizance of all vices that the law lets slip. You are given to sexual excesses ; very well, you shall have the dropsy. You indulge in debauchery ; you shall have consumption. You open wide your doors to scoundrels, and live amongst them ; you shall be betrayed, made mock of, despised. The best thing is to be resigned to the fairness of these sentences, and to say to oneself " you deserved that " ; to shake one's ears and either correct one's faults or remain as one is, but on the aforesaid conditions.

I : You are right.

He : And besides, I don't invent any of those unkind stories ; I stick to the role of tale-bearer. They say that some days ago, about five in the morning, a fearful uproar was heard ; all the bells were ringing ; cries sounded, the broken, indistinct cries of a man who's being smothered : " Help, help, I'm choking, I'm dying." These cries issued from the patron's room. They went to his rescue. Our stout lady, who'd quite lost her head, who'd lost her sight, who had passed out, as one does at such times, went on speeding up her movements, lifting herself up on both hands as high as she could and then letting fall onto the Treasurer of the *Parties Casuelles* her full weight of two or three hundred pounds, with all the velocity imparted to it by the frenzy of pleasure. It was a hard job getting him free. A

queer fancy that, for a little hammer to put itself underneath a heavy anvil !

I : You're a filthy fellow. Let's speak of something else.
Since we've been talking I've had one question on the tip
of my tongue.

He : Why did you keep it there so long ?

I : Because I feared it might be indiscreet.

He : After what I've just disclosed to you, I don't know
what I could keep secret from you.

I : You are well aware of my opinion of your character ?

He : Perfectly. I'm an abject, despicable wretch in your
eyes, and sometimes in my own too ; but not often. I
congratulate myself on my vices more often than I blame
myself for them. You are more constant in your contempt.

I : That's true ; but why reveal your full villainy to me ?

He : First, because you were already acquainted with a
good part of it, and I saw there was more to be gained than
lost by confessing the remainder to you.

I : How's that, if you please ?

He : If there's one quality in which it's essential to attain
sublimity, it is wickedness. A petty thief gets spat upon ;
but a great criminal can't be refused some sort of admiration. His courage astonishes you. His cruelty makes you
shudder. Consistency of character is always appreciated.

I : But you haven't got it yet, this desirable consistency
of character. From time to time, you seem to me to
vacillate in your principles. It's not clear whether you owe
your wickedness to nature or to study, and whether study
has carried you as far as it might.

He : I agree with you ; but I've done my best. Have I
not been modest enough to recognize more perfect beings
than myself ? Have I not spoken of Bouret with the deepest
admiration ? Bouret is the world's greatest man, to my
mind.

I : But you come next, immediately after Bouret.

He : No.

I : Palissot, then ?

He : Palissot, but not Palissot alone.

I : And who can be found worthy to share the second rank with him ?

He : The renegade of Avignon.

I : I've never heard tell of this renegade of Avignon ; but he must be a most astonishing man.

He : So he is.

I : The history of great men has always interested me.

He : I can well believe it. This man used to live with a good, honest descendent of Abraham, one of those who were promised to the Father of all believers in number as many as the stars.

I : With a Jew ?

He : With a Jew. He had won first the Jew's pity, then his goodwill, finally his whole-hearted trust. For that's the way it always is. We rely so much on our good deeds, that we seldom withhold our confidence from the man on whom we have showered kindnesses. How can we expect men not to be ungrateful, when we offer them the opportunity to be so without punishment ? This is a wise thought which did not occur to our Jew. So he confided to the renegade that his conscience would not allow him to eat pork. You shall see how a fertile mind took advantage of this confession. A few months went by, during which our renegade displayed an ever-increasing attachment. When his Jew seemed to him thoroughly touched, thoroughly captivated, and thoroughly convinced, by his attentions, that he had no better friend among all the tribes of Israel . . . admire the circumspection of this man. He made no haste. He allowed the pear to ripen before he shook the branch. Too much enthusiasm might ruin his plan. You see, it is generally the case that greatness of character is due to a natural balance between several contrary qualities.

I : Oh, let your reflections alone, and go on with your story.

He : That cannot be. There are certain days when I have to reflect. It's a disease that must run its course. Where had I got to ?

I : To a well-established intimacy between the Jew and the renegade.

He : Then the pear had ripened. . . . But you're not listening to me. What are you thinking about.

I : I'm thinking about the unevenness of your tone, sometimes lofty, sometimes base.

He : How can a vicious man maintain an even tone ? . . . Well, one evening he came up to his kind friend, looking terrified, his voice broken, his face pale as death, trembling in every limb. " What is the matter ? " " We are lost." " Lost ? How is that ? " " Lost, I tell you, hopelessly lost." " What do you mean ? " " One moment, let me recover from my terror." " Come, come, be calm," said the Jew to him, instead of saying, " You're an arrant knave ; I don't know what you have to tell me, but you're an arrant knave ; you're acting terror."

I : And why ought he to have spoken thus to him ?

He : Because the man was deceiving him, and had gone too far. That's quite clear to me, so don't interrupt me any more. " We are lost, hopelessly lost." Don't you feel the affectation of the repeated " lost " ? " A traitor has denounced us to the Holy Inquisition, you as a Jew, me as a renegade, an infamous renegade." Notice how the traitor unblushingly used the most odious terms. It takes more courage than you'd think to call oneself by one's right name. You don't know what it costs to reach that point.

I : I certainly don't. But this infamous renegade ? . . .

He : Was a deceiver ; but a very skilful one. The Jew takes fright, begins tearing his beard, rolls on the ground. He sees the police-spies at his door ; he sees himself arrayed in the *sanbenito* ; and sees his *auto-da-fé*[12] being made ready. " My friend, my dear friend, my only friend, what are we to do ? " " To do ? Why, let ourselves be seen about, assume an air of complete security, behave just as usual. This tribunal proceeds secretly, but slowly. We must take advantage of its delays to sell everything. I'll go and hire a boat, or get someone else to hire it ; yes, someone else will be best. We'll deposit your fortune in it, for it's your fortune they're after ; and we will go, you and I, to seek beneath another sky the freedom to serve our God and to follow unmolested the law of Abraham and of our conscience. In the dangerous situation we are in, the important point is to do nothing rash." No sooner said than done. The boat is hired, and provided with foodstuffs and with sailors. The Jew's fortune is put on board. Next day at dawn they are to set sail. They may sup cheerfully and sleep in safety. Next day they are to escape from their persecutors. During the night the renegade gets up, robs the Jew of his pocket-book, his purse and his jewels ; goes on board and makes off. And do you think that's all ? Well, you're quite wrong. When I was told this story, I guessed what I've concealed from you to test your shrewdness. It's just as well you are an honest man ; you'd have made a very poor rogue. Up till now, that's all the renegade was—a wretched knave whom nobody would want to resemble. But he achieved sublimity in his wickedness by himself informing against his good friend the Israelite, who was seized by the Holy Inquisition when he awoke, and of whom a fine bonfire was made a few days later. And thus it came about that the renegade enjoyed untroubled possession of the fortune of that accursed descendant of those who crucified Our Lord.

I : I don't know which I think more horrible—the villainy of your renegade or the tone in which you speak of it.

He : That's just what I was telling you. You cannot be merely contemptuous of a deed of such atrocity ; and that's the reason for my sincerity. I wanted to show you the high degree of excellence I'd attained in my art ; to compel you to confess that I was at least original in my degradation, to take up my place, in your mind, in the rank of great rascals, and then to cry : *Vivat Mascarillus, fourbum Imperator* ! Come on, then, master philosopher, join in the chorus : *Vivat Mascarillus, fourbum Imperator.**

And with that he began to sing a most remarkable fugue. The melody was now grave and majestic, now light and playful ; one moment he would imitate the bass ; the next, one of the treble parts ; he suggested the sustained passages by stretching out his arm and his neck ; and thus he made and played for himself a triumphal song, which clearly showed that he knew more about good music than about good morals. As for myself, I did not know whether to run or to stay, whether to laugh or to be revolted. I stayed, intending to turn the talk on to some topic that might drive from my mind the horror that possessed it. I began to find intolerable the presence of a man who discussed a horrible deed, a loathsome crime, as a connoisseur of painting or poetry would examine the beauties of a work of art ; or as a moralist or a historian might pick out and praise the details of a heroic action. I grew gloomy, in spite of myself. He noticed it, and said :

He : What's the matter with you ; are you feeling ill ?

I : Yes, somewhat : but it will pass.

He : You have the anxious look of a man who is haunted by an unpleasant thought.

I : That's just it.

After a moment's silence on his part and on mine, during which he walked up and down whistling and singing, I said, to bring him back to where his talent lay :

I : What are you composing nowadays ?

He : Nothing.

I : That must be tedious.

He : I was stupid enough already. I went to hear that

* Molière, *L'Etourdi.*

music of Duni's and our other young composers, and that was the end of me.

I : You admire that style, then ?

He : Of course.

I : And you find beauty in these new songs ?

He : Beauty ? I should say so ! What recitative ! How true, how expressive !

I : Every imitative art has its model in nature. What model does the musician take when he writes a song ?

He : Why not start further back ? What is a song ?

I : I must confess that question is beyond my powers. That's the way we all are ; we retain in our memories only terms that we think we understand, through using them frequently and perhaps applying them correctly ; we have in our minds only vague conceptions of their meaning. When I utter the word " song," I have no clear conception, any more than you and most of your fellows have when you say reputation, blame, honour, vice, virtue, modesty, decency, shame, absurdity.

He : Song is an imitation of the sounds of the physical world or of the accents of passion, by means of the notes of a scale invented by art or inspired by nature, as you please, and rendered either by the voice or by an instrument ; and you see that, if certain terms are changed, the definition holds good for painting, rhetoric, sculpture and poetry. Now, to come to your question : what is the model for the musician or his song ? Speech, if the model is a living thinking being ; sound, if the model is inanimate. Speech must be considered as one line, and song as another which twines itself about the first. The stronger and truer the speech, which is the basis of the song, and the greater the number of points at which the intertwining song touches it, the more convincing and beautiful will the song be. And that is what our young musicians have grasped very well. When you hear : *Je suis un pauvre diable** you fancy you hear

* I am a poor devil.

300

a miser complaining; if he did not sing, he would speak in the same tones to the earth when he entrusts his gold to it and says *O terre, reçois mon trésor*.* And the little girl who feels her heart throb, who blushes and is distressed and begs his lordship to let her go, would she express herself otherwise? These compositions include every sort of character, an infinite variety of speech. It's sublime, you may take my word for it. You should go and hear the piece where the young man who feels himself dying cries: *Mon coeur s'en va.* Listen to the song: listen to the symphony, and then you shall tell me what difference there is between the true voice of a dying man and the phrases of this song. You will see if the line of the melody doesn't entirely coincide with the line of the speech. I haven't mentioned rhythm, which is yet another of the conditions of song; I've confined myself to expression; and nothing is truer than this saying, which I've read somewhere: *Musices seminarium accentus*; accent is the nursery of melody. You may judge from this how difficult and important it is to be able to write good recitative. There's no fine tune from which a fine recitative cannot be made, and no fine recitative from which a clever man could not extract a fine tune. I wouldn't like to affirm that whoever recites well will sing well; but I'd be much surprised if a man who sang well could not recite well. And you may believe all that I'm telling you; for it is true.

I : I'd ask nothing better than to believe you, if there were not one little obstacle that prevents me.

He : And that is?

I : That if this music is sublime, then that of the divine Lulli, of Campra, Destouches and Mouret, and even, between ourselves, that of your dear uncle, must be a little dull.

Whispering in my ear, he answered me:

He : I don't want to be overheard, for there are many

---

* O Earth! receive my treasure.

people here who know me ; but that's just what it is. I
don't care about my dear uncle, since that's what you call
him—he's a man of stone ; if he saw me with my tongue
hanging out a foot, he wouldn't offer me a glass of water ;
but let him go on making the devil's own din with his
hon-hon, hin-hin, tu-tu-tu, turelu-tutu in octaves and sevenths ;
those who are beginning to know something about it and
who don't any longer mistake mere noise for music, will
never put up with that. There ought to be a police regula-
tion forbidding anyone, whatever his rank or position, to
perform Pergolesi's *Stabat*. That *Stabat* should have been
burnt by the public executioner. Good Lord, those damned
Bouffons[13] with their *Servante Maîtresse* and their *Tracollo*
have given us a good kick in the backside. Formerly such
things as *Tancrède, Issé, Europe galante, les Indes, Castor,
les Talents Lyriques*, would play for four, five, six months.
There was no end to the performances of *Armide*. And
now they're toppling over like card castles. And so Rebel
and Francœur are in the wildest rage. They say that all's
lost, that they are ruined ; that if we put up with this
low market-place music any longer, the nation's music is
done for ; and that the Royal Academy of the blind-alley[14]
will have to shut up shop. There's certainly some truth
in that. The old fogies who have gone there every Friday
for thirty or forty years, instead of enjoying themselves as
they used to, are bored and yawn without quite knowing why.
They ask themselves why, and can't answer. Why don't
they ask me ? Duni's prophecy will be fulfilled ; and at
the rate things are going, I'll stake my life that in four or
five years from the *Peintre amoureux de son modèle* there won't
be a cat left in the famous blind-alley.[14] Those worthy
folks ! They gave up their own symphonies in order to
play Italian symphonies ; they thought their ears would
grow accustomed to these and yet their vocal music remain
unaffected ; as though symphony did not bear to song the
same relation—except for a certain freedom engendered by

the range of the instrument and the mobility of the player's fingers—as song to real speech. As though the violin did not ape the singer, who may one day, when the beautiful has given place to the difficult, ape the violin ; the first man who played Locatelli was the apostle of the new music. Let them tell their tale to somebody else ! What, once we've become accustomed to the imitation of the accents of passion or of natural phenomena—for that is the whole scope of music's objective—shall we retain our liking for flights, lances, glories, triumphs, victories ? " *Va t'en voir s'ils viennent, Jean.*"* They imagined that they could weep and laugh at scenes of tragedy and comedy set to music, that they could listen to the accents of fury, hatred, jealousy, the true lamentations of love, the ironies and witticisms of the French or Italian theatre, and yet remain admirers of *Ragonde* and *Platée.* Stuff and nonsense, I'd say !—that they could continually experience with what facility, flexibility, and softness the harmony, prosody, ellipses and inversions of the Italian tongue lend themselves to the art of song, to its movement, its expression, its phrases, and to the measured value of sounds, and that they could still remain unaware how stiff, dead, clumsy, heavy, pedantic and monotonous is their own. Well, well ! They persuaded themselves that after mingling their tears with those of a mother mourning her son's death, after shuddering to hear a tyrant give orders for a murder, they would not find tedious their fairy tales, their insipid mythology, their little sugary madrigals, that are not more indicative of the poet's bad taste than of the wretched state of an art that puts up with them. Worthy folks ! It is not so, and it never can be. The true, the good and the beautiful have their rights. These may be contested, but they will be admired in the end. Anything which does not bear this stamp, though it may be admired for a while, will set you yawning in the end. Yawn, then, gentlemen, yawn as much as you please.

* Get along, John, see if they're coming !

Don't hesitate to yawn. The rule of nature, and of my trinity, against which the gates of hell will never prevail—the true which is the father, and which engenders the good which is the son, whence proceeds the beautiful which is the Holy Spirit—is being quietly established. The strange god takes his place humbly on the altar, beside the national idol; little by little he becomes more firmly settled there; one fine day, he gives his neighbour a shove with his elbow, and crash, there goes the idol. They say that's the way the Jesuits implanted Christianity in China and in India. And in spite of all the Jansenists say, this political method that goes towards its goal, without noise or bloodshed, with no martyrs made and not a single tuft of hair torn out, seems to me the best.

I : All this you've been saying is fairly reasonable.

He : Reasonable ? All the better. Devil take me if I'm trying to be ! It just comes as it pleases. I'm like those musicians in the blind-alley were when my uncle appeared ; if I make a lucky hit, it's because a charcoal-burner's apprentice will always speak better about his trade than a whole academy and all the Duhamels in the world.

And then he began to walk about, humming in his throat some of the airs from the *Ile des fous,* the *Peintre amoureux de son modèle,* the *Maréchal ferrant,* the *Plaideuse,* and from time to time he exclaimed, raising his hands and eyes to heaven : " And isn't that beautiful ? Good God, can a man have ears in his head and yet ask such a question ? " He began to get excited and to sing to himself. As his passion grew he raised his voice ; then came gestures, facial grimaces and bodily contortions ; and I said, " Good, now he's losing his head and we shall have some fresh scene " ; and so it was ; he burst forth, " *Je suis un pauvre misérable. . . . Monseigneur, monseigneur, laissez-moi partir. . . . O terre, reçois mon or : conserve bien mon trésor. . . . Mon âme, mon âme, ma vie ! O terre. . . . Le voilà le petit ami ; le voilà . . . le petit ami ! . . . Aspettare e non venire. . . . A Zerbina penserete. . . . Sempre in contrasti con te si sta. . . ."*

He mixed up in confusion thirty tunes, Italian, French, tragic, comic, of every sort and character ; now in a bass voice he sank down to the underworld, now he screamed shrilly ; and mimicked the walk, carriage and 'gestures of the different characters singing ; by turns furious, pacified, imperious, sneering. Now he plays a young girl in tears, and reproduces all her mincing airs ; now he becomes a priest, a king, a tyrant, threatening, commanding, flying into a rage ; now he is a slave and obeys. He grows calm, he laments, he complains, he laughs ; never out of tune or time, never losing the sense of the words nor the character of the air. All the chess-players had left their boards and gathered round him. The windows of the café were filled outside by the passers-by who had stopped to hear the noise. There were shouts of laughter fit to raise the roof. But he noticed nothing ; he went on, in a state of mental aberration and ecstasy so near to madness, that it seemed doubtful whether he would recover, whether he should not be hastily put into a carriage and taken straight to the asylum. Singing a fragment of Jomelli's *Lamentations* he repeated the finest passages of each piece with incredible precision, truth and fire ; during that fine accompanied recitative in which the prophet paints the desolation of Jerusalem he shed a torrent of tears that set us all weeping. Everything was in it, refinement of singing, expressive power, and grief. He stressed the passages which revealed particularly the composer's greatness ; he would leave the vocal score to take up the instrumental part, which he would suddenly abandon in order to return to the voice ; intermingling one with the other so as to preserve the connections and the unity of the whole ; seizing hold of our souls, and holding them in suspense, in the most extraordinary situation I have ever known. . . . Was it admiration I felt ? yes, it was admiration ; was it pity ? yes, it was pity ; but a certain tinge of absurdity was fused with these feelings and changed their nature. But you would have burst out laughing at the way he mimicked the various instruments. With his cheeks puffed out and swollen, on a harsh gloomy note, he reproduced the horns and bassoons ; he assumed a shrill nasal tone for the oboes ; hurrying his voice at an incredible speed, for the stringed instruments, whose smallest intervals he sought to render ; he whistled for the piccolo, he cooed for the flutes ; shouting, singing, flinging himself about like a madman ; playing all by himself the parts of dancers and singers, male and female, of a whole orchestra and a whole operatic company, dividing himself into twenty different roles, running, stopping short, with the look of one possessed, his eyes flashing, foaming at the mouth. It was terribly hot ; and the sweat that ran in the furrows of his brow and along his cheeks, mingled with the powder from his hair, streamed down and streaked the top of his coat. What did I not see him do ? He wept, he laughed, he sighed, he gazed ; now tender, now tranquil, now furious ; he was a woman swooning from grief ; an unfortunate wretch a prey to despair ; a towering temple ; birds hushing their song at sunset ; waters murmuring in a cool and lonely spot, or falling in torrents from a high mountain ; now a storm, a tempest, where the cry of those about to perish mingles with the whistling of the wind and the crash of thunder. Now he was night with its gloom, now darkness and silence, for even silence may be painted with sounds. He had gone quite out of his mind. . . . Tired out, like a man emerging from a deep sleep or a prolonged fit of abstraction, he stayed motionless, stupefied, bewildered. He gazed around him, like one who has lost his way and tries to recognize the place where he is. He was waiting to recover his strength and his wits ; mechanically he wiped his face. Like a man waking up to see a crowd of people round his bed ; forgetting entirely, or completely unaware of what he had done, he cried out at first : " Why, gentlemen, what is the matter ? What's the reason for your laughter and astonishment ? What is the matter ? " Then he added : " There's real music for you, and a real musician. And yet, gentlemen, certain pieces by Lulli are not to be despised. I defy anyone to improve on the scene beginning ' *Ah, j'attendrai* ' without altering the words. Certain passages of Campra are not to be despised, nor my uncle's airs for the violin, nor his gavottes, his entries of priests, soldiers, and sacrificers. . . . *Pâles flambeaux, nuit plus affreux que les ténèbres.* . . . *Dieu du Tartare, Dieu de l'Oubli.* . . ." Here he swelled his voice and sustained his notes ; the neighbours came to their windows ; we thrust our fingers into our ears. He added : " That's where lungs are needed, a powerful organ, a great volume of breath. But soon we shall be greeting the Assumption ; Lent and the Epiphany are over. They don't yet know what should be set to music, nor consequently, what suits a musician. Lyric poetry is not born yet. But they'll come to it ; by dint of hearing Pergolesi, the Saxon, Terradeglias, Traetta, and the others ; by dint of reading Metastasio, they'll have to come to it."

I : What ? So Quinault, La Motte and Fontenelle didn't know their business ?

He : Not the new style. There are not six consecutive lines in all their charming poems that could be set to music. There are ingenious maxims, light, tender, delicate love-poems ; but if you would know how useless all that is for our art, the most violent of all, not excepting that of Demosthenes, let these verses be recited to you and see how cold, how languid, how monotonous they seem. There's nothing in them you see, that can serve as a model for song. I'd as soon have to set to music La Rochefoucauld's *Maxims* or the *Pensées* of Pascal. The line that's to suit us must be dictated by the animal cry of passion. We need expressions hurrying after one another ; the short phrase, its sense broken, suspended ; the musician must have the whole and each of its parts at his disposal, must be able to omit or repeat a word, add one that's lacking, turn the phrase round and round without destroying it, like a polypus ; all of which makes it far harder to write lyric poetry in French than in languages that allow inversions, and that actually present all these advantages. . . . *Barbare, cruel, plonge ton poignard dans mon sein. Me voilà prête à recevoir le coup fatal. Frappe. Ose*. . . . *Ah! je languis, je meurs*. . . . *Un feu secret s'allume dans mes sens*. . . . *Cruel amour, que veux-tu de moi ?* . . . *Laisse-moi la douce paix dont j'ai joui*. . . . *Rends-moi la raison* . . .* We need strong passions ; the tenderness of the musician and the lyric poet must be exaggerated. The aria almost always winds up the scene. We need exclamations, interjections, pauses, interruptions, affirmations, denials ; we call, invoke, cry, moan, weep and laugh frankly. No wit, no epigrams ; none of your pretty thoughts. All that is too far from plain nature. Don't go and think, now, that the acting and declamation of stage-players can serve as models for us. No, no. We need something more vigorous, less mannered, more sincere. The more monotonous and unaccented our language, the more essential to us are the plain speech and common utterances of passion. The cry of animal impulse or of human emotion provides the accent that is lacking.

While he spoke thus, the crowd that surrounded us, either failing to understand or taking no interest in what he was saying, had drawn back, since generally children, like men, and men, like children, would rather be amused than instructed ; each had gone back to his game ; and we remained alone, in our corner. Sitting on a bench, leaning

* " Ah, cruel barbarian, plunge thy dagger into my breast. See I am ready to receive the fatal blow. . . . Strike. . . . Dare. . . . Ah! I am falling, I am dying. . . . A hidden fire enflames my senses. . . . Cruel love, what do you demand of me ? Leave me the quiet peace which I have enjoyed. . . . Let me be sane once more. . . ."

his head against the wall, his arms dangling, his eyes half shut, he said : " I don't know what's the matter with me ; when I came here, I was fresh and lively ; now I'm beaten, broken, as though I'd walked ten leagues. It's come over me all of a sudden."

I : Would you like to drink something ?
He : With pleasure. I feel hoarse and weak, and my chest is sore. This happens almost every day, I don't know why.
I : What would you like ?
He : Whatever you please. I'm not particular. Poverty has taught me to like anything.

We were served with beer and lemonade. He filled a great glass and emptied it twice or thrice in succession. Then, like a man revived, he coughed loudly, began to throw himself about and to speak once more :
He : But in your opinion, my lord philosopher, is it not a very queer thing that a foreigner, an Italian, like Duni, should come and teach us how to accent our music, how to make our song comply with every sort of movement, of rhythm, of interval, of speech, without offending prosody? It wasn't such a formidable task, after all. Anyone who had listened to a beggar asking for alms in the street, or a man in a fit of anger, a jealous woman raging, a lover in despair, or a flatterer, yes, a flatterer softening his tone, drawling his syllables, speaking in a honeyed voice ; in a word, to any passion, no matter what, provided that by its energy it is worthy to serve as model for a musician— must have noticed two things ; first, that there is no fixed length for syllables, long or short, nor even any fixed proportion between their lengths ; next, that passion deals with prosody almost as it pleases, that it can compass the widest intervals, and that the man who exclaims at the climax of his distress, " Ah, unfortunate wretch that I am," rises

on the interjectory syllable to the highest and shrillest note, and sinks on the others to the deepest and gravest notes, compassing an octave or an even greater interval, and giving to each sound the quantity that suits the turn of the melody, without offending the ear, although neither the long nor the short syllables will keep the length or brevity they had in unimpassioned speech. What a long way we have travelled since the days when we cited as prodigies of musical declamation the parentheses from *Armide*: " *Le vainqueur de Renaud (si quelqu'un le peut être)* "* and the " *Obéissons sans balancer* "† from the *Indes galantes*! To-day such prodigies make me shrug my shoulders in pity. At the pace art is progressing, I don't know where it will end up. Meanwhile let's have a drink.

He had two or three without knowing what he was doing. He would have drowned himself, as he had exhausted himself, without noticing, if I had not shifted the position of the bottle for which he was groping absent-mindedly. Then I said :

I : How comes it that with such fine judgment and great sensitiveness in regard to the beauties of the art of music, you should be so blind to what is beautiful in moral matters, and so insensitive to the charms of virtue ?

He : Because, apparently, these require a sense that I don't possess ; a fibre that has not been granted me, a slack string that is plucked in vain, that won't vibrate ; or perhaps because I have always lived among good musicians who were bad men ; whence it happens that my ear has become very sensitive and my heart deaf. And then there's something hereditary in it. My father's blood and my uncle's are the same blood. The paternal molecule was hard and obtuse ; and that cursed paternal molecule has assimilated all the rest.

* " The conqueror of Renaud (if anyone can be)."
† " Let us obey without hesitation."

I : Do you love your child ?

He : Do I love him, the little rascal ? I'm mad about him.

I : Won't you seriously endeavour to check the effect of that cursed molecule in him ?

He : I think such an endeavour would be quite useless. If he is destined to be a good man, I shall not prevent him. But if the molecule has determined that he is to be a rogue like his father, the trouble I should have taken to make a decent man of him would do him a great deal of harm ; his education continually thwarting the tendency of the molecule, he would be pulled by two contrary forces, and would walk all awry along the path of life, as I see an infinite number of men doing, equally at sea in right and wrong ; they are what we call " creatures," which is the most to be dreaded of all epithets, since it indicates mediocrity, and the utmost degree of disdain. A great rogue is a great rogue, but is not a " creature." Before the paternal molecule had gained the upper hand again, and had brought him to the state of perfect baseness which I have reached, an infinite time would have passed ; he would waste his best years. I'm doing nothing about it just now. I let him grow ; I examine him. He is already greedy, artful, a thief, an idler, a liar. I'm very much afraid he's a chip off the old block.

I : And you'll make a musician of him, so that nothing shall be lacking in the resemblance ?

He : A musician ! a musician ! sometimes I look at him, grinding my teeth, and say : " If you ever get to know a single note, I think I'll wring your neck."

I : And pray, why ?

He : It leads to nothing.

I : It leads to everything.

He : Yes, when one excels at it ; but who can promise himself that his child will excel ? There are ten thousand chances to one that he'd never be more than a wretched string-scraper like myself. Do you know that it might well be easier to find a child fit to govern a kingdom, to become a great king, than a great fiddler?

I : It seems to me that pleasing talents, even though second-rate, amid a people without morals and sunk in debauchery and luxury, carry a man quickly forward in the path of fortune. I myself have heard the following conversation between a sort of patron and a sort of protégé. The latter had been advised to apply to the former, as being an obliging man who might help him. " Monsieur, what do you know? "—" I know mathematics tolerably well."—" Well, then, teach mathematics ; after you've covered yourself with mud on the pavements of Paris for ten or twelve years, you'll have three or four hundred *livres* a year."—" I've studied law, and I am well-versed in jurisprudence."—" If Puffendorf and Grotius came back into the world they would die of hunger, propped up against a milestone."—" I have a good knowledge of history and geography."—" If there were any parents who took their children's education seriously, your fortune would be made, but there aren't any."—" I'm a fairly good musician."—" Well ! Why didn't you say that at first ? And to show you what profit can be got from that talent, I have a daughter. Come every day, from half-past seven till nine in the evening ; you shall give her lessons, and I will give you twenty-five *louis* a year. You shall breakfast, dine, lunch and sup with us. The rest of your day will be your own ; you may dispose of it to your own advantage."

He : And what became of this man ?

I : If he had been wise, he'd have made his fortune, which apparently is the only thing you have eyes for.

He : Undoubtedly. Gold, gold. Gold is everything, and all the rest, without gold, is nothing. And so, instead of stuffing his head with fine maxims, which he'd have to forget on pain of being nothing but a beggar, when I possess a sovereign, which doesn't happen often, I stand in front of him. I pull the sovereign from my pocket,

I show it to him with admiration. I raise my eyes to heaven. I kiss the sovereign in front of him. And to make him understand still better the importance of the sacred coin, I speak to him in a lisping voice, I point out with my finger all that one can buy with it, a pretty frock, a pretty cap, a nice cake. Then I put the sovereign in my pocket. I walk about proudly ; I lift up the flap of my waistcoat ; I pat my pocket with my hand ; and that's how I make him understand that the self-confidence he sees in me springs from the sovereign that's in there.

I : Nothing could be better. But if it should happen that, deeply impressed with the value of the sovereign, one day. . . .

He : I follow you. One must shut one's eyes to that possibility. There's no moral principle but has its disadvantage. At the worst, it means a bad quarter of an hour and then all's over.

I : Even from your point of view, so wise and courageous, I persist in believing that it would be a good thing to make a musician of him. I know no quicker method of getting into touch with those in power, of serving their vices and putting one's own to profit.

He : True ; but I have schemes for a swifter and surer success. Ah ! if only he were a girl ! But just as one doesn't do what one pleases, so one has to accept what comes ; to profit by it as much as possible ; and to that end one should not be so foolish as to give a spartan education to a child destined to live in Paris, like so many fathers, who could do nothing worse if they planned disaster for their children. If my child's education is bad, that is the fault of my country's morals, and not mine. Let who can be responsible. I want my son to be happy ; or, what comes to the same thing, to be honoured, rich and powerful. I have some knowledge of the easiest ways to attain this end ; and I'll teach him these early. If you blame me, all you wise men, the crowd and my success will absolve me.

He will have gold, you may take my word for it. If he has enough of it, he'll lack nothing, not even your esteem and your respect.

I : Maybe you're wrong.

He : Or else he'll do without them, like many others.

In all this, there were a great many of those things that people think, and according to which they act, but which they never say. To tell the truth, that was the most marked difference between this fellow and most of those around us. He admitted the vices that he had, and that others have ; but he was no hypocrite. He was neither less nor more abominable than they ; he was only franker and more consistent, and sometimes profound in his depravity. I shuddered to think what his child would become, under such a teacher. It is certain that, brought up according to ideas so strictly modelled on our morality, he was bound to go far, unless something checked his progress prematurely.

He : Oh, you needn't be afraid. The important and difficult point to which a good father must pay particular attention is, not so much to give his child vices that will make him rich, ridiculous ways that will win him the favour of great folks—every one does that, if not syste-matically like myself, at all events in practice and by precept—but to indicate to him just how far to go, the art of avoiding shame, dishonour and the penalty of the law ; such discords in the social harmony need careful placing, preparing and resolving. There's nothing so dull as a series of perfect harmonies. Something is needed to add savour, to divide up the beam and scatter its rays.

I : Very good. By this comparison, you bring me back from morals to music, which I had left against my will ; and I thank you for that, since, to be honest with you, I like you better as a musician than as a moralist.

He : And yet I'm quite an inferior musician, and quite a superior moralist.

I : I have my doubts about that ; but even if it were so, I am a decent man, and my principles are not yours.

He : So much the worse for you. Ah ! if only I had your talents !

I : Leave my talents out of it ; and let's get back to yours.

He : If only I could express myself like you ! But I talk a damned ludicrous jargon, belonging half to society and literary folk and half to the market-place.

I : I speak badly. I can only tell the truth ; and that doesn't always succeed, as you know.

He : But it's not in order to tell the truth, it's in order to tell lies well that I covet your talents. If only I knew how to write, how to fling a book together, write a dedication, make a fool drunk with his own merit, wheedle my way into women's favour !

I : And you can do all that a thousand times better than I can. I should not be worthy even to take lessons from you.

He : So many great qualities wasted, and their value unsuspected by you !

I : I get back to the full such value as I set on them.

He : If that were so, you would not be wearing that rough coat, that waistcoat of coarse cloth, those woollen stockings, those thick shoes, that ancient wig.

I : Quite so. A man must be most unskilful, if he doesn't get rich though he goes to any length to become so. But, you see, there are people like myself who don't consider wealth as the most precious thing on earth ; queer people.

He : Most queer. One can't be born with that turn of mind. One acquires it ; for it's not found in nature.

I : Not in human nature ?

He : Not in human nature. Everything that lives, without exception, seeks its own well-being at another's expense ; and I'm certain that if I left my little rascal to grow

315

up, without telling him about anything, he would want to be richly clad, a favourite among men, beloved by women, and to grasp to himself all the joys of life.

I : If the little savage were left to himself, if he preserved all his foolishness and combined the violent passions of a man of thirty with the lack of reason of a child in the cradle, he'd wring his father's neck and go to bed with his mother.

He : That proves the necessity of a good education, and who disputes that ? And what is a good education, if not that which leads to every sort of pleasure, without danger and without difficulty ?

I : I'm not far from agreeing with you ; but let us avoid making ourselves plain.

He : Why ?

I : Because I fear our agreement is only apparent, and that, if once we embarked on a discussion of the dangers and difficulties to be avoided, we should no longer understand one another.

He : And what does that matter ?

I : Let's leave that alone, I tell you. I could not teach you what I know on that subject ; and you will find it easier to teach me what you do know, and I do not, about music. Dear Rameau, let us talk about music, and you tell me how it happens that with such a gift for appreciating, remembering and reproducing the finest passages from great masters, with all the enthusiasm that they inspire in you and that you communicate to others, you have composed nothing worthwhile.

Instead of answering me, he began to shake his head, and pointing his finger to the sky, exclaimed : " What about the stars ? When nature created Leo, Vinci, Pergolesi, Duni, she smiled. She assumed a solemn and imposing air when she created my dear uncle Rameau, who'll be known as the great Rameau for about ten years, and then will be heard of no more. When she threw together his nephew, she made a grimace, and then another, and then yet another." And as he said these words he was making all sorts of faces, expressive of contempt, disdain and irony; and he seemed to be kneading a lump of dough between his fingers and laughing at the absurd shapes he gave it. When he had done this, he threw the grotesque image away and said:

"That's how she made me and flung me beside other grotesques, some apoplectic, with great wrinkled bellies, short necks, great eyes starting out from their heads; others with crooked necks; some dried-up, bright-eyed, hook-nosed; all began to burst with laughter when they saw me; and I put my hands on my ribs and burst with laughter on seeing them; for fools and lunatics are amused by one another; they seek out and attract each other. If, once I'd got there, I hadn't found ready to hand the proverb that says "a fool's money is a clever man's heritage," I'd have invented it. I felt that nature had put my birthright in the purse of those grotesque puppets and I thought up a thousand ways of regaining possession of it."

I : I know those ways; you've told me of them and I have much admired them. But amongst so many expedients, why did you not try that of a fine work of art?

He : That's what a man of the world said to the abbé Le Blanc. . . . The abbé said: "The Marquise de Pompadour takes me up in her hand, carries me to the threshold of the Academy, and there withdraws her hand, and I tumble down and break both my legs." The man of the world replied: "Well, abbé, you must get up again and burst open the door with your head." The abbé retorted: "That's what I tried to do; and do you know what I got from it? A bump on the forehead."

After this little tale, my friend began to walk about with his head bent, with a pensive and downcast air; he sighed,

317

wept, lamented, raised his hands and his eyes, beat his head with his fist till he almost broke his brow or his fingers, and added : " And yet it seems to me there's something inside there ; but I knock it and shake it in vain, nothing comes out." Then he began to shake his head and beat his brow harder than ever, and said : " Either there's no one in, or they won't answer." The next moment he assumed a haughty air, lifted his head, laid his right hand on his heart, and walked about saying : " I can feel, yes, I can feel." He imitated a man growing angry, growing indignant, moved to tenderness, commanding, beseeching, and improvised speeches expressing wrath, commiseration, hatred and love ; he sketched the character of these passions with surprising subtlety and truth. Then he added : " That's it, I think. Now it's coming ; that's what comes of finding a midwife who knows how to stimulate and hasten the birthpangs, and to bring forth the child. When I'm alone, I take up my pen, I want to write, I bite my nails, I scratch my forehead. Nothing doing, the god is not at home. I had persuaded myself that I had genius ; and at the finish of my line I read that I'm a fool, a fool, a fool. But how is one to feel, to be uplifted, to paint with power, when one frequents such people as those whom one has to see in order to live ; with the kind of talk one makes and listens to going on all around, and such gossip as : ' To-day the boulevard was delightful. Have you heard the " little monkey " ? She acts enchantingly. Monsieur So-and-So has the finest dapple-grey carriage-horses you can imagine. Beautiful Madame What-not is beginning to fade. At forty, fancy doing one's hair that way ! Young Miss What's-her-name is covered with diamonds which cost her hardly. . . . You mean that cost her dear ? . . . No, no. . . . Where did you see her ? . . . At *L'Enfant d'Arlequin perdu et retrouvé*. The scene of despair is played as it never was before. The Punchinello at the *Foire* theatre has a voice, but no subtlety, no soul. Madame So-and-so has given birth to two children at once. Each father can have his own. . . .' And do you think that this, said again and again and listened to every day, can fire one and lead one to great things ? "

I : No. It would be better to shut oneself up in one's attic, drink water, eat dry bread, and search one's own soul.

He : Possibly ; but I haven't the courage for that ; and then, why sacrifice one's happiness to an uncertain success ? And think of the name I bear ! Rameau ! It's embarrassing to be called Rameau. Talent is not like nobility, which is transmitted and which grows more illustrious as it passes from grandfather to father, from father to son, from son to grandson, without any merit being required on the descendant's part ! The old stock branches out into an enormous collection of fools ; but what matter ? It's not the same with talent. To win merely the same fame as one's father, one must be cleverer than he. One must inherit something of his fibre. That fibre was lacking in me ; but my wrist has got supple, the bow is plied and the pot boils. There's soup, if there's no glory.

I : In your place, I wouldn't take it for granted ; I should try.

He : And do you think I haven't tried ? I wasn't fifteen when I said to myself for the first time : " What's the matter with you, Rameau ? You're dreaming. And what are you dreaming about ? That you'd like to have done, or to do, something that excites the admiration of the universe. Well ! it's as easy as winking ! Just whistle and snap your fingers and they'll come to you ! " At a later age I repeated what I'd said as a child. To-day I still repeat it ; and yet I remain beside the statue of Memnon.

I : What do you mean by the statue of Memnon ?

He : Surely that's quite plain. Around the statue of Memnon there were an infinite number of others, on which

the sun's rays fell equally ; but his was the only one that
uttered sounds. There's one poet, Voltaire, and who else ?
Voltaire ; and the third, Voltaire ; and the fourth,
Voltaire. There's one musician, Rinaldo da Capua ; there's
Hasse ; there's Pergolesi ; there's Alberti ; there's Tartini ;
there's Locatelli ; there's Terradeglias ; there's my uncle ;
there's that little Duni who has neither looks nor presence,
but who has feeling, good God, who has the gift of song
and of expression. The rest, beside these few Memnons,
are like so many pairs of ears stuck on the end of a stick.
And so we're beggars, too wretched for any words. Ah,
master philosopher, poverty's a terrible thing. I see it
crouching down with its mouth agape to catch a few drops
of the icy water that escapes from the barrel of the Danaïdes.
I don't know if it quickens the wit of the philosopher ;
but it chills the poet's head confoundedly. You can't sing
well underneath that barrel. Even so, he's a lucky man who
can get there at all ; I've been there, and I wasn't able to
stay there. I'd been guilty of that folly once before. I've
travelled in Bohemia, in Germany, in Switzerland, in
Holland, a devil of a long way.

I : Underneath the leaking barrel ?

He : Underneath the leaking barrel ; there was a wealthy
and extravagant Jew who loved music and my crazy ways.
I made music to have pleased the gods. I played the fool ;
I lacked nothing. My Jew was a man who knew his law,
and who observed it with the utmost rigidity, sometimes amongst friends, always amongst strangers. He got
himself into a tiresome scrape that I must tell you about,
for it's amusing. There was at Utrecht a charming courtesan. He desired this Christian ; he dispatched a secret
agent to her, with a bill of exchange for a considerable sum.
The queer creature refused his offer. The Jew was in despair
about it. The agent said to him : " Why distress yourself
thus ? You want to go to bed with a pretty woman ?
Nothing is easier, and even to go to bed with one who's

prettier than the one you're after—with my wife, whom I'll let you have at the same price." No sooner said than done. The agent keeps the bill of exchange and the Jew goes to bed with the agent's wife. The bill falls due. The Jew lets it be claimed and disputes its validity. There is a lawsuit. The Jew said to himself : " This man will never dare say on what conditions he has my bill, and I shan't pay it." In court he cross-questions the agent. " From whom did you get this bill ? "—" From yourself." —" Was it for money lent ? "—" No."—" For merchandise provided ? "—" No."—" For services rendered ? " —" No, but that's nothing to do with the matter. I have got it. You signed it, and you shall pay it."—" I did not sign it."—" Am I a forger then ? "—" You, or some other whose agent you are."—" I am base, but you are a knave. I tell you, you'd better not drive me too far. I shall tell everything. I shall dishonour myself, but I shall ruin you." The Jew made light of the threat ; and the agent revealed the whole affair at the next session. Both of them were found guilty ; and the Jew was condemned to pay the bill of exchange, the value of which was spent on the relief of the poor. Then I parted company with him. I came back here. What was I to do ? for I must either die of poverty or do something. All sorts of schemes then passed through my head. One day I was on the point of going off to join some provincial company of actors, where I'd be equally good or bad on the stage or in the orchestra ; next day, I contemplated getting one of those pictures painted that they fix on the end of a pole and stick up at a street crossing, and standing there shouting at the top of my voice : " This is the town where he was born : here he is taking leave of his father the apothecary ; here he is arriving at the capital, seeking his uncle's house ; here he is at the feet of his uncle, who drives him away : here he is with a Jew, etc., etc." Next day, I was fully determined to throw in my lot with street-singers ; that might not have been a bad thing to do ; we'd have given a concert under my dear uncle's windows, and he'd have died of rage. I took another course.

Here he stopped, and assumed, first, the attitude of a man holding a violin, tuning the strings with a twist of his arm, and next, that of a poor wretch worn out with fatigue, whose strength fails him, whose legs are shaking, who'll die unless someone gives him a bit of bread ; he indicated his dire need by pointing his finger at his half-opened mouth ; then he added : " You understand. They'd throw me a morsel. We'd fight for it, three or four of us, starving creatures. And now, think your great thoughts, create your beautiful works in the midst of such distress ! "

I : It would be difficult.

He : Tossed hither and thither, I'd landed yonder at last. I was in clover there. I'm out of it. Now I shall have to saw cat-gut once more, and start pointing my finger at my gaping mouth again. There's nothing stable in this world. To-day we're on the top, to-morrow at the bottom of the wheel. We're led by cursed circumstance, and led very badly.

Then, drinking a draught that was left at the bottom of the bottle, and addressing his neighbour : " For pity's sake, Sir, a small pinch. That's a fine snuffbox you have. You don't happen to be a musician ? . . .—No. . . .—All the better for you ; for they're a most unfortunate set of wretches. Fate decreed that I should be one ; whereas perhaps, at Montmartre, there is in a mill, a miller or a miller's boy who'll never hear any other sound than that of his clapper, and who might have invented the finest songs. To the mill, Rameau ! to the mill, that's where you belong."

I : Whatever man undertakes, he was destined to it by nature.

He : She makes some strange blunders. For my part I don't see things from that height at which the man who prunes a tree with shears is indistinguishable from the caterpillar that nibbles its leaves, and whence you only see two different animals each fulfilling its duty. Take up your perch on the epicycle of Mercury ; and from there, if you like, imitate Réaumur, and as he divides the genus of flies into those that sew, those that roam, and those that scythe, you may divide the human species into joiners, carpenters, couriers, dancers and singers. That's your own business. I won't meddle with it. I'm in this world, and I mean to stop here. But if it's natural to have an appetite —for I always find myself coming back to appetite, to the sensation that's ever-present with me—I think things are ordered very badly if one sometimes has nothing to eat. What a devil of a system ! Some men enjoying a superabundance of everything, while others have a stomach as insistent as theirs, a hunger that renews itself like theirs, and nothing to get their teeth into. Worst of all is the constrained attitude that want imposes on us. The needy man doesn't walk straight like his fellows ; he jumps, he crawls, wriggles, creeps along ; he spends his life taking and holding poses.

I : What are poses ?

He : Go and ask Noverre. The world provides far more than his art can imitate.

I : And so you, also, to use your own expression or Montaigne's, have taken up your ' perch on the epicycle of Mercury,' and contemplate the varied pantomime of the human race ?

He : No, no, I tell you. I'm too heavy to rise so high. I leave to the cranes their home in the clouds. I stick to the earth. I look around me ; and I take up my poses, or I amuse myself watching the poses others take up. I'm an excellent mime, as you shall judge.

Then he began to smile, and to imitate the sycophant, the suppliant, the time-server ; with his right foot forward, his left drawn back, his back bent, his head raised, his eyes apparently fixed on other eyes, his mouth a little open, his arms stretched out towards some object ; he awaits an order, he receives it ; he is off like a dart, he comes back, he has done his errand and gives his account of it. He attends to everything ; he picks up things that fall ; he puts a cushion or a footstool under someone's feet ; he holds a saucer ; he draws up a chair ; he opens a door ; he shuts a window, draws curtains ; he watches the master and mistress ; he stands motionless, arms dangling, legs together ; he listens ; he seeks to read faces ; and then adds : " That's my pantomime, and it's about the same as and that of all flatterers, courtiers, lackeys and beggars."

This man's crazy tricks, the tales of the abbé Galiani[15] and the extravagant fantasies of Rabelais have sometimes set me musing deeply. These three storehouses have furnished me with ludicrous masks which I put on the faces of the gravest personages ; and I see a prelate as Pantaloon, a president as a satyr, a monk as a hog, a minister as an ostrich and his chief secretary as a goose.

I : But, according to you (I said to him,) there are many beggars in this world ; and I know no one who is not acquainted with some steps of your dance.

He : You are right. There is in the whole kingdom only one man who walks straight, that's the Sovereign. All the others take up poses.

I : The Sovereign ? You can't be too sure about that ; don't you think he sometimes has by his side some little foot, some little cluster of curls, some little nose that compels him to do a bit of play-acting ? Whoever needs somebody else, is poor and takes up a pose. The king takes a pose before his mistress, and before God ; he performs his pantomime steps. The minister performs as courtier, flatterer, lackey or beggar before his king. The crowd of climbers assume your poses as they perform before the minister, in a hundred ways, each one viler than the other ; so does the abbé in his bands and long gown, once a week at least, before the official who controls the list of livings. I tell you, what you call the beggars' pantomime is the way the whole world goes. Every one has his little Hus and his Bertin.

He : That comforts me.

But while I was speaking, he was mimicking the poses of the people I mentioned, in the most comical fashion ; for instance, for the little abbé, he held his hat under his arm, and his breviary in the left hand ; with the right, he lifted up the tail of his coat ; he walked with his head slightly bent over one shoulder, his eyes downcast, playing the hypocrite so perfectly that I seemed to see the author of the *Réfutations* before the Bishop of Orléans. When I spoke of flatterers and climbers he fell prostrate ; behold Bouret at the Comptroller-general's !

I : That's a fine performance (I said), but yet there is one being who has no need to play your pantomime. That is the philosopher, who has nothing and who asks for nothing.

He : And where is such a creature to be found ? If he has nothing, he must suffer ; if he begs for nothing, he'll get nothing, and he'll go on suffering.

I : No. Diogenes laughed at wants.

He : But he had to be clothed.

I : No ; he went naked.

He : Sometimes it was cold in Athens.

I : Less so than here.

He : But people ate there.

I : Of course.

He : At whose expense ?

I : At nature's. Who provides for the savage ? Why, the earth, the animals, fishes, trees, herbs, roots and streams.

He : That's a poor dinner-table.

I : It's a large one.

He : It is badly served.

I : Yet we despoil it to supply our own tables.

He : But you'll admit that the industry of our cooks, pastry-cooks, chefs, restaurant-keepers and confectioners contributes something ! On so austere a diet, your Diogenes cannot have had very rebellious organs.

I : You're wrong there. In those days the Cynic's robe was the same as our monk's gown, and its virtue was much the same. The Cynics were the Carmelites and Franciscans of Athens.

He : I've got you there. Diogenes must therefore have played the pantomime too ; if not before Pericles, at least before Laïs and Phryne.

I : You're wrong again. Though others paid a high price for the courtesan she'd give herself to him for pleasure.

He : But if it happened that the courtesan was busy and the Cynic in a hurry. . . .

I : He went back to his tub and did without her.

He : And you'd advise me to imitate him ?

I : On my life, it would be better than to cringe, to degrade and prostitute oneself.

He : But I need a good bed, good food, warm clothes in winter, cool clothes in summer ; rest and money and many other things ; and I'd rather owe them to someone's kindness than acquire them by hard work.

I : That's because you are an idler, a glutton, a base and grovelling soul.

He : I think I told you as much.

I : The good things in life have their price, no doubt ; but you don't know the price of what you are sacrificing in order to obtain them. You play your base pantomime, as you always have done and as you always will do.

He : It's true. But that has cost me little, and now costs me nothing. And that's why I'd be wrong to assume a different demeanour, which would be uncomfortable for me and which I should not keep up. But I see from what you tell me that my poor little wife was a sort of philosopher. She was as brave as a lion. Sometimes we went without bread and hadn't a penny. We'd sold almost all our clothes. I would fling myself across the foot of the bed and there rack my brains trying to find someone who'd lend me a crown, which I should not pay back ; while she, merry as a grig, would sit down to her harpsichord, and sing to her own accompaniment. She had a voice like a nightingale ; I'm sorry you never heard her. When I was to perform at any concert I'd take her along with me. On the way I'd say : " Come on, madame, make them admire you ; display your talent and your charms ; carry them away, bowl them over." We'd arrive ; she'd sing, she'd carry them all away, bowl them over. Alas, I've lost her, poor darling ! Besides her talent, she had a mouth so small you could hardly put your little finger in it ; teeth like a row of pearls ; such eyes, such feet ; such a skin, such cheeks, such breasts, such slim legs like a gazelle, and thighs and buttocks fit for a sculptor's model. Sooner or later she'd have the Farmer-General at least. What a walk, what buttocks, oh, my goodness, what buttocks !

Then he began to imitate his wife's walk ; he tripped along, carrying his head high, flirting with a fan, waggling his backside ; it was the funniest and most absurd caricature of our little coquettes.

Then resuming the thread of his discourse, he added : " I took her walking everywhere, in the Tuileries, in the Palais-Royal. I could never have kept her. When she crossed the street of a morning, bareheaded, in her short jacket, you'd have stopped to watch her, and you might have encircled her with four fingers without squeezing her. Those who followed her, who watched her tripping along on her little feet, and studied that plump bottom outlined under her light petticoats, quickened their steps ; she'd let them catch her up ; then she'd swiftly turn on them those two great brilliant black eyes of hers ; that made them stop short. The front of the medal was as good as the back. But alas, I've lost her, and all my hopes of fortune have vanished with her. I'd taken her with that sole end in view, I'd confided all my schemes to her ; and she had too much shrewdness not to see their certainty of success, and too much wisdom not to approve of them."

And then he began to sob and weep, saying :
" No, no, I shall never get over her loss. Since then I've taken to a priest's skull-cap and bands."
I : Out of grief ?
He : If you like. But really to carry my bowl about on my head. . . . But do look what time it is, for I must go to the opera.
I : What's being played ?
He : Something of Dauvergne's. There are quite good things in his music ; it's a pity he wasn't the first to say them. Among the dead, there are always some who distress the living. It can't be helped. *Quisque suos [non] patimur manes.** But it's half-past five. I hear the bell ringing vespers for the abbé of Canaye and for myself. Good-bye, master philosopher. Isn't it true that I am always the same ?
I : Alas, yes, unfortunately.
He : May that misfortune last another forty years. He laughs best who laughs last.

(1762–1773)

---

* *Quisque suos patimur manes.* Virgil. *Æneid* VI, 743. The usual transla-tion is : " Each of us suffers his appropriate punishment in the next world."

NOTES

I

THE INDISCREET TOYS

[1] Diderot is sketching here part of the argument and demonstration that the soul, spirit, or mind is a product of nature, in that it develops and manifests itself parallel to and intertwined with the development of the physical body. As the organism becomes more highly organized physically so the behaviour indicating the emergence of mind, consciousness, becomes more complex, developing to the full consciousness of the fully developed human organism. By pushing the argument back beyond the fœtus, where Mirzoza starts, to the most primitive germ cells, the development of the faculty of sensation into consciousness, mind, is still more clearly seen to be intimately linked with the increasing complexity of the physical organization. (See the *Conversation between d'Alembert and Diderot*, p. 51 *et seq.*)

[2] Referring to Galileo (1564–1642), one of the founders of experimental science, and his well-known experiments at the Leaning Tower of Pisa. The story of his conflict with the Pope and the Inquisition, their attempts to prevent his work and the development of his teaching, in their suppression of intellectual liberty is well described in *Makers of Science* by Ivor B. Hart (1924), pp. 103–24. See also J. W. Draper's *History of the Conflict between Religion and Science.*

[3] Referring to the invention of the barometer by Torricelli (1608–47) and Viviani (1622–1703) pupils of Galileo, and the demonstration by Pascal (1623–62) that the height of a column of mercury which the weight of the atmosphere could support decreased as the barometer was carried to higher altitudes up a mountain, thereby decreasing the weight of air above it. (See Hart, op. cit., p. 179.)

[4] Referring to the optical experiments of Newton (1642–1727) particularly the dispersion of white light into its component colours by a prism, thus founding the science of spectrum analysis. (See Hart, op. cit. pp. 138–72.)

II

ON THE INTERPRETATION OF NATURE

1 The disarming opening clauses and the final paragraph which enclose the clear exposition of Diderot's evolutionary hypothesis in Section LVIII, *Questions*, were no doubt deliberately designed to escape the censor. Luppol has discussed (*Diderot*, 1936, p. 157) the appearance in Diderot's writing so late as 1754 of references to an " eternal God," etc., which have permitted some writers to find traces of a belief in God and in the immortality of the soul in these thoughts *On the Interpretation of Nature*. Luppol concludes that such references were deliberately introduced to mislead the censorship. In 1754 Diderot had already had one book burnt and the permit for the *Encyclopedia* had been withdrawn and the first two volumes suppressed, although the interdict was later raised by d'Argenson. " It was therefore dangerous to express himself clearly not only for his personal security but also for the fate of the *Encyclopedia* as a whole. However he had to give a sort of methodological guide to his collaborators . . . The thoughts *On the Interpretation of Nature* are precisely this guide drawn up for a limited number of initiates. As for the Jesuits, in order to distract their attention, Diderot could well consent to utilize the ' Eternal.' " (Luppol. op. cit., p. 158.)

This was clearly understood for example, by Naigeon, Diderot's close friend and literary executor, who referred to this passage of the *Interpretation of Nature* as follows : " The authors of the *Catechism of the Cacouacs* and the *Comedy of the Philosophers* [two Jesuit anti-Encyclopedist works—Ed.] were far from suspecting that in this work by Diderot there was a passage where he silently undermines the basis of the evidence drawn from the order and arrangement of the universe. He did not state formally that this evidence signified nothing ; one sees even that he wraps up his meaning and that he fears to be understood by those who might proscribe him, but none of those for whom he was writing, the philosophers, was deceived by it, and that was precisely what he wished." (Naigeon. *Memoires*, p. 166.)

III

CONVERSATION BETWEEN D'ALEMBERT AND DIDEROT

1 Diderot has written about the composition of the *Conversation between d'Alembert and Diderot* and *D'Alembert's Dream* in letters to Sophie Volland which enable the date for the writing of them to be fixed. He wrote : " Since there are no new books to review, I am making extracts of books which do not yet exist, while waiting for someone to write them. When this resource, which is very fertile, fails me, I have another, which is the composition of some small writings. I have made a Dialogue between d'Alembert and myself ; we chat in it pretty gaily, and even pretty clearly, despite the dryness and obscurity of the subject. To this Dialogue there succeeds another, much more extensive which serves to illuminate the first ; this is called *D'Alembert's Dream*. The speakers in it are d'Alembert dreaming, Mlle. de l'Espinasse, the friend of d'Alembert, and Dr. Bordeu. If I had wanted to sacrifice the richness of the background to the elevation of style, Democritus, Hippocrates and Leucippus would have been my characters ; but verisimilitude would have restricted me to the narrow confines of the ancient philosophy, and I should have lost too much thereby. It is of the highest extravagance, and yet at the same time contains most profound philosophy. There is some skill in having put my ideas into the mouth of a dreaming man : it is often necessary to give wisdom an air of folly in order to procure a hearing. I would rather it were said, ' But that is not so absurd as one might think,' than to say, ' Listen to me ; here are some very wise things.' " (*Œuvres Complètes*, Vol. XIX, p. 320. *Letters to Sophie Volland*, No. 125, 11 September, 1769.)

2 " *Un Etre* " : a Being ; the Creator, Divine Spirit, God, or Superhuman Intelligence in idealist philosophy. The cleavage between idealism and materialism in philosophy is thus characterized by Engels : " Thus the question of the relation of thinking to being, the relation of spirit to nature—the paramount question of the whole of philosophy—has, no less than all religion, its roots in the narrow-minded and ignorant notions of savagery. But this question could for the first time be put forward in its whole acuteness, could achieve its full significance, only after European society had awakened from the long hibernation of the Christian Middle Ages. The question of the position of thinking in relation to being, a question which, by the way, had played a great part also in the scholasticism of the Middle Ages, the question : which is primary, spirit or nature—that question, in relation to the Church, was sharpened into this : ' Did God create the world or has the world been in existence eternally ? '

" The answers which the philosophers gave to this question split them into two great camps. Those who asserted the primacy of spirit to nature, and, therefore, in the last instance, assumed world creation in some form or other—(and among the philosophers, Hegel, for example, this creation often becomes still more intricate and impossible than in Christianity)—comprised the camp of idealism. The others, who regarded nature as primary, belong to the various schools of materialism.

" These two expressions, idealism and materialism, primarily signify nothing more than this ; and here also they are not used in any other sense. What confusion arises when some other meaning is put into them will be seen below." (F. Engels. *Ludwig Feuerbach*, p. 31.)

[3] Faculty of sensation, sensitiveness. Diderot uses the word " *sensibilité*." See *Elements of Physiology*, p. 137, and the corresponding note. (p. 350.)

Helvétius discussed the question of the " faculty of sensation " as follows : " I shall be asked perhaps what is the faculty of sensation (*faculté de sentir*) and what produces this phenomenon in us ? Here is what a famous English chemist thinks concerning the souls of animals : ' We recognize in bodies, (he says) ' two kinds of property ; those whose existence is permanent and unalterable ; these make impenetrability, weight, mobility, etc. These qualities belong to general physics.'

' There are also in these same bodies other properties, the fugitive and transient existence of which are turn by turn produced and destroyed by certain combinations, decompositions or movements in the internal parts. These kinds of properties make the different branches of natural history and chemistry etc. ; they relate to special branches of physical science.

' Iron, for example, is a compound of phlogiston* and a particular mineral. In this state of combination it is subject to the attractive power of the magnet. Let the iron be chemically altered, and this property is destroyed. The magnet has no action on a ferrous mineral deprived of its phlogiston. When one combines the metal with another substance such as sulphuric acid, the combination similarly destroys in the iron the property of being attracted by the magnet.

' Fixed alkali (soda) and nitric acid have each an enormous number of specific properties ; but there remains no vestige of these properties when they are combined together, forming saltpetre.

' At ordinary temperature nitric acid combines with fixed alkali with

*Phlogiston : The phlogiston theory (Becher, Stahl) explained the oxidation of iron as a loss of phlogiston. The theory was finally refuted by the experiments of Lavoisier. (See F. J. Moore. *History of Chemistry*, Chaps. 4–6.) This does not affect the validity of the argument of Helvétius.

the greatest ease. Let this compound be heated sufficiently to melt it, and let there be added any combustible material, and the nitric acid will abandon the fixed alkali to unite with the combustible substance, and in this act of union is produced that elastic force whose effects are so surprising in gunpowder.

'All the properties of the soda are destroyed when it is combined with sand to form glass, whose transparency, insolubility, electrical properties, etc., are, if I may say so, so many new creations, produced by the combination, and which are destroyed by the decomposition of the glass.

'Now in the animal world, why should not organization equally produce this singular quality which is called the faculty of sensation? All the phenomena of medicine and natural history evidently prove that this power in animals is only the resultant of the structure of their bodies, that this power begins with the formation of their organs, is present so long as they exist and is lost at last by the dissolution of these same organs. If the metaphysicians ask me what then becomes of this faculty of sensation in the animal, I shall answer them : ' Just what becomes of the property of being attracted by the magnet, in chemically altered iron.' " (Helvétius. *De l'Homme*, 1773. Tome I, pp. 108–10, footnote *b*.)

It has not been possible to trace the " English chemist " to whose *Treatise on the Principles of Chimistry* Helvétius refers. Plekhanov (*Essays in the History of Materialism*, p. 91) quotes a similar passage from the English scientist Joseph Priestley (1733–1804, the discoverer of oxygen) : " To make my meaning if possible better understood, I will use the following comparisons. The power of cutting in a razor depends upon a certain cohesion and arrangement of the parts of which it consists. If we suppose this razor to be dissolved in any acid liquor, its power of cutting is certain to be lost, or cease to be, though no particle of the metal that constituted the razor be annihilated by the process ; and its former shape, and power of cutting, etc., may be restored to it after the metal has been precipitated. Thus when the body is dissolved by putric action, its power of thinking entirely ceases." (*A Free Discussion of the Doctrine of Materialism*, London, 1778, pp. 82–3.)

[4] *Animate force and inanimate force*, i.e. kinetic energy and potential energy. For example, the kinetic energy of a fly-wheel, or a flowing stream ; and the potential energy of a compressed gas, an explosive, a coiled spring.

[5] Falconet was a celebrated sculptor with whom Diderot had a long correspondence (*Œuvres Complètes*, Vol. XVIII).

Diderot and Falconet discussed, among many other things, whether consideration for the view of posterity would lead to the undertaking of the noblest actions and the production of the best works of art. Falconet held that it would not ; hence Diderot's reference.

Huez, of the Academy of Sculpture ; he made a statue of Maupertuis Senior, of which Grimm said : " It will not give M. Huez the immortality which he gives to the father of Maupertuis."

⁶ Making marble eatable. The chemical and biological steps in the transformation of inorganic or mineral matter into organic material, which Diderot brilliantly uses in this passage to support his completely materialist standpoint as against the idealist standpoint put forward by d'Alembert in his opening lines, were subsequently worked out in detail by soil microbiologists many years later.

⁷ " So, then, I make flesh, or soul, as my daughter said, an actively sensitive substance," (*Je fais donc de la chair ou de l'âme, comme dit ma fille, une matière activement sensible*). In a letter to Sophie Volland (10 August, 1769) Diderot wrote : " I could hardly write this afternoon, and when at last I wanted to do so, my daughter prevented me ; she claims that when I am not alone I must be with her. Oh ! What fine progress the child has made, and all quite alone ! Some days ago I asked her what the soul was. ' The soul,' she answered, ' well, the soul is made when flesh is made.' " (*L'âme ! me répondit-elle, on fait de l'âme quand on fait de la chair.*)

⁸ Jean-le-Rond d'Alembert (1717–83) was the illegitimate son of the Marquise de Tencin, and the Chevalier Destouches. He was exposed on the steps of St. Jean-le-Rond, whence his name, sent to nurse in Picardy by the police who found him, traced by his father and placed in the care of a glazier's wife, Madame Rousseau, as described by Diderot. He became a famous mathematician and collaborated with Diderot as co-director of the *Encyclopedia*.

⁹ The metaphysical and dialectical modes of thought may be described in connection with this passage where Diderot solves a metaphysically " insoluble " problem, dialectically, and in so doing gives a brilliant germinal conception of biological evolution.

" Which came first, the hen or the egg ? " is a classic example of the " insoluble " problems posed by metaphysical (as against dialectical) thinking. So long as the rigid, fixed proposition that eggs came from hens and hens from eggs is adhered to, which is the metaphysical mode of outlook, the problem is indeed insoluble. Yet it has been " solved " by nature, since there are hens and hen's eggs ; nature did not get involved in the vicious circle which metaphysicians cannot break. Diderot solves this dialectically, indicating the natural solution, namely, that before there were hens and eggs there was something else from which the hen-egg system was evolved and goes on to sketch a theory of evolution.

Engels's discussion of the metaphysical and dialectic modes of outlook may be quoted here to show the subsequent development of conscious materialist dialectics after Diderot:

" The old method of investigation and thought which Hegel calls 'metaphysical,' which preferred to investigate *things* as given, as fixed and stable, a method the relics of which still strongly haunt peoples' minds,* had a good deal of historical justification in its day. It was necessary first to examine things before it was possible to examine processes. One had first to know what a particular thing was before one could observe changes going on in connection with it. And such was the case with natural science. The old metaphysics which accepted things as finished objects arose from a natural science which investigated dead and living things as finished objects. But when this investigation had progressed so far that it became possible to take the decisive step forward of transition to the systematic investigation of the changes which these things undergo in nature itself, then the last hour of the old metaphysics sounded in the realm of philosophy also. And in fact, while natural science up to the end of the last century [eighteenth, *Ed.*] was pre-dominantly a *collecting* science, a science of finished things, in our own century [nineteenth, *Ed.*] it is essentially a *classifying* science, a science of the processes, of the origin and development of these things, and of the inter-connection which binds all these natural processes into one great whole." (F. Engels. *Ludwig Feuerbach*, p. 55.)

The contrast between the metaphysical and dialectical modes of outlook is further clearly described by Engels in the following passage : " When we reflect on nature, or the history of mankind, or our own intellectual activity, the first picture presented to us is of an endless maze of relations and interactions, in which nothing remains what, where and as it was, but everything moves, changes, comes into being and passes out of existence. This primitive, naïve, yet intrinsically correct conception of the world was that of ancient Greek philosophy, and was first clearly formulated by Heraclitus : everything is and also is not, for everything is in *flux*, is constantly changing, constantly coming into being and passing away. But this conception, correctly as it covers the general character of the picture of phenomena as a whole, is yet inadequate to explain the details of which this total picture is composed ; and so long as we do not understand these details, we must detach them from their natural or historical connections, and examine each one separately, as to its nature, its special causes and effects, etc. This is

*A modern example of the metaphysical mode of outlook still ' haunting peoples' minds ' is given by the following : " Which came first, the hen or the egg ? Who knows the right answer to the ancient riddle ? It is like the unending controversy over the economic relations of producers and consumers."—(T. W. Mercer. *Reynolds News*, 4 April, 1936.)

primarily the task of natural science and historical research ; branches of science which the Greeks of the classical period, on very good grounds, relegated to a merely subordinate position, because they had first of all to collect materials for these sciences to work upon. The beginnings of the exact investigation of nature were first developed by the Greeks of the Alexandrian period, and later on, in the Middle Ages, were further developed by the Arabs. Real natural science, however, dates only from the second half of the fifteenth century, and from then on it has advanced with constantly increasing rapidity. The analysis of nature into its individual parts, the grouping of the different natural processes and natural objects in definite classes, the study of the internal anatomy of organic bodies in their manifold forms—these were the fundamental conditions of the gigantic strides in our knowledge of nature which have been made during the last four hundred years. But this method of investigation has also left us as a legacy the habit of observing natural objects and natural processes in their isolation, detached from the whole vast interconnection of things ; and therefore not in their motion, but in their repose ; not as essentially changing, but as fixed constants ; not in their life but in their death. And when, as was the case with Bacon and Locke, this way of looking at things was transferred from natural science to philosophy, it produced the specific limitations of the last century, the metaphysical mode of thought.

" To the metaphysician, things and their mental images, ideas, are isolated, to be considered one after the other, apart from each other, rigid, fixed objects of investigation given once for all. He thinks in absolutely irreconcilable antitheses. ' His communication is Yea, yea, Nay, nay, for whatsoever is more than these cometh of evil.' For him a thing either exists, or it does not exist ; it is equally impossible for a thing to be itself and at the same time something else. Positive and negative absolutely exclude one another ; cause and effect stand in an equally rigid antithesis to one another. At first sight this mode of thought seems to us extremely plausible, because it is the mode of thought of so-called sound common sense. But sound common sense, respectable fellow as he is within the homely precincts of his own four walls, has most wonderful adventures as soon as he ventures out into the wide world of scientific research. Here the metaphysical mode of outlook, justifiable and even necessary as it is in domains whose extent varies according to the nature of the object under investigation, nevertheless sooner or later reaches a limit beyond which it becomes one-sided, limited, abstract, and loses its way in insoluble contradictions. And this is so because in considering individual things it loses sight of their connections ; in contemplating their existence it forgets their coming into being and passing away ; in looking at them at rest it leaves their motion out of account ; because it cannot see the wood for the trees. For everyday purposes we know, for example, and can say with certainty, whether an animal is alive or not ; but when we look more closely we find that this is often an extremely complex question, as jurists know very well. They have cudgelled their brains in vain to discover some rational limit beyond which the killing of a child in its mother's womb is murder ; and it is equally impossible to determine the moment of death, as physiology has established that death is not a sudden, instantaneous event, but a very protracted process. In the same way every organic being is at each moment the same and not the same ; at each moment it is assimilating matter drawn from without, and excreting other matter ; in fact, within a longer or shorter period the matter of its body is completely renewed and is replaced by other atoms of matter, so that every organic being is at all times itself and yet something other than itself. Closer investigation also shows us that the two poles of an antithesis like positive and negative, are just as inseparable from each other as they are opposed, and that despite all their opposition they mutually penetrate each other. It is just the same with cause and effect ; these are conceptions which only have validity in their application to a particular case as such, but when we consider the particular case in its general connection with the world as a whole they merge and dissolve in the conception of universal action and interaction, in which causes and effects are constantly changing places, and what is now or here an effect becomes there or then a cause, and *vice versa*.

" None of these processes and methods of thought fit into the frame of metaphysical thinking. But for dialectics, which grasps things and their images, ideas, essentially in their interconnections, in their sequence, their movement, their birth and death, such processes as those mentioned above are so many corroborations of its own method of thought. Nature is the test of dialectics, and it must be said for modern science that it has furnished extremely rich and daily increasing materials for this test, and has thus proved that in the last analysis nature's process is dialectical, and not metaphysical." (F. Engels. *Anti-Dühring*, pp. 27–9.)

The Conversation between d'Alembert and Diderot and *D'Alembert's Dream* are rich with examples of Diderot's dialectical view of nature, which will be obvious after reading the above description of materialist dialectics. In the field of natural science Diderot was far ahead of his contemporaries in the realization of the dialectic character of natural phenomena.

[10] In connection with this conception of evolution see also the excerpt from *On the Interpretation of Nature*, LVIII, 2, quoted on p. 48 and the extract from the *Letter on the Blind*, p. 28.

[11] Another example of Diderot's dialectic conception of nature.

337

Cf. Engels's : " the whole vast interconnection of things." (*Anti-Dühring*, p. 28 ; see note 9.)

[12] The two substances, i.e., matter and mind.

[13] Lenin, in *Empirio-Criticism* (pp. 17–19) quotes the subsequent passages from the *Conversation between d'Alembert and Diderot* (pp. 57–61 of this translation) as showing the materialist position in the relation of matter with sensation, consciousness, mind : " The doctrine consists not in the derivation of sensation from the movement of matter or in the identification of sensation with the movement of matter, but in the recognition that sensation is one of the properties of matter in motion." (Lenin. *Materialism and Empirio-Criticism*, Collected Works, Vol. XIII, p. 28.)

[14] René Descartes (1596–1650), mathematician (creator of analytical geometry), metaphysician and physicist. The following extracts from Marx's analysis of French materialism in *Die Heilige Familie* serve to characterize Descartes as a philosopher :

" . . . there are two tendencies in French materialism, of which one derives its origin from Descartes and the other from Locke. The latter is pre-eminently an element of French culture and flows directly into socialism. Both tendencies intersect in the course of development. The former, mechanical materialism, merges into French natural science proper. We do not need to deal more closely with the French materialism coming direct from Descartes, any more than with the French school of Newton and the development of French science in general.

Therefore, only this must needs be said : in his physics Descartes had invested matter with self-creative power and had conceived of mechanical motion as its vital art. He had completely separated his physics from his metaphysics. Within his physics matter is the sole substance, the sole basis of being and knowledge.

French mechanical materialism attached itself to the physics of Descartes in contrast to his metaphysics. His disciples were by profession anti-metaphysicians, viz., physicians [i.e., in the sense of physicist —Ed.].

This school begins with the physician Leroy ; it reaches its acme with the physician Cabanis. The physician Lamettrie is its centre. Descartes was still living when Leroy transferred the Cartesian conception of animals to the human soul, as, similarly, Lamettrie did in the eighteenth century—and declared the soul to be a mode of the body and ideas to be mechanical motions. Leroy even believed Descartes had concealed his real opinions. Descartes protested. At the end of the eighteenth century Cabanis completed Cartesian materialism in his work *Connection between the Physique and Morality of Man*.

" The metaphysics of the seventeenth century, as represented in France particularly by Descartes, had materialism as an antagonist from the hour of its birth. This antagonism to Descartes was personified in Gassendi, the restorer of Epicurian materialism. French and English materialism always remained in close relationship to Democritus and Epicurus. Cartesian metaphysics had another opponent in the English materialist Hobbes. Gassendi and Hobbes vanquished their opponent long after their deaths at the very moment when Cartesian metaphysics already ruled as the official power in all French schools. . . .

" In the seventeenth century metaphysics was still saturated with profane content (see Descartes, Leibnitz, etc.). It made discoveries in mathematics, physics and other exact sciences which appeared to belong to it. By the beginning of the eighteenth century this semblance had already been destroyed. The positive sciences had separated themselves from it and had marked off their independent domain. The whole wealth of metaphysics now consisted in nothing but thought entities and heavenly things, at precisely the time when real entities and earthly things began to concentrate all attention upon themselves. Metaphysics had become stale. Helvétius and Condillac were born in the same year that Malebranche and Arnould, the last great French metaphysicians of the seventeenth century, died." (Engels. *Ludwig Feuerbach*, pp. 81-3.)

" A combination of Cartesian and English materialism is to be found in the writings of Lamettrie. He uses the physics of Descartes to its minutest detail. His *L'homme machine* [Man-machine—Ed.] is a performance on the model of the *Tier Maschine* [Animal Machine] of Descartes." (Engels. *Ludwig Feuerbach*, p. 87.)

It is clearly seen therefore how Diderot criticized the *mechanical* materialism of Descartes, and of his contemporaries (Lamettrie, Cabanis), and avoided it while still retaining the fundamental materialist basis. In this he was far in advance of his contemporaries, and was moving towards a *dialectical* materialism. It is *mechanical* materialism which many modern biologists criticize, thinking they thereby criticize the materialist interpretation of nature. *Dialectical* materialism is the modern development of Diderot's conception. (See, for example, Marcel Prenant, *Biologie et Marxisme*. Paris, 1936.)

[15] " . . . the faculty of sensation as a general property of matter or a product of its organization." (See notes 3 and 13.)

[16] The translation from Diderot given in the English translation of Lenin's *Materialism and Empirio-Criticism* (pp. 17-19) has defects. In particular the sentence " *Mais si je me dèpars de cette cause ?* " is incorrectly rendered : " And if I will take this cause as a starting point ? " (p. 19.)

[17] George Berkeley (1685–1753) denied that it was possible to pass

from the perceived qualities of various kinds, sensations received from without, to the underlying substratum or substance, matter, as the materialists held. Diderot said of Berkeley : " Those philosophers are termed idealists who, conscious only of their own existence and of a succession of external sensations, do not admit anything else. An extravagant system which should to my thinking have been the offspring of blindness itself. And yet, to the disgrace of the human mind and philosophy this system though the most absurd, is the most difficult to combat." (Diderot. *Œuvres Complètes*, Vol. I, p. 304.)

[18] Cf. Engels's criticism of Dühring's " formal principles, derived from *thought* and not from the external world, which are to be applied to nature and the realm of man, and to which therefore nature and the realm of man have to conform. But whence does thought obtain these principles ? From itself ? No, for Herr Dühring himself says : the realm of pure thought is limited to logical schemata and mathematical forms (the latter, moreover, as we shall see, is wrong).

" Logical schemata can only relate to *forms of thought* ; but what we are dealing with here are forms of *being*, of the external world, and these forms can never be created and derived by thought out of itself, but only from the external world. But with this the whole relationship is inverted : the principles are not the starting-point of the investigation, but its final result ; they are not applied to nature and human history, but abstracted from them ; it is not nature and the realm of humanity which conform to these principles, but the principles are only valid in so far as they are in conformity with nature and history. That is the only materialistic conception of the matter. . . ." (F. Engels. *Anti-Dühring*, pp. 43-4.)

[19] Compare F. Engels. *Anti-Dühring*, p. 102-104.

[20] Compare, " It is no longer a question anywhere of inventing interconnections from out of our brains, but of discovering them in the facts." (F. Engels. *Ludwig Feuerbach*, p. 69.) Diderot appeals to the criterion of *practice*.

[21] " Seduced by analogy." Compare Lenin's notes : *Elements of Dialectics* : " 1. *Objectivity* of observation. Not ' examples,' not unrepresentative forms. The thing in itself." (Quoted in T. A. Jackson. *Dialectics*, p. 635.)

[22] Buridan's ass. Another metaphysically " insoluble " problem : the ass that died of hunger between two equally attractive bundles of hay, unable to choose between them ; posed by Jean Buridan, Rector of Paris University about A.D. 1327, derived from Aristotle. (See T. A. Jackson. *Dialectics*, pp. 198-9.)

D'ALEMBERT'S DREAM

D'Alembert's Dream offers particular difficulties in translation because Diderot had to employ a certain limited number of words to describe several different genetic, embryological and histological phenomena, of which a clear conception did not then exist in science, and for which the requisite precise technical terms were therefore not available. Diderot was reaching forward and suggesting hypotheses in connection with these ideas, which were then no doubt the subjects of discussion among the scientists among whom Diderot moved. In the light of later scientific development it is possible to understand what were the conceptions which Diderot was seeking to express. In the text the terminology has been left as Diderot wrote it ; and the notes can indicate the different senses in which Diderot used the same few non-technical words.

[1] " I believe I have told you that I had made a dialogue between d'Alembert and myself. On re-reading it, it took my fancy to make a second one, and it has been done. The characters in it are d'Alembert who dreams, Bordeu and the friend of d'Alembert, Mlle. de l'Espinasse. It is called *D'Alembert's Dream*. It isn't possible to be more profound and more extravagant. I added afterwards five or six pages that would make my lover's hair stand on end ; but, however, she will never see them ! But this will surprise you very much, that there's not a word about religion and not a single improper word. After that I defy you to guess what it can be." (*Œuvres Complètes*, Vol. XIX, p. 315. *Lettres à Mlle. Volland*, No. 124, 2 September, 1769.)

The " five or six pages " that would make Sophie Volland's " hair stand on end." refers to the *Continuation of the Conversation* (pp. 118–126).

[2] Diderot says : " *Une molécule sensible et vivante se fond dans une molécule sensible et vivante.*" It is best to translate *molécule* here as particle.

[3] " *Life is the mode of existence of albuminous substances,* and this mode of existence essentially consists in the constant self-renewal of the chemical constituents of these substances. The term albuminous substance is used in the sense used by modern chemistry, which includes under this name all substances constituted similarly to ordinary white of egg, otherwise also known as protein substances. The name is inappropriate, because ordinary white of egg plays the most lifeless and passive role of all the substances related to it, since, together with the yolk, it is merely food for the developing embryo. But while so little is as yet known of the chemical composition of albuminous substances, this name is yet better than any because it is more general.

" Everywhere where we find life we find it associated with an albuminous body, and everywhere where we find an albuminous body not in process of dissolution, there also, without exception, we find the phenomena of life. . . ."

" But what are these universal phenomena of life which are equally present among all living organisms ? Above all, an albuminous body absorbs other appropriate substances from its environment and assimilates them, while other, older parts of the body are consumed and excreted. Other, non-living, bodies also change, and are consumed or enter into combinations in the course of natural processes ; but in doing this they cease to be what they were. A rock worn away by atmospheric action is no longer a rock ; metal which oxidizes rusts away. But what with non-living bodies is the cause of destruction, with albumen is *the fundamental condition of existence*. From the moment when the uninterrupted metamorphosis of its constituents, this constant alternation of nutrition and excretion [cf. Diderot's " continual action and reaction " —*Ed.*], no longer takes place in an albuminous body, from that moment the albuminous body itself comes to an end and decomposes, that is, dies. Life, the mode of existence of albuminous substance, therefore, consists primarily in the fact that at each moment it is itself and at the same time something else ; and this does not take place as the result of a process to which it is subjected from without, as is the way in which this can occur in the case of inanimate bodies. On the contrary, life, the exchange of matter which takes place through nutrition and excretion, is a self-completing process which is inherent in and native to its medium, albumen, without which it cannot exist." (F. Engels. *Anti-Dühring*, pp. 94–6.)

(By albuminous substance Engels does not mean a protein in its modern sense as a pure crystalline chemical substance, but the complex of chemicals that underlie protoplasm : proteins, carbohydrates, lipides, salts.—*Ed.*)

[4] The " Eel-man " ; name given by Voltaire to Needham (1713–1781), an English biologist and Catholic divine, who believed in the spontaneous generation of little " eels " from fermenting flour. He really saw the micro-organisms which were causing the fermentation. In 1745 Needham published " *An Account of some Microscopical Discoveries founded on an Examination of the Calamary and its Wonderful Milt vessels.*"

[5] Diderot uses the word " *atome* " obviously not in the chemical sense.

[6] Cf. Engels's discussion of time and space in *Anti-Dühring*. He first quotes Kant's antinomy concerning time and space. *The First Antinomy of Pure Reason* has as thesis : The world has a beginning in time and is limited also with regard to space. Kant then gives the proof of it. He then states and proves the contrary thesis : the world can have no beginning in time and no end in space. (Kant *Critique of Pure Reason*, Part I, Section II, Book II, Div. II, §2. English tr. Max Müller,

p. 344, 346). In this he finds the antinomy, the insoluble contradiction, that the one thesis is just as demonstrable as the other. Engels continues : " The problem itself has a very simple solution. Eternity in time, infinity in space, mean from the start, and in the simple meaning of the words, that there is no end in *any* direction, neither forwards nor backwards, upwards or downwards, to the right or to the left. This infinity is something quite different from that of an infinite series, for the latter always starts out from one, with one first term. . . . " (*Anti-Dühring*, pp. 60–61.)

Engels then discusses " infinite series " in space and time : " It is clear that the infinity which has an end but no beginning is neither more nor less infinite than that which has a beginning but no end. The slightest dialectical insight . . . [would show] . . . that beginning and end are necessarily interconnected like the North Pole and the South Pole, and that if the end is left out, the beginning just becomes the end —the *one* end which the series has ; and *vice versa*. The whole fraud would be impossible but for the mathematical usage of working with infinite series. Because in mathematics it is necessary to start from definite, finite terms in order to reach the indefinite, the infinite, all mathematical series, positive or negative must start from 1, or they cannot be used for calculation. The abstract requirements of a mathematician are, however, very far from being a compulsory law for the world of reality. . . .

" Infinity is a contradiction, and is full of contradictions. From the outset it is a contradiction that an infinity is composed of nothing but finites, and yet this is the case. The finiteness of the material world leads no less to contradictions than its infiniteness, and every attempt to get over these contradictions leads . . . to new and worse contradictions. It is just *because* infinity is a contradiction that it is an infinite process, unrolling endlessly in time and space. The removal of the contradiction would be the end of infinity." (*Anti-Dühring*, p. 62.)

" From the dialectical standpoint, the possibility of expressing motion in its opposite, in rest, presents absolutely no difficulty. To dialectical philosophy the whole contradiction, as we have seen, is only relative ; there is no such thing as absolute rest, unconditional equilibrium, and the motion as a whole puts an end to the equilibrium. When therefore rest and equilibrium occur they are the result of arrested motion, and it is self-evident that this motion is measurable in its result, and can be expressed in it, and can be resorted out of it again in one form or another." (*Anti-Dühring*, p. 74.)

[7] Epicurus (341–271 B.C.) was one of the great Greek materialists. He developed and extended the theories of Democritus. The work of Epicurus dominates the history of early materialism. Besides relatively

fragmentary remains of Epicurus's writings, the best exposition of his ideas is given in the poem *De Rerum Natura* (Concerning the Nature of Things) by the Latin poet Lucretius (*c.* 97–55 B.C.)

Epicurus founded a science of the universe with a materialist basis, eliminating the powers and activities of spirits, without supernatural laws and without any " heavenly justice " towards man.

The theory of knowledge of Epicurus established the primacy of the external world in opposition to philosophic idealism, particularly that of Plato. Knowledge, perception, is an " action " of the external world on man, although the mind is not entirely passive before it.

On this basis Epicurus constructed his physics. He took over from Democritus the atomic conception of all that exists ; the motion of the hard, indivisible atoms, as they move to occupy the non-resisting void between them, creates the universe ; a conception of the world where everything happens by virtue of mechanical casuality, chance and finality being excluded. Epicurus developed this doctrine in relation to the properties and movements of the atoms. He attributed weight to the atoms, limited and not unlimited shapes, and a contingent source of motion, " declination," in addition to motion as a result of juxtaposition to unresisting void. Epicurus envisaged a universe without finality, without providence or destiny, where only mechanical causes operated and where the soul even, and the gods, were described as complex structures of material atoms.

For a recent description of the materialism of Democritus, Epicurus and Lucretius, which provided the starting-point for Diderot's philosophic materialism, the book *Les Materialists de l'Antiquité* by Paul Nizan, should be consulted.

[8] No case of supposed spontaneous generation of living organisms from non-living matter has yet been proved ; alleged cases have been shown to be due to fortuitous infection by micro-organisms. This was demonstrated in particular by Pasteur, in experiments designed to show that alleged cases of spontaneous generation did not take place under sterile conditions. Nevertheless, modern science believes in the chemical origin of life at a definite period in the Earth's development.

" Through combination of modern biochemical knowledge with astrophysical and geological considerations about the early atmosphere of the planet, we can make a plausible picture of the origin of life by purely chemical means, and no other hypothesis for its origin can be put forward which will stand the slightest rational examination." (J. D. Bernal. *Engels and Science.*)

[9] Father Castel's ribbon. This was an instrument, an " ocular clavecin " invented by Father Castel in which multicoloured ribbons were combined in colour harmonies by striking a keyboard.

10 Compare with Lenin's *Elements of Dialectics* :
" 2. *Totality* of the manifold *relations* of the things to others.

. . .

" 8. The *relations* (of the thing or appearance) not only manifold but *general, universal.* Everything (appearance, process, etc.) is connected with *every other*." (Quoted in T. A. Jackson. *Dialectics*, p. 635.)

11 Cf. Note 3.

12 " The gross developments of a network (*réseau*) that forms itself, increases, extends, and throws out a multitude of imperceptible threads (*fils*)," i.e., the development of the nervous system.

13 The subsequent passage where Bordeu is speaking is not easy to understand. It is evident, however, that Diderot is attempting to describe the development of the fertilized egg-cell and subsequent cell-differentiation. With this is intermingled a conception of the development of the nervous system. To express these conceptions only a few non-technical words were used by Diderot :

(*a*) " . . . that speck became a loose thread, then a bundle of threads," (*ce point devint un fil délié, puis un faisceau de fils*). The " bundle of threads " here suggests the collection of cells at early stages of growth of the germ-cell, rather than an allusion to nerve fibres, which is the sense in which it is used again later.

(*b*) " Each of the fibres of the bundle of threads (*chacun des brins du faisceau de fils*) was transformed, solely by nutrition and according to its conformation (*par la seule nutrition et par sa conformation*) into a particular organ ; exception being made of those organs in which the fibres of the bundle are metamorphosed, and to which they give birth," (*abstraction faite des organes dans lesquels les brins du faisceau se métamorphosent, et auxquelles ils donnent naissance*). This appears to refer to the organs, the gonads, where the germ-cells themselves are reproduced. The word " brin " meaning literally shoot, sprig, blade (of grass), stick, bit, is clearly used to mean a sub-division of thread (*fil*). The use of " brin " also meaning the *staple* (of rope, etc.) gives a clue justifying translation as *fibre*, which we have used, as being the unit from which a thread is made, by taking many fibres together.

(*c*) " The bundle is a purely sensitive system." The bundle (*faisceau*) here seems to refer to the nervous system.

(*d*) " Fibre " (*brin*) here refers to the various nerves.

(*e*) " . . . bundle with a peculiar fibre which would give rise to an organ unknown to us." (*un faisceau avec un brin singulier qui donnerait naissance à une organe qui nous est inconnu.*)

(*f*) " . . . two fibres which characterize the two sexes." (. . . *les deux brins qui charactérisent les deux sexes.*)

If the " fibres " (*brins*) in phrases *e* and *f* are thought of in this context as the chromosomes of the cells, which control the subsequent development and sex of the organism, the whole passage may be looked upon as another example of the way in which Diderot was seeking to develop a purely materialist hypothesis, entirely on theoretical grounds in advance of scientific knowledge, to account for the " mysteries " of biological development. All this has a surprisingly modern ring.

(g) Here " fibre " (brin) refers once more to the nerve fibres.

[14] Diderot is suggesting how interference with the germ-cells or embryo might alter the structure of the adult. If the subsequent passage, dealing with abnormalities, etc., is read also bearing in mind the chromosome conception (the chromosomes being the cell structures which carry the genes controlling the development of the organism, the genetic material) then this passage is seen to be a brilliant foreshadowing, purely theoretical at that time, of subsequent ideas of biological development and heredity.

[15] The remarks in the previous note, about the germ-cells and chromosomal control of the adult structure apply here also.

The French is : " Pour fair un enfant on est deux, comme vous savez. Peut-être qu'un des agents répare le vice de l'autre, et que le réseau défectueux ne renaît que dans le moment où le descendant de la race monstrueuse prédomine et donne le loi à la formation du réseau. Le faisceau de fils constitue la différence originelle et première de toutes les espèces d'animaux. Les variétés du faisceau d'une espèce font toutes les variétés monstrueuses de cette espèce."

In this passage, if the " bundle of threads "(faisceau de fils) is understood as the chromosomes of the germ-cells, Diderot's genetical hypothesis is quite straightforward. The " leaps " could be mutations.

[16] " . . . balloons under his feet." In tabes dorsalis, the soles of the feet lack sensation, and hence there is the feeling of an inert layer between where feeling ends in the foot and where the sole actually touches the ground.

" ' They call ut " Locomotus attacks us," ' he sez, ' bekaze ' sez he, ' ut attacks us like a locomotive, if ye know fwhat that manes. An' ut comes,' sez he, lookin' at me, ' ut comes from being called Love-o'- Women.'

" ' You're jokin, docthor,' I sez.

" ' Jokin' ! ' sez he. ' If iver you feel that you've got a felt sole in your boot instid av a Governments bull's-wool, come to me,' he sez, ' an I'll show you whether 'tis a joke.' " (Rudyard Kipling. " Love-o'- Women," in Many Inventions.)

[17] Sensibilité seems best translated by sensibility or feeling here, since it is referring to a general, temperamental or intellectual condition, and not to the specific sensitiveness of living matter.

[18] This is a brilliant " interpretation of dreams."

[19] " The concepts of number and form have not been derived from any source other than the world of reality. The ten fingers on which men learnt to count, that is, to carry out the first arithmetical operation, may be anything else, but they are certainly not a free creation of the mind. Counting requires not only objects that can be counted, but also the ability to exclude all properties of the objects considered other than their number—and this ability is the product of a long historical evolution based on experience. Like the idea of number, so the idea of form is derived exclusively from the external world, and does not arise in the mind as a product of pure thought. There must be things which have shape and whose shapes are compared before anyone can arrive at the idea of form. . . .

" Before it was possible to arrive at the idea of deducing the *form* of a cylinder from the rotation of a rectangle about one of its sides a number of real rectangles and cylinders, in however imperfect a form, must have been examined. Like all other sciences, mathematics arose out of the *needs* of men ; from the measurement of land and of the content of vessels, from the computation of time and mechanics. . . .

" The ideas of lines, planes, angles, polygons, cubes, spheres, etc., are all taken from reality, and it requires a pretty good portion of naïve ideology to believe the mathematicians—that the first line came into existence through the movement of a point in space, the first plane through the movement of a line, the first solid through the movement of a plane and so on. Even language rebels against such a conception. A mathematical figure of three dimensions is called a solid body, *corpus solidum*, hence even in Latin a tangible object ; it has therefore a name derived from sturdy reality and by no means from the free imagination of the mind." (F. Engels. *Anti-Dühring*, pp. 47–9.)

IV

PHILOSOPHIC PRINCIPLES ON MATTER AND MOTION

[1] *Nisus.* Means literally a pressing or pressure ; striving, exertion, effort ; in labour.

Hence *in nisu* is used by Diderot in the sense of a dynamic equilibrium, or a state of potential energy, as against translatory motion of a body, kinetic energy.

The idea is developed in the following : " The real progenitor of English materialism is Bacon. To him natural philosophy is the only true philosophy, and physics based upon the experience of the senses is the chiefest part of natural philosophy. Anaxagoras and his *homæomeria*, Democritus and his atoms, he often quotes as his authorities. According to him the senses are infallible and the source of all knowledge. All science is based on experience, and consists in subjecting the data furnished by the senses to a rational method of investigation. Induction, analysis, comparison, observation, experiment are the principal forms of such a rational method. Among the qualities inherent in matter, motion is the first and foremost, not only in the form of mechanical and mathematical motion, but chiefly in the form of an impulse, a vital spirit, a tension—or a ' qual ' to use a term of Jacob Böhme's—of matter." (From *Die Heilige Familie*, by K. Marx ; quoted by F. Engels in *Ludwig Feuerbach*, pp. 84–5.)

" *Qual* " is a philosophical play upon words. " *Qual* " literally means torture, a pain which drives to action of some kind ; at the same time the mystic Böhme puts into the German word something of the meaning of the Latin *qualitas* ; his " *qual* " was the activating principle arising from, and promoting in its turn, the spontaneous development of the thing, relation or person subject to it, in contradistinction to a pain inflicted from without.

2 Molecule. Diderot uses the word *molécule* in the sense of an extremely small particle greater than an atom. The modern chemical use of the term molecule was not defined until Avogadro (1776–1856) distinguished between atoms and molecules. In this translation *molécule* has usually been translated as molecule where the meaning would not conflict with its modern usage, otherwise as particle.

3 This whole passage on matter and motion should be compared with the following : "*Motion is the mode of existence of matter.* Never anywhere has there been matter without motion, nor can there be. Motion in cosmic space, mechanical motion of smaller masses on the various celestial bodies, the motion of the molecules as heat or as electrical or magnetic currents, chemical combination or disintegration, organic life —at each given moment each individual atom of matter in the world is in one or other of these forms of motion, or in several forms of them at once. All rest, all equilibrium, is only relative and only has meaning in relation to one or another definite form of motion. A body, for example, may be on the ground in mechanical equilibrium, may be mechanically at rest ; but this in no way prevents it from participating in the motion of the earth and in that of the whole solar system, just as little as it prevents its most minute physical parts from carrying out the oscillations determined by its temperature, or its atoms from passing through a chemical process. Matter without motion is just as unthinkable as motion without matter. Motion is therefore as uncreatable and as indestructible

as matter itself; as the older philosophy (Descartes) expressed it, the quantity of motion existing in the world is always the same. Motion therefore cannot be created; it can only be transferred. When motion is transferred from one body to another, in so far as it transfers itself, is active, it may be regarded as the cause of motion, in so far as the latter is transferred, is passive. We call this active motion *force*, and the passive, the *manifestation of force*. In this it is as clear as daylight that the force is equal to its manifestation, because in fact it is the *same* motion which takes place in both." (F. Engels. *Anti-Dühring*, pp. 71-2.)

"The basic distinction between the materialist and the idealist is that the materialist takes sensation, perception, conception and, in general, human consciousness as the copy of objective reality. The world is the movement of this objective reality reflected in our consciousness. To the movement of ideas, perceptions, etc., corresponds the movement of matter outside us. The notion of matter expresses nothing but objective reality which is given us in sensation. Therefore to separate matter from motion would be the same as separating thought from objective reality, the same as separating sensation from the external world—in a word, would be equivalent to joining the idealist camp. This ruse of recognizing motion without matter in order to deny more effectively materialism is only possible because of the silence which is kept about the relation of matter to thought." (Lenin. *Materialism and Empirio-Criticism*, pp. 226-7.)

For a discussion on this point in relation to modern physics see T. A. Jackson. *Dialectics*, pp. 251-273.

V

ELEMENTS OF PHYSIOLOGY

[1] Beings, in the French: *Être*, meaning "existing things."

[2] *Mécontents*: literally dissatisfied; hence: unsuited, ill-adapted, misfits.

[3] Cf. *Motion is the mode of existence of matter*. Never anywhere has there been matter without motion, nor can there be . . . all rest, all equilibrium, is only relative, and only has meaning in relation to one or another definite form of motion. . . .

"Matter without motion is just as unthinkable as motion without matter." (Engels. *Anti-Dühring*, p. 71.) See Section IV. Note 3, above.

[4] "*Mechanical Motion*. Among natural scientists movement is always understood as mechanical motion, change of place. This is a legacy from the pre-chemical eighteenth century and greatly impedes a clear concep-

tion of phenomena. Movement in application to matter is *change in general*. . . . This does not mean that each of the higher forms of movement is not always and necessarily connected with real mechanical motion (external or molecular) just as the higher forms of movement produce other forms of movement at the same time. Chemical action is impossible without changes in temperature and electricity. Organic life is impossible without mechanical, molecular, chemical, thermal, electrical and other changes. But the presence of these accessory forms does not exhaust the essence of the chief form in each case. Some day we shall certainly experimentally ' reduce ' thinking to molecular and chemical motions in the brain ; but does this exhaust the essence of thought ? " (Engels. *Dialectics and Nature*, quoted in Rudas, *Dialectical Materialism and Communism*, pp. 20–1.)

[5] Sensitiveness, in the French, *sensibilité*. In the present translation this has been translated as sensitiveness, or faculty of sensation, rather than by " feeling," since the latter word in English now often has a less technical and more figurative meaning, as in " a man of feeling " or " to hurt anyone's feelings." Diderot almost invariably uses *sensibilité* in the sense of the faculty of sensation pertaining to matter in general, or to matter organized in a certain way, as in living matter ; the property of being able to feel impressions on it caused by other portions of matter ; sensitiveness. This is made clear in Diderot's note.

See the quotations from Helvétius about the " *Faculté de sentir* " and from Joseph Priestley on pp. 332–3. Section III. Note 3.

[6] Diderot here and elsewhere in the *Elements of Physiology* uses *molécule* somewhat in the sense of cell. At the time he was writing the discovery of the cell as the unit of living matter had not been made. This was the fundamental contribution of Schleiden and Schwann in 1838.

VI

SUPPLEMENT TO BOUGAINVILLE'S ' VOYAGE '

[1] Louis Antoine de Bougainville (1729–1814) was at first a mathematician and barrister and entered the army in 1753. He became secretary at the French Embassy in London, but left the diplomatic service to go with Montcalm to Canada, where he became a colonel and showed great bravery. After the peace of 1763 he took service in the navy and obtained permission to found a colony in the Falkland Islands. Three years later the French Government sold the colony to the Spanish. The

great voyage to which his name is attached lasted from 1766-9, and allowed him to explore a great part of the Archipelago of Oceania including Tahiti. The record of his voyage round the world, the first by a Frenchman, was published in 1771 and had a great success. Diderot wrote a review of it the same year. Bougainville distinguished himself in the American War of Independence. He received a naval command at Brest in 1790, retired, and entered the Institut Français and the Bureau of Longitudes. Napoleon I made him a senator and count. Diderot's *Supplement* was written in 1772 and was circulated in manuscript copies ; it was not published until after the Revolution, in 1796.

Diderot's *Supplement* was really aimed at the corruption of morals in France, and the mask with which this criticism was covered caused no illusions to the philosophers. The celebration of the " state of nature " was a satirical criticism ; it was not believed that the " noble savage " really existed in the perfection ascribed to him in the *Supplement*. Diderot's reference in the *Conversation between the Abbé Barthélemy and Diderot* to the savages encountered by Bougainville shows that he did not believe this (see p. 200). Besides the contemporary social criticism, the *Supplement* is remarkable for its surprisingly modern treatment of social and sexual problems.

[2] Roman Campagna : at that time a notoriously unhealthy, marshy district.

[3] Beauce : a very fertile corn-growing district in France, between Paris and Orleans.

[4] Almoner : priest probably acting as ship's chaplain.

[5] Diderot is here criticizing in effect the developing system of the bourgeoisie itself, thus outstripping ideologically the very class whose revolutionary aspect he reflected. Compare with this extract from the *Manifesto of the Communist Party* by K. Marx and F. Engels (1848) :

" In proportion as the bourgeoisie, i.e., capital, is developed, in the same proportion is the proletariat, the modern working class, developed —a class of labourers who live only so long as they find work, and who find work only so long as their labour increases capital. These labourers, who must sell themselves piecemeal, are a commodity, like every other article of commerce, and are consequently exposed to all the vicissitudes of competition, to all the fluctuations of the market." (p. 15.)

[6] The dialectical character of all natural phenomena. Compare : " When we reflect on nature, or the history of mankind or our own intellectual activity, the first picture presented to us is of an endless maze of relations and interactions, in which nothing remains what, where and as it was, but everything moves, changes, comes into being and passes out of existence. This primitive, naïve, yet intrinsically correct conception of the world was that of ancient Greek philosophy,

and was first clearly formulated by Heraclitus : everything is and also is not, for everything is in *flux*, is constantly changing, constantly coming into being and passing away." (F. Engels. *Anti-Dühring*, p. 27.)

[7] Only now has Diderot's "utopian" vision of State responsibility for all children and aged people, for all citizens, become an integral part of any social fabric, namely in the U.S.S.R., where employment is a right guaranteed by the State, and every citizen is a social asset. unlike capitalist countries where the unemployed working class is frankly looked upon as " scrap."

[8] A clear recognition of the primary role of the labourer in commodity production.

[9] Compare Diderot's analysis of the marriage relation with the following : " The bourgeoisie has torn away from the family its sentimental veil and has reduced the family relation to a mere money relation." (*Manifesto of the Communist Party*. K. Marx and F. Engels. 1848. p. 11.)

" But you Communists would introduce community of women, screams the whole bourgeoisie in chorus.

" The bourgeois sees in his wife a mere instrument of production. He hears that the instruments of production are to be exploited in common, and naturally, can come to no other conclusion than that the lot of being common to all will likewise fall to the women.

" He has not even a suspicion that the real point aimed at is to do away with the status of women as mere instruments of production.

" For the rest, nothing is more ridiculous than the virtuous indignation of our bourgeoisie at the community of women, which, they pretend, is to be openly and officially established by the Communists. The Communists have no need to introduce community of women ; it has existed almost from time immemorial.

" Our bourgeois, not content with having the wives and daughters of their proletarians at their disposal, not to speak of common prostitutes, take the greatest pleasure in seducing each other's wives.

" Bourgeois marriage is in reality a system of wives in common and thus, at the most, what the Communists might possibly be reproached with is that they desire to introduce, in substitution for a hypocritically concealed, an openly legalized community of women. For the rest it is self-evident that the abolition of the present system of production must bring with it the abolition of the community of women springing from that system, i.e., of prostitution both public and private." (*Manifesto of the Communist Party*. K. Marx and F. Engels. 1848. pp. 27–8.)

[10] See note 7.

[11] Characters in Diderot's stories : *This is not a story* and *On the Inconsistency of Public Judgment on Private Behaviour*.

VII

CONVERSATION BETWEEN THE ABBÉ BARTHÉLEMY AND DIDEROT

[1] D'Holbach was one of the great French materialists. He was a close friend of Diderot. At his houses (he was a rich man) he provided a meeting-place for the philosophers. He contributed many scientific articles to the *Encyclopedia*, and published many other works which he either wrote, edited or translated. (See W. H. Wickwar. *Baron d'Holbach*; G. V. Plekhanov. *Essays in the History of Materialism*.)

[2] See the quotation from the *Letter on the Blind*, p. 28.

[3] By Montesquieu.

IX

CONVERSATION OF A PHILOSOPHER WITH THE MARÉCHALE DE X.

[1] This was first published in 1776 in the *Correspondence Secret* of Métra. According to a tradition reported by Naigeon, friend and literary executor of Diderot, the Maréchale de X. was the Maréchale de Broglie.

In the *Correspondence Secret*, the name Diderot is used throughout in place of Crudeli.

An English translation of this *Conversation* by "E.N." was published in 1875 by Thomas Scott, who was a theist, critical of bible-worship and dogma. He published at his own expense, from his private address, about two hundred pamphlets and leaflets, constituting in the mass "a liberal education on religious questions." (J. M. Robertson. *History of Free Thought in the Nineteenth Century*, II, p. 399.)

[2] The Hôpital was the Salpêtrière, place of imprisonment for prostitutes; the Bicêtre a prison.

[3] Jansenists were Catholics, followers of the teaching of Cornelius Jansen (1585–1638). While the orthodox Roman Catholic admitted a mysterious collaboration of the human will and the Divine Spirit in the work of salvation, Jansen suppressed the role of the human will and taught predestination, which separated the elect from the damned for ever, by an absolute and irrevocable decree of God.

X

RAMEAU'S NEPHEW

[1] To take pleasure in *Rameau's Nephew* it is unnecessary to know anything about the writing of the *Encyclopedia* or of the quarrel about the " Bouffons." Nevertheless some knowledge of these things increases the pleasure of the reading. The writing of the *Encyclopedia*, and the attacks on the " philosophers " have been mentioned in the introduction and indicate the historical setting of the satire. Without annotations about all the personalities named, it is clear enough usually to which camp they belonged. More complete annotation would be an academic exercise, adding nothing to the universal qualities of Diderot's satire, and impeding the appreciation of its dialectic brilliance.

This translation is made from the editions of Billy and of Hilsum (see bibliography) which reproduce the complete text of an autograph manuscript published for the first time by Georges Monval in 1891. The following is a letter of Marx to Engels on *Rameau's Nephew*.

" London, April 15
" 1869.

" To-day I have discovered by accident that we have two copies of the *Neveu de Rameau* in our house and I am therefore sending you one. This unique masterpiece will give you fresh pleasure again. Old Hegel says about it : ' The mocking laughter at existence, at the confusion of the whole and at itself, is the disintegrated consciousness, aware of itself and expressing itself, and is at the same time the last audible echo of all this confusion. . . . It is the self-disintegrating nature of all relations and their conscious disintegration. . . . In this aspect of the return to self the *vanity of all things* is the self's *own* vanity, or the self is itself vanity . . . but as the indignant consciousness it is aware of its own disintegration and by that knowledge has immediately transcended it. . . . Every part of this world either gets its mind expressed here or is spoken of intellectually and declared for what it is. The *honest consciousness* (the role which Diderot allots to himself in the dialogue) takes each lement [a] for a permanent entity and does not realize in its uneducated thoughtlessness that it is doing just the opposite. But the disintegrated consciousness is the consciousness of reversal and indeed of absolute reversal : its dominating element is the concept, which draws together the thoughts that to the honest consciousness lie so wide apart ; hence the brilliance of its language. Thus the contents of the mind's speech about itself consist in the reversal of all conceptions and realities : the universal deception of oneself and others and the shamelessness of declaring this deception is therefore precisely the greatest truth. . . . To the quiet consciousness, which in its honest way goes on singing the melody of the True and the Good in even tones, i.e., on one note, this speech appears as " a farrago of wisdom and madness," ' *b* etc. (a passage from Diderot follows).

" More amusing than Hegel's commentary is that of Mr. Jules Janin *c* from which you will find extracts in the appendix to the little volume. This *cardinal de la mer* [sea-cardinal] feels the lack of a moral in Diderot's *Rameau* and has therefore set the thing right by the discovery that all Rameau's contrariness arises from his vexation at not being a ' born gentleman.'

" The Kotzebue-ish rubbish which he has piled up on this cornerstone is being performed as a melodrama in London. From Diderot to Jules Janin is no doubt what the physiologists call regressive metamorphosis. The French intellect as it was before the Revolution and under *Louis Philippe* ! . . ." (Letter of K. Marx to F. Engels. *Marx-Engels Correspondence*, Letter 123, p. 259.)

[Notes to the above Letter :
a element ; each element in the dialectical movement, process of becoming ; in German, *moment*.

b The passage from Hegel is from the *Phänomenologie des Geistes*.

c Janin, Jules (1804–74) ; French bourgeois author and literary critic with a popular reputation in bourgeois circles.]

2 In the French, *Cagniard* : a haunt of beggars in Paris on the left bank of the Seine, on the river's edge.

3 Palissot, Fréron : anti-Encyclopedist writers. Palissot was author of the *Comédie des Philosophes*, a satirical play against Diderot and his circle. Both Palissot and Fréron were writers used by the Jesuits who are remembered now only in connection with their abuse of the Encyclopedists.

4 Author of a poem on *The Pox* ; hence the remark about him on p. 283.

5 Bergier : a theological enemy of Diderot and the " philosophers."

6 Children from orphanages with uniforms of these colours.

7 Cf. " The workingmen have no country" (K. Marx and F. Engels, *Manifesto of the Communist Party*, 1848. p. 28.)

8 Calas was tortured and broken on the wheel on a charge of having murdered his son to prevent his becoming a Catholic. Voltaire had his innocence established and the Calas family compensated. It is to this Diderot is referring.

9 Bouret : a farmer-general, i.e., one of the chief tax-collectors to whom that lucrative office had been farmed out. The farmers-general were allowed to keep all they could extract in taxes above a certain fixed sum which they paid for the office. At the Revolution the hatred of the people for the farmers-general found expression.

[10] *Comedy of the Philosophers*, by Palissot. See note 3.

[11] Helvétius, Claude (1715-71). One of the great triumvirate of eighteenth-century French materialists : Diderot, d'Holbach and Helvétius. Helvétius was author of *De l'Esprit* (a punning title meaning On Wit, or On Mind, Spirit), and *De l'Homme* (On Man). See G. V. Plekhanov *Essays in the History of Materialism.*

Diderot may have assisted in the composition of *De l'Esprit*, and he wrote a long critical commentary on *De l'Homme*. (*Œuvres Complètes*, Vol. II, p. 275.)

[12] *Sanbenito.* Under the Spanish Inquisition confessed and penitent " heretics " (i.e. anyone not a Roman Catholic) were made to wear a yellow cloak-like garment having a St. Andrew's cross in red before and behind. Heretics who refused to be converted were made to wear a similar black garment, painted with flames and devils, when walking to the place of execution by burning—the *auto-da-fé*. Literally the latter means " act of the faith."

[13] *Bouffons.* The company of the " Bouffons " were Italian singers and dancers playing the new Italian opera-bouffes of Pergolesi, Latilla, Ciampi, Jomelli, Leo, etc. Their appearance in Paris in 1752 crystallized opinion which was feeling the need for new and freer development in music, as against the scholastic and rule-bound French productions of the time. The " philosophers " (Diderot and his circle) supported the new Italian music, which was violently attacked by critics of the reactionary camp, and a lively pamphleteering battle developed between them. The quarrel about the *bouffons* represented one aspect of the general ideological fermentation ; the Encyclopedists, supporters of new ideas, new hopes, freer and wider developments, against the reactionaries led by the Jesuit writers (Fréron, Palissot, Cazotte).

[14] Royal Academy of the blind-alley (*Academie Royale du cul-de-sac*). The public queued up in the blind-alley (*cul-de-sac*) at the Opera before admittance. This was often the scene of disputes between rival groups.

[15] The Neapolitan abbé Galiani was a close friend of Diderot and the "philosophers." Diderot collaborated with him in his *Dialogues sur le commerce des blés.*

BIBLIOGRAPHY

DIDEROT. *Œuvres Complètes.* Edited by J. Assézat and M. Tourneux. 20 volumes. Paris, 1875–79 (Garnier).

An excellent selection of Diderot's writings, in French, is that edited by André Billy : *Bibliothèque de la Pléiade.* Paris, 1935 (*Nouvelle Revue Française*), 1 vol., 1005 pages. Also 3 vols. in the series *Génie de la France,* Paris (Hilsum).

The above have been used for the translations.

BABELON, ANDRÉ. Editor of Diderot's *Lettres à Sophie Volland,* Paris, 1930 (Librairie Gallimard), 3 vols.

BERNAL, J. D. *Engels and Science,* 1935, Labour Monthly Pamphlet, No. 6.

BILLY, ANDRÉ. *Diderot.* Paris, 1932 (Les Editions de France).

DRAPER, J. W. *History of the Conflict between Religion and Science,* London (Watts).

ELLIS, HAVELOCK. *The New Spirit,* 1926 (4th ed.), London (Constable).

ENGELS, FREDERICK. *Herr Eugen Dühring's Revolution in Science (Anti-Dühring),* London (Lawrence & Wishart).

ENGELS, FREDERICK. *Ludwig Feuerbach and the Outcome of Classical German Philosophy.* London (Lawrence and Wishart).

HART, IVOR B. *Makers of Science.* London, 1924 (Oxford University Press).

JACKSON, T. A. *Dialectics.* London, 1936 (Lawrence and Wishart).

KIPLING, RUDYARD. *Many Inventions.* London (Macmillan).

LENIN, V. I. *Materialism and Empirio-Criticism.* Collected Works, Vol. XIII. London (Lawrence & Wishart).

LENIN, V. I. Quoted in Ralph Fox, *The Novel and the People,* 1937 (Lawrence & Wishart), p. 33.

LUC, JEAN. *Diderot.* II. Paris (Editions Sociales Internationales).

LUPPOL, I. K. *Diderot.* Paris, 1936 (Editions Sociales Internationales).

MARX, K. and ENGELS, F. *Manifesto of the Communist Party.* London (Lawrence & Wishart).

MARX, K. and ENGELS, F. *Selected Correspondence, 1846–95.* Ed. Dona Torr. London, 1934 (Lawrence & Wishart).

MOORE, F. J. *History of Chemistry.* New York, 1918 (McGraw-Hill).

MORLEY, JOHN. *Diderot.* 1886 edition, 2 vols. London (Macmillan).

BIBLIOGRAPHY

NIZAN, PAUL.   *Les Matérialistes de l'Antiquité.   Démocrite-Epicure-Lucrèce.*
Paris, 1936.   (Editions Sociales Internationales).

PLEKHANOV, G. V.   *Essays in the History of Materialism.*   Tr. Ralph Fox.
London, 1934 (John Lane).

PRENANT, MARCEL.   *Biologie et Marxisme.*   Paris, 1936 (Editions Sociales
Internationales).

RESTIF DE LA BRETONNE.   *Monsieur Nicolas, ou Le Coeur Humain Dévoilé.
Memoires Intimes.*   Edition of Isidore Liseux.   Paris, 1883, 14 vols.

ROBERTSON, J. M.   *A History of Free Thought in the Nineteenth Century.*
2 vols., London, 1929 (Watts).

RUDAS, L.   *Dialectical Materialism and Communism.*   3rd Edition, 1934.
Labour Monthly Pamphlet, No. 4.

WICKWAR, W. H.   *Baron d'Holbach ;   A Prelude to the French Revolution.*
London, 1935 (Allen and Unwin).